The Handbook for Legal Innovation

NICOLA SHAVER

Commissioning editor
Alex Davies

Managing director
Sian O'Neill

The Handbook for Legal Innovation
is published by

Globe Law and Business Ltd
3 Mylor Close
Horsell
Woking
Surrey GU21 4DD
United Kingdom
Tel: +44 20 3745 4770
www.globelawandbusiness.com

The Handbook for Legal Innovation

ISBN 9781787429130
EPUB ISBN 9781787429147
Adobe PDF ISBN 9781787429154

To Jenefer and Peter,
Who have supported me in every way possible
And instilled in me a life-long love of learning.

Contents

Chapter 4: Planning for the future

Chapter 5: Building a portfolio of initiatives

Chapter 6: Determining priorities

Chapter 7: Creating and growing an innovation function

PART 2: Methodologies for Change

Chapter 8: Supercharging your strategy

Chapter 9: Change management

Chapter 10: Communications and storytelling

Chapter 11: Creative problem-solving and process improvement

About the author

Nicola Shaver has been working at the forefront of change in the legal industry for the past ten years. She is the CEO and co-founder of Legaltech Hub, the foremost educational platform for insights and analysis on legal innovation, digital transformation, and legaltech procurement, combined with the most comprehensive directory of legal technology solutions globally.

Nicola has 20 years of experience in the legal industry, including ten years of practice experience with top tier firms and Fortune 500 companies and close to a decade of global experience as a senior innovation leader with international firms. In 2020, the same year that her department at Paul Hastings LLP was named Innovator of the year, the International Legal Technology Association named her Innovative Leader of the Year. Nicola developed a curriculum on legal technology for summer associates that was shortlisted by the *Financial Times* Innovative Lawyers Awards for the Future of Law category. In 2021, she became a Fastcase 50 honoree and a Fellow of the College of Law Practice Management. In 2022, the ABA named her one of its Women of Legaltech.

In addition to her work with Legaltech Hub, Nicola is the host of Luminate+ series The Innovation Edge, and an adjunct professor at Cardozo Law School, where she developed and teaches the school's inaugural course on legal technology and the business of law. She is a frequent advisor to law firms, corporate legal departments, and legaltech companies. She has been invited to speak at conferences in Australia, Canada, the United States, Latin America, and Europe, on topics such as digital transformation and technology adoption. She is a regular contributor to publications including Law360, ALM Legaltech News, *Modern Lawyer*, and *Legal Business World*, and a passionate advocate for positive change in the legal industry.

Foreword

Why should lawyers at the top of their game change the way they work? After all, they already lead the market, and if it ain't broke...

True leaders know that the only constant is change and that, to stay at the top of the market, they need to improve the way they work because there's always someone coming up behind them. But reminiscent of what we used to hear in response to climate change, some people simply deny that change exists. Or others acknowledge the need for change but choose not to act because the consequences of inaction aren't immediate while the complexities and the efforts demanded to address it are. Market leaders understand the danger of not changing, and they get to work.

Change is hard. Especially when you're dealing with smart and busy people, who work in a risk-averse environment. Innovation is the language of change, and by definition, innovation involves failure. When trying new approaches, there is no guarantee of success. Since the current mode of work – despite occasional client frustration with the business model – continues to drive high profits, it's hard to get lawyers to modify it – until they realize they have to.

Cynics will claim that despite recent record investments in LegalTech and ongoing calls for the "death of the billable hour model", not much has actually changed in the practice of law. But change comes in many forms. Think about the taxi industry, which was very stable for many year. In a short period, Uber transformed that market *without changing the core service* – you're not zapped through space or transported by drones and you still need to get in a car and get through traffic from point A to point B. What Uber innovated was the buying experience, bringing clarity and transparency to the customer. You don't need to seek a driver on the street. You don't need to know how to get where you're going, or even where you are. You know the price up front. Holders of traditional taxi medallions have struggled to catch up and compete with this more-evolved competition. As things stand today, leading partners at high-end law firms without an innovation strategy are analogous to yellow cab medallion holders.

In her *Handbook for Legal Innovation*, Nikki Shaver – a leading legal innovator herself – offers insightful and practical guidance for those tasked with leading transformation in law firms or legal organizations. In this essential guide, Nikki offers a step-by-step outline for running a legal innovation program, reflecting her decades-long experience supporting knowledge management and innovation initiatives in law firms across Australia, Canada, and the US, and drawing on her involvement in the Legal Innovation and Design group (L.I.D.) she founded and the global LegalTech community of which she is an influential member.

The first part of the *Handbook* offers practical tips, tools, and inspiration for the cultural change needed to help organizations address internal barriers to revising the processes and the ways they deliver services to clients. It also provides the framework for building a strategy and prioritizing potential initiatives. Finally, it talks about the people you need in order to get things done – the common roles and organizational charts of the departments and groups that support knowledge and innovation initiatives, as well as the character traits most common among successful innovation staff.

The second part of the *Handbook* dives deeply into change management strategies and offers examples of ways to engage with the broader audience who needs to adopt the new modes of working. Nikki translates these common-sense principles into easy-to-follow steps that can provide a path to success.

You've probably heard the saying, "Technology won't replace lawyers, but lawyers who *use* technology *will* replace those who don't". If you believe there's a better way to deliver legal services to clients, read on to find out what it takes.

Oz Benamram
Chief knowledge and innovation officer at
Simpson Thacher and Bartlett LLP

Introduction

Legal practice has undergone significant change over the past five to ten years, and it will continue to undergo change at an exponentially high rate. The increasing pace of disruption means that the business model of many law firms is likely to shift significantly during the careers of the generation of young lawyers just now graduating. It is the kind of change that will affect everyone in legal, and those who are not prepared for it or who are not ready to embrace it will be left behind.

Law societies and organizations across the world have recognized this. In 2016, for example, the Australian College of Law created the Centre for Legal Innovation[1] to act as an innovation-focused think tank. In the UK, the Government has invested hugely in legal innovation, contributing over two million pounds in 2018 and 2019 to the digital transformation of the UK's legal sector and to boost lawtech.[2] In the United States, the American Bar Association (ABA) offers a Legal Technology Resource Center[3] and releases an annual Tech Survey.[4] Even more significantly, the ABA has formally recognized the importance of all lawyers understanding technology in practice. In 2012, the ABS approved an amendment to the Model Rules of Professional Conduct, and specifically to Model Rule 1.1, which deals with maintaining competence. The amendment, Comment 8, reads:

> *"To maintain the requisite knowledge and skill, a lawyer should keep abreast of changes in the law and its practice,* including the benefits and risks associated with relevant technology, *engage in continuing study and education and comply with all continuing legal education requirements to which the lawyer is subject."*[5]

This rule has become known as the *duty of tech competency* and it has – at the time of writing – been adopted in 40 states across America.[6] The tech competency rule acknowledges that new skills are becoming important for lawyers, including a knowledge and understanding of technology-assisted practice.

In spite of these changes, only 50 percent of law schools in the United States offer courses on legal innovation, legal technology, or the business of law.[7] More disappointing is the fact that only approximately 15 percent of law students register to take those courses and study these topics at law school. Lack of awareness might be one reason for this low enrolment rate, but another is that large law firms, in particular, have not adapted their recruitment practices to the changing context of legal practice. Typically, large law firms still seek out candidates from top law schools, with academic rankings towards the top of their class. Although many firms recognize the increasing importance of new skills for legal practice, this understanding has not affected hiring practices. Neither law schools nor law firms are making it known during traditional on-campus recruitment exercises that associates who have an understanding of the way the profession is changing, and an openness to embracing that change, are more likely to succeed in the profession, or that these candidates are preferred. And yet it is a fact that associates who are able to remain flexible and adaptable when it comes to the way that they work are the ones who will succeed in the legal market of the future.

Changing market conditions

Over the past decade or so, the legal market and the forces influencing it have altered considerably. Where large, top tier law firms used to exclusively dominate the market for high value commercial legal work, there are now new competitors at play (see Figure 1). Alternative legal service providers (ALSPs), NewLaw model firms[8] (often spin-offs from large law that operate technology- driven practices with fixed fee arrangements), and the Big Four accounting firms are just some of the new forces increasing competition in the market.

Moreover, as deregulation or re-regulation of the industry occurs globally, even in places like the United States where this would have seemed impossible just a few years ago, the market will continue to change and evolve.

Consider the increasing market share cornered by ALSPs, or law companies. Not long ago, it would have been unheard of for large law to feel threatened by ALSPs. When they initially emerged, it was anticipated that their focus would remain squarely on high volume, low value work such as document review and litigation support – but this type of company is growing more significantly than anticipated. Where ALSPs constituted $8.4bn of legal work in 2015, they now command over $14bn.[9] Leadership of a large law firm in the United States recently admitted that the ALSP

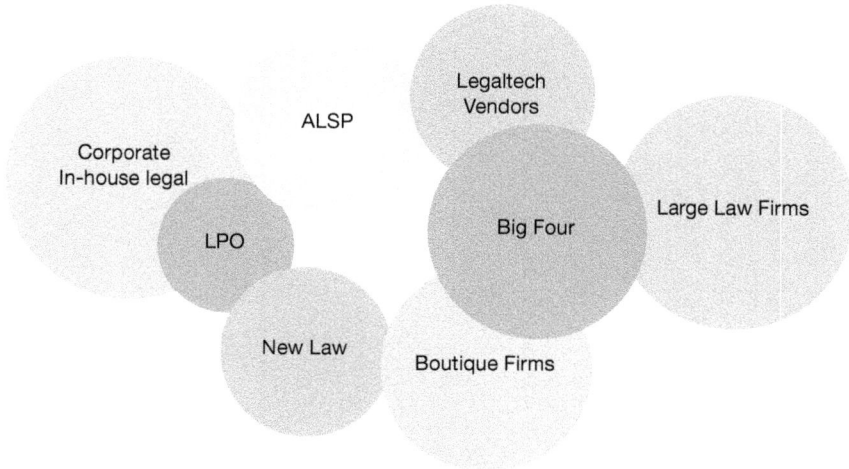

Figure 1: Competitors for commercial legal work.

market had stolen eight percent of its firm's annual revenue for two years running. These figures are likely to grow.

The unexpected competitiveness of ALSPs results partly from the growth of corporate in-house legal departments working with ALSPs, but in fact use of ALSPs by law firms has now outstripped that of corporate legal departments (see Figure 2).[10] The growth in market share is also indicative of the fact that ALSPs have started evolving to offer more sophisticated services to their clients. Technology-enabled services have always allowed ALSPs to provide greater value for high volume work, but as the technology and ALSP sophistication evolves, they have been able to take on higher value work and more complex tasks. Many ALSPs are developing proprietary systems to gain sustainable competitive advantage, such as state-of-the-art artificial intelligence systems.[11]

Core to the growing success of ALSPs lies the fact that they adopt business models allowing for rapid innovation, with much of the work that they do being supported by considerable technology investment. As a result, ALSPs are able to get work done quickly and charge lower prices for it, making these entities an attractive prospect for clients who are trying to reduce spend on outside legal.

It is still largely the case that non-lawyers may not run law firms in the United States, but in countries where deregulation has happened, for example Australia and the UK, new-law firms owned and run by non-lawyers and the Big Four accounting firms are beginning to take market share from large, established law firms. In Spain, for example, the Big Four now take up four spaces on the list of top ten law firms by revenue.[12] This

US law firms using ALSPs

US corporations using ALSPs

2016 (n=160)	2018 (n=336)	2020 (n=372)	2016 (n=112)	2018 (n=182)	2020 (n=214)
51%	72%	79%	61%	70%	71%

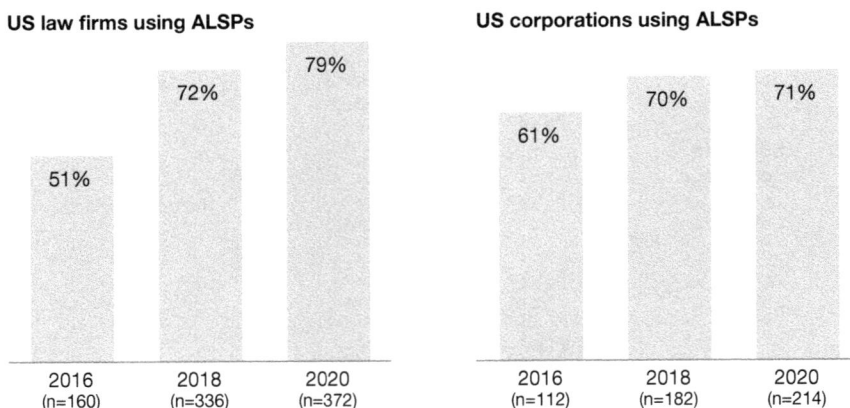

Figure 2: Growth of ALSP market, 2016-2020. Source: 2021 ALSP Report.[13]

kind of intervention by non-traditional law practices has historically been considered unlikely in the United States, but it shouldn't be. Fresh ground was broken in 2021 in Utah when Law on Call opened as the first fully non-lawyer owned law practice in the United States.[14] The amendment to Model Rule 5.4 that made this possible is now under consideration by working groups in various other states, and similar changes in regulation have already occurred in Arizona.[15]

Every year, Altman Weil undertakes a study of transformation in the legal industry. In recent years, the study has pointed to a fascinating trend. Participating firms were asked whether they were losing business to any providers of legal services in the market, other than their direct competitors. In addition to ALSPs and the Big Four, law firms responded that they were losing market share to their own clients. In fact, clients are seizing more work from firms than any other competitors in the market, both because they have been keeping more work in-house (and sending less to outside counsel) and because they are actively using technology tools that reduce the need for outside counsel.[16] Over 53 percent of corporate legal departments have reduced spend on outside legal counsel over the past three years, and that number is set to increase.[17] The result of this trend is that there is simply less market share to go around, and law firms have to fight harder with new tools in order to retain their client base or grow it.

As part of learning about the market to help communicate the need for change, I have spoken to a wide network of in-house counsel to understand better what their needs are and what they are doing themselves to improve the way their teams practice. What I have heard is hardly surprising – corporate legal departments are beginning to use technology to streamline their own work. More sophisticated and better resourced legal departments are undertaking broad automation exercises, and many client organizations read enough about the market to understand what solutions are available to law firms to help them reduce costs, streamline work, offer packaged services, and improve value to clients. The fact that corporate legal departments are considered a cost center and often do not have the budget for significant technology investment themselves does not mean that corporate counsel are unaware of changes in the market or what types of technology are available to support legal practice. The rise of legal operations and organizations like CLOC[18] has seen a greater understanding of technology-assisted practice on the corporate side. Even before these developments, long before "legal innovation" became a buzzword, certain types of clients (such as large financial institutions) were automating workflows. Technology companies such as Google, Amazon, and Meta not only have legal operations departments but also dedicated legal technology teams producing proprietary software solutions to support their lawyers. For these companies, if their firms are markedly less modern in their work practices than they are, it is problematic.

Those working in large, top tier law firms – the type of firm that is called "White Shoe" in the United States, or that Bruce MacEwan and Janet Stanton have called maroon firms[19] – often point out that their clients aren't talking with their feet. In other words, in spite of all the new competitive forces in the market, in spite of the regulatory changes and the growing sophistication of clients vis-à-vis technology, most clients aren't yet protesting against the billable hour or insisting on changes to the traditional model of legal service delivery. For these types of firms, some argue, the reputation of the firm is king.[20] They are "destination" law firms.[21] Clients of these firms don't care how much they pay for services, because they are paying for a name.[22] They aren't showing any inclination towards walking away from their top tier panel firms – regardless of how averse those firms might be to adopting modern technology and methods of practicing. This may be true, for the moment. For some maroon firms at the very top of the market, that may even continue to be true for some time. But those firms make up one percent of the market. They do not represent the standard. The bottom line is that, for the vast majority of firms, if their lawyers are not starting to explore and avail themselves of the technology and resources that are available to offset the prohibitive costs of the traditional model of legal work, an increasing number of clients will recognize this and eventually move on to instruct more progressive firms.

The boom in legal technology

Perhaps in part as a response to the market changes that have caused legal institutions to open up to the concept of digital transformation, legal technology has boomed over the past decade. A recent browse on Legaltech Hub shows close to two thousand tools developed specifically for the commercial legal market, more than one thousand of which have been developed in the United States alone.[23] This is an extraordinary wealth of solutions in a market that looked completely different just five years ago.

In addition to the rise of legaltech companies, we have seen significant growth in the amount of investment in these start-ups. Legaltech start-ups didn't used to attract venture capital funding – in fact, it was widely reported before 2015 that investors had no interest in the legal technology space.[24] In 2018, however, US VC firms invested over $136bn in legaltech across nearly 10,000 transactions, representing a five-fold increase from 2009.[25] Average transaction values rose to almost $14m in 2018, double the figure in 2014.[26] In 2021, legaltech investment had topped $41bn by the middle of the year.[27] Innovation is broadly touted as the response that law firms must take to increased competition in the market. Without context or definition, innovation is an empty word, but often when we refer to it in commercial legal it is adjacent to a discussion of legal technology.

We'll get to defining innovation more specifically later in the book, but for now, let's contextualize it. When we talk about innovation in law, we generally talk not just about technology, but also about people and processes. People, because staffing legal matters with alternative time-keepers, or with multi-disciplinary professionals as well as traditional lawyers, is another way to be innovative. Process, because looking at our legal processes and refining them through legal project management, or by eliminating unnecessary steps, is an additional way to innovate in the practice of law. Technology is an obvious response to the boom we are seeing, especially as there are so many tools available now that we can use to effectively augment legal practice, to cut out some of the dull repetitive work lawyers used to do, and to help improve efficiency in practice.

Beyond people, process, and technology you will often also hear legal innovators talk about data. Data in law might seem like an anomaly, but actually, legal documents are data, and they are filled with other types of data – like clauses, for example, and legal concepts. By structuring data, we can get more out of technology, and by using other sources of larger amounts of data – such as litigation data, or financial data about the business of law – we can leverage analytics to gain insights that help drive meaningful decisions in legal practice.

There is more to legal innovation, though, even when one includes data in the mix. To truly disrupt and transform the industry we need to look at both traditional and new business models in law. And we need to examine the way that these might and should change, both in private practice and in corporate legal departments, in order to better serve the industry. There is no better time than the present to jump headfirst into the effort that many of us are engaged in, to transform the way law has traditionally operated and ensure that clients – or customers – are better served everywhere that law is practiced.

Leading innovation

In 2018, I moved from Toronto to New York City to take up a role at Paul Hastings, a large AmLaw 100 firm. I became responsible for overseeing and running global teams tasked with supporting research and knowledge needs and driving innovation efforts across all practices and offices of the firm. Perhaps most daunting, however, was the responsibility of instilling a culture of innovation within a traditional law firm model, in a firm whose partners (like most large law firm partners) were kept busy round-the-clock billing time.

Change is difficult at the best of times. Driving change across a 2,000-person organization with 21 global offices and a conservative corporate culture was even more challenging. Nevertheless, we dug in and I developed a strategy for change along with a truly audacious vision for the team: by the end of 2020, just two years after we implemented that strategy, the firm would be recognized as one of the most innovative in North America.

The firm was already doing some interesting things, but a scan of various indices indicated that it wasn't viewed in the industry – or by clients – as one that was particularly innovative. One of the sticking points, I soon learned, was the absence of any obvious incentive for lawyers to change anything about their way of working, especially in larger office locations like New York. As Richard Susskind has said, there is folly in suggesting to a group of millionaires that they should change the way they're doing things.[28] Unlike in many legal markets across the globe, large law firms in major US cities have not experienced any significant downturn in availability of work over the past few years – even during COVID-19. Clients continue to pay the high fees and to stomach the annual rate increases charged by these firms, and profit-per-equity partner continues to rise. In the absence of obvious marketplace incentives, where does one start in trying to generate forward-thinking momentum? In the dichotomy of the carrot-and-stick approach, it appeared neither was available.

I had moved to the States from Canada, where the market is quite different. There, market share is smaller and discrete – what there is, is what there is.[29] As the Canadian Bar Association has commented, there is low or no growth in many areas of practice.[30] In order to increase market share, firms are therefore under pressure to steal a piece of the pie from other firms. To do so, a firm must prove that it is able to offer better value – a higher or at least equal quality of service for less money – or to provide new and better ways of servicing clients. In legal, where less money means less time, these firms are forced to reflect upon their work and explore new, more efficient ways of doing things in order to stay in business.[31]

What I realized in New York, with a Sisyphean effort ahead, is that while innovation roles in legal have proliferated significantly over the past years, and though there is a lot of talk about innovation in the market – there is very little out there by way of guidance for how to "do" innovation in firms. We may discuss our projects, we might share wins, but there wasn't a book or a program that identified methodologies and pulled them together with practical tips to give those who lead innovation at firms a blueprint – or choice of blueprint – to follow in order to achieve culture change.

The true story of L.I.D. and identifying a need in the industry

In 2019, after speaking with many peers and recognizing that there was a need in the industry for an organization that provided support and resources to those tasked with leading innovation in commercial legal organizations, I founded the Legal Innovation and Design group (L.I.D.)[32] to do just that. I reached out to my network and, along with a small, intrepid group of legal innovators, set out to find a model that would work for the group and provide genuine utility to those involved. We used design thinking to determine the format, cadence, and programming for group meetings, throwing colorful post-its on the glass windows of a fancy conference room on the client floor in a midtown law firm on Park Avenue, and decided that each meeting should have a component of "doing" rather than just speaking. We wanted participants and members to learn experientially, and we wanted meetings to involve facilitated workshops and presentations about different methodologies for innovation – not just in legal, but across industries. We set up a LinkedIn group and quickly developed global interest from people who wanted to start their own regional chapters of L.I.D.

When the pandemic hit, it required us to quickly iterate on our original plan. We took L.I.D. virtual and starting using online white-boarding and brainstorming tools like Miro and Mural to perform the "doing" aspect of our meetings. One of the benefits of the new format was that it allowed people from all over the world to participate, and we were soon holding meetings that involved participation not just from across the United States but also Canada, Europe, Latin America, Asia, and Australia. Our LinkedIn membership rose to over 500 people, including not just law firm innovation leaders but also in-house counsel, legal operations professionals, consultants, lawyers working at the Big Four accounting firms, and more. I realized that there had been a real thirst for facilitated brainstorming to help people find new ways to successfully drive culture change and innovation initiatives in law firms and legal departments. That lightbulb moment led to the research I undertook for this book, a text designed to help people explore different ways of driving active change in commercial legal environments.

Who this book is for

In 2020, the law firm I had joined in 2018 won the most prestigious award globally for legal innovation and was named Innovator of the Year by the International Legal Technology Association. We had met the big hairy audacious goal we set two years earlier. Culture change and innovation in any organization is a team effort, and we didn't wish this result into action simply by dreaming big. We had developed a multi-disciplinary team of outstanding, creative professionals who worked together effectively to establish methodologies and execute on high-value projects that caught the eye of the industry in an opportune moment. During that multi-year process, in providing learning resources to the team and enabling them to fail and pivot and try new things, in co-developing the L.I.D. programming and hearing what worked for others, I managed to learn a bit along the way about what it takes to successfully lead change in commercial legal organizations.

This book is for people who are wondering, as I did, what it takes to successfully drive widespread culture change across an organization, and how to set about undertaking that herculean task. It's for those who occasionally feel alone as they encounter hurdle after internal hurdle and recognize that being mandated with innovating within a traditional business model can be a thankless task. We need external support because sometimes internal support is hard to come by. The work of future-proofing law will never be "done" – innovation is a constant push towards adaptation and disruption.

Change efforts should make you feel uncomfortable, because by definition they involve moving people out of the status quo and into unknown territory. It will sometimes feel chaotic. That doesn't mean that those of us driving change need to feel constantly uncomfortable while doing so.

This book is intended as a handbook that you can dip in and out of, to inspire yourself and your team to try new things, to remind yourself that there are change agents and chaos pilots everywhere rebelling against the norm, pushing the envelope a little more every day. Like the L.I.D programming, in addition to practical advice about growing or starting an innovation effort in law firms, it is also intended to offer suggestions from outside of the legal industry, because law – as we all know – is late to the game when it comes to digitization and true business model disruption, and there's a lot we can learn from those who have blazed paths before us. Hopefully, this book will provide some guidance for those entering the profession who are looking for advice on how to create change, as well as some useful reminders and prompts for those who have been doing this for a while. As well as theory and background on various methodologies, the book provides practical tips and tools, giving you some concrete suggestions for getting unstuck, overcoming obstacles, and moving forwards.

Legal is an industry desperately in need of change – I firmly believe this. You can be part of something bigger than just a few projects at your firm; you can be part of changing a profession so that fewer people suffer from depression and addiction, so that it is actually responsive to client needs, so that inefficiency is not rewarded, and people's lives aren't reduced to six-minute units. Just as the number of innovation roles in law firms is growing, so are legal operations roles in-house. If you consider each of us leading innovation as a flame in a dark stadium, think about how those flames are multiplying. You're not the only light out there. We are knitting a blanket of lights that will ultimately bond together so that the stadium we occupy together looks entirely different.

Strive on, chaos pilot – together, we can do this.

A note on terminology

There are regional variations in the terminology used to describe innovation teams and initiatives in law firms and corporate legal departments. In some jurisdictions (notably the United Kingdom and Australia), innovation is almost always a separate team entirely distinct from the knowledge management (KM) team. In Canada and the United States, innovation has generally evolved out of KM initiatives and the innovation team will often continue to be called KM. The title "chief knowledge and innovation officer" is now common, but there are still many firms where a chief knowledge officer or KM director has full oversight of innovation at the firm, and where there are no titles that contain the actual word "innovation". Some firms and legal departments refer to these types of initiatives as digital transformation efforts. In law firms where responsibility for innovation still falls to part of the IT department, there may therefore be a chief digital officer instead of a chief innovation officer. In corporate legal departments, there are rarely any innovation titles, and this type of work instead falls under legal operations. Some law firms have now also started using the term legal operations to refer to this type of work internally.

In short, there is no consistency of terminology in the industry. In this book, for the sake of clarity, the term "Innovation" will be used throughout, though there are references as well to knowledge management titles and roles. For your purposes, consider the guidance in this book to be relevant to any initiatives you are leading that focus on growth through transformation, regardless of what your role or your function might be called.

References

1   www.cli.collaw.com/about-cli/overview
2   www.gov.uk/government/news/
    tech-nation-to-support-growth-of-uk-lawtech-with-2-million-of-government-funding
3   www.americanbar.org/groups/departments_offices/legal_technology_resources
4   www.americanbar.org/news/abanews/aba-news-archives/2019/10/
    aba-releases-2019-techreport-and-legal-technology-survey-report-/
5   Comment 8 to model rule 1.1, www.americanbar.org/groups/professional_
    responsibility/publications/model_rules_of_professional_conduct/
    rule_1_1_competence/comment_on_rule_1_1/.
6   www.lawnext.com/tech-competence
7   www.geeklawblog.com/2019/10/the-geek-in-review-ep-55-the-legal-tech-and-
    innovation-pipeline-can-law-schools-and-law-firms-better-the-process.html
8   Consultant Eric Chin defined NewLaw in 2013 as "any model, process, or tool
    that represents a significantly different approach to the creation or provision of
    legal services than what the legal profession traditionally has employed." https://
    centurionlgplus.com/newlaw-guid-what-is-new-law/. As applied to law firms,
    NewLaw means firms that embrace new ways of practicing, including entirely new
    business models.
9   www.thomsonreuters.com/en/press-releases/2021/february/
    alternative-legal-service-providers-are-quickly-becoming-mainstream-for-law-firms-
    and-corporations-creating-a-14-billion-market.html
10 2021 ALSP Report, https://www.thomsonreuters.com/en-us/posts/wp-content/
    uploads/sites/20/2021/07/ALSP_2021-Report_FINAL-1.pdf
11 See, for example, Axiom's spin-off, Orgaimi: www.legaltechnologyhub.com/vendors/
    orgaimi-by-axiom/.
12 www.leadersleague.com/en/news/
    nine-of-spain-s-ten-biggest-law-firms-increased-revenue-last-year

13 www.thomsonreuters.com/en-us/posts/wp-content/uploads/sites/20/2021/07/ALSP_2021-Report_FINAL-1.pdf

14 www.abajournal.com/news/article/first-law-firm-owned-entirely-by-nonlawyers-opens-in-utah

15 www.reuters.com/legal/legalindustry/practice-innovations-non-lawyer-ownership-law-firms-are-winds-change-coming-rule-2022-03-31.

16 www.altmanweil.com//dir_docs/resource/474829CC-0945-4A99-B321-2BFD3DAB146D_document.pdf

17 https://abovethelaw.com/2017/10/right-sizing-your-legal-operations-for-scale/

18 https://cloc.org/

19 In a series of articles published in 2019, Bruce MacEwan and Janet Stanton defined a new way of segmenting the legal market, not by size of firm but by firm type. They describe maroon firms as those that have such strong reputations in the market for bet-the-company type work that they don't need to increase efficiency or concern themselves with how much they charge their clients. Their clients will return to them regardless of cost for the high value work they send these firms. Gray firms, on the other hand, operate in the more competitive space of run-the-company type work. These firms must improve service delivery models, employ efficiency and productivity tools, and adjust pricing models to maintain and grow their client base. Most firms are gray firms. https://adamsmithesq.com/2019/06/introducing-the-maroons-the-grays-part-1

20 https://adamsmithesq.com/2019/06/introducing-the-maroons-the-grays-part-1/

21 *Ibid.*

22 *Ibid.*

23 www.legaltechnologyhub.com/

24 https://abovethelaw.com/2018/07/200m-in-two-months-says-investors-no-longer-snubbing-legal-tech/?rf=1

25 https://news.bloomberglaw.com/bloomberg-law-analysis/analysis-2019-legal-tech-investments-top-1b-after-strong-q3

26 *Ibid.*

27 https://legal.fronteousa.com/2021/11/18/legal-technology-has-record-vc-investment-in-2021/; www.law360.com/pulse/articles/1458718/legal-tech-smashed-investment-records-in-2021

28 www.forbes.com/sites/davidparnell/2014/03/21/richard-susskind-moses-to-the-modern-law-firm/?sh=2d1d49833d94

29 www.cba.org/CBAMediaLibrary/cba_na/PDFs/CBA%20Legal%20Futures%20PDFS/trends-isssues-eng.pdf

30 *Ibid.*

31 *Ibid.*

32 www.innovatinglegal.com/

Part 1:
Establishing and Building your Innovation Function

Part one of this book provides practical guidance and advice for setting up an innovation function at a law firm or within a corporate legal department (where it might form part of a legal operations function). It is for people who want to work in legal innovation, those already working in it, and those who are in the process of moving into more senior roles. It's also for lawyers and law firm leaders who want to know what this kind of function might look like if it was established at their firm, and how to go about doing so.

I have had many people early in their legal innovation journey turn to me and ask questions like:

- *"Why do I need a strategy? I was a lawyer once, I know what they need!"*
- *"What does a business plan look like? Can you show me an example?"*
- *"I have approval for one more headcount but I don't know what type of role I need."*
- *"What sorts of skills should I be looking for when hiring to make sure I develop the right team?"*
- *"How do I know which projects to pursue first?"*

This first part of the book is designed to answer all of these questions.

Here, you will find practical guidance for how and why to establish a vision for your team, how to develop a strategy for innovation (and adoption), how to identify and prioritize projects, how to develop a business plan that targets innovation goals across multiple time-spans, and how to build and grow your team. Keep in mind that innovation means different things depending on context, and that it will evolve as your firm and the market changes. Establishing these fundamentals is not a once-and-done effort. Coming back on a regular cadence to review the firm's vision for the future, to update strategic goals, and to review project prioritization will benefit your team and the firm as a whole.

Chapter 1:
The impetus for change

Why change, why now?

Although change in the legal industry has been heralded with great fanfare for a number of years, it is only now that we are reaching a tipping point. As recent surveys have indicated, use of innovative technology has become one of the most important reasons clients continue to retain law firms, and the absence thereof is one of the reasons clients cite for switching outside counsel. The Wolters Kluwer Future Ready Lawyer Survey, released in September 2022, revealed that clients were not only interested in using advanced technology themselves to improve the operation of their legal departments, but that they also expected their law firms to be able to support them in this work.[1] And yet, few law firms are really equipped to support clients in their digital transformation efforts. The survey also showed that clients are increasingly willing to review their panel law firms if they feel those firms are not delivering efficient and effective services.[2]

To put it succinctly: clients will walk away from law firms that are not modernizing their services in line with market demand. The law firms that want to survive in the future must be making these changes now.

When I started working in legal innovation in 2013, it was widely assumed that AI technology would transform the industry within the following five years. ROSS Intelligence was launched the same year, the first legal start-up entitled (after a competition at the University of Toronto) to use IBM Watson as its AI backbone.[3] For the first time, lawyers were confronted with the prospect that they, or at least some percentage of lawyers, might be rendered obsolete by technology. The fear that "we may all be replaced by robots" started to feel real, and many change efforts had to begin with reassurances that process optimization or automation would merely improve the way that lawyers work, rather than eliminate the work altogether.

Here we are now in 2022, and although AI is being used widely in law firms and law departments, not a lot about the fundamental business model of legal practice has been transformed. The billable hour has endured in spite of a push towards flat fees and alternative fee arrangements. Law firm hierarchies are alive and well. The lawyer / non-lawyer divide remains entrenched, and continues to be expressed through pay inequity, inconsistent benefit entitlements, and relative status. Incremental changes have occurred in the way that lawyers work and the way legal services are delivered to clients, but the traditional structures around legal practice remain mostly stagnant.

And yet, clients are clamoring for change. Upon choosing new panel firms, clients have in the past focused first on the representative work and past experience of a firm, the types of matters it has successfully run, and the expertise of its lawyers. It used to be that a few RFPs or tenders a year would ask questions about the actual service delivery model for legal services, the diversity of a firm's legal teams, and the technology used by a firm to conduct its legal work. Now, almost all RFPs include questions of this nature (the Wolters Kluwer Future Ready Lawyers survey revealed that 91 percent of clients already were or intended to ask these questions of their panel law firms in the next year).[4] The legal expertise of a firm and its lawyers is considered a given – it's assumed that the legal work itself will be high quality, particularly among the top echelon of firms within any given market. The differentiators now are instead related to the way the work is conducted, the processes used to deliver it, and the people who conduct it. Questions about diversity are near-ubiquitous, with the Mansfield Certification[5] initiative run by American general counsels having refocused conversations about legal spend to put diversity and inclusion front and center. Over the past three years, RFP questions about innovation and technology have also become commonplace. In most cases, these questions are relatively general, asking for lists or examples of the technologies a firm uses to advance legal practice. Increasingly, however, the questions are specific and require the firm to outline, for example, instances where the firm has been able to help client in-house teams solve internal problems and streamline work.

During the time I have worked in legal innovation, I've attended conferences all over the world. The best conferences are those that include corporate legal departments as well as law firms, and potentially law schools and other verticals in legal, all coming together to discuss or workshop topics of change from multiple perspectives. At these conferences, I have frequently heard in-house lawyers complain about the lack of initiative displayed by their panel law firms.

"My bank sends me marketing materials and surveys all the time," said one corporate lawyer at a large accounting firm. *"Why doesn't my law firm ever pick up the phone to ask me if their customer service is up to scratch?"*

Another said they would love it if their law firms took the initiative and informed them about some of the innovation initiatives they were running in-house – but this had never happened. Yet another commented that they would like to meet some of the business professionals who worked alongside lawyers at their panel firms, but they rarely had the opportunity to do so.

I started bringing these client voices back to the firm, letting partners know when it was their clients who were saying these things. Actually writing down these quotes verbatim and emailing them to relevant decision-makers at the firm was one of the ways I could gradually influence culture. Another was developing and cultivating relationships with in-house lawyers and legal operations professionals and learning more about what our clients were doing on the innovation side. I learned that one financial client had undertaken a year-long global project to bring consistency to loan documents and the processes around generating those documents, and had then automated all loan documents using cutting-edge technology. The message I was able to bring back to the firm is that our clients are actively undertaking large-scale process optimization and document automation exercises. How can we sell our services to these clients if we aren't at least as sophisticated as they are in the execution of our services?

The reason innovation teams and titles are proliferating at law firms is that most firms recognize the need for change. Although change has been incremental and seems slow, it is happening, and firms will have to continue to change if they want to stay in the game. Investment in a team of people whose job it is to understand what technologies and methodologies are available to accelerate and implement change is an indication that firm leadership understands the need for future-proofing. Any firm wishing to succeed into the future must be investing now in innovation, taking a hard look at their internal processes and at the way that they deliver services to clients. Firms that have already invested in change professionals are in a position to offer new services to clients, or to offer legal services in new ways that work better for clients. They have teams of outstanding multi-disciplinary professionals serving clients holistically. This team-oriented client work will become the norm in law,[6] and firms who are only just now starting out on this journey have some catching up to do.

Nevertheless, it's imperative that firms take the leap and start the hard work of instilling modern methodologies both internally and with their clients. Investing in these teams is the first step towards future-proofing a firm, but it is not the only step that must be taken. In too many firms, money is devoted to building innovation, KM, or technology teams but they are expected to work within the traditional structure and business model of the firm – making their work almost impossible. The mere existence of a multi-disciplinary change team doesn't mean that internal barriers or hurdles to change have been alleviated. Instead, the team is commonly tasked with pushing change across the organization in spite of the traditional structures that remain in place. Firms should be investing in more than personnel – they should be re-evaluating the business model of law and shifting the structures that make change so difficult. Without altering the way that legal matters and client work is defined, without accepting that professionals without law degrees have value to offer, without being willing to entertain new ways of billing and working with clients, firms will have a difficult time truly ingraining the new practices developed by any innovation team. Until these structural hurdles are addressed, leading change or working in innovation in any firm is an uphill battle, and one for which you need stamina, resilience, vision, and a strategy.

References

1 Wolters Kluwer 2022 *Future Ready Lawyer Survey*: www.wolterskluwer.com/en/news/new-future-ready-lawyer-survey-finds-increasing-pressures-on-legal-professionals

2 *Ibid.*

3 www.rossintelligence.com/about-us

4 Wolters Kluwer 2022 *Future Ready Lawyer Survey*.

5 In 2017, general counsel across the US collectively drafted a document called the Mansfield Rule, requiring law firms to use a minimum of 30 percent women and attorneys of color in leadership roles and in hiring practices and promotions to partner. Firms who were able to prove this level of diversity could become "Mansfield Certified". The rule has now evolved, with version 5.0 launched in July 2021, requiring diversity across a greater spectrum of areas. www.diversitylab.com/pilot-projects/mansfield-rule-legal-department-3-0-edition/

6 See Adam Curphey's excellent book on this subject: Curphey, Adam (2022). *The Legal Team of the Future: Law+ Skills*. London: London Publishing Partnership.

Chapter 2:
Establishing a vision

This book assumes that you have either been set the task of leading innovative change in a commercial legal environment, you are part of a team undertaking this work, or you are interested in innovation and want to know what it would take to bring change to your legal organization. For the many firms that are just now recognizing there is a need for this kind of initiative, it can be difficult to know where to start. Although leaders are beginning to see that change is important, they haven't yet understood the significance of it. Rather than hiring expert professionals or dedicating the funds necessary to build a strong team with real force behind it, firms are appointing people internally – a partner who has an interest in technology, for example, or a lawyer who has been supporting their practice rather than actively billing – as innovation leaders and handing them the difficult task of creating a roadmap to the future. If you are one of these individuals, you may feel you have been left without the resources, know-how, or support to succeed. Even if you are someone who has been hired from the outside to build an innovation team or to develop an existing function into something bigger, it can be difficult to know where to start.

Although it's tempting to dive straight into projects that seem like low hanging fruit, or obvious opportunities, there is value in taking a more planned, structured approach. This is not to say that you can't or shouldn't also start with a low-hanging-fruit project once you have the perspective and resources to do so but taking the time first to gain some perspective and ensure you are approaching things appropriately for the organization is critical. All too often, innovation efforts fail because they have started in the wrong way. Adoption is a challenge commonly cited as one of the most significant problems for innovation and technology teams in legal organizations – and yet the cause of this problem is not well understood. Adoption problems are often a matter of timing. Trying to solve an adoption problem after the technology is already rolled out is like putting a band-aid on a wound: too little, too late. If you approach your innovation and change efforts in the right way, taking adoption into account from the very beginning, you are much less likely to need to deal with poor adoption issues at a later stage. It's vital, therefore, that before you jump in to undertake ad hoc projects, you pause to think carefully about what you and your team want to achieve. This means establishing a vision that is in step with the goals of the entire organization.

Beginning with a strong vision will provide you with a significant goal that you can use to develop your strategy, your team, and your priorities. This goal is not one that should be easy or straightforward to achieve. It should be a clear, vivid picture that is also significant and exciting – a Big Hairy Audacious Goal (or BHAG). A BHAG is a goal that is challenging, and big enough to excite the people on your team.[1] A BHAG is not to be confused with a strategy – a strategy is a roadmap for success, but it doesn't necessarily define success. In order to create a successful strategy, you first need to understand what success means to you, your team, and your organization. As a leader, a key part of your initial role is to create a clear vision and a sense of purpose for your department so that everyone working with your team understands why they exist and what the department seeks to do both within the organization and beyond.

Have you ever asked your innovation or legal operations professionals what they believe their purpose is in the organization? Many innovation teams have mission statements, or a version thereof. Similar to a tactical innovation strategy, a common failing is to put the emphasis of this mission statement on external factors. These aspects of a mission statement might refer to streamlining legal work, for example, or improving efficiency, or reducing costs.

If your mission is focused on specific actions, however, what happens when the dial turns on change and the emphasis of your mission has to shift, too? For example, one of the most powerful ways to execute on innovation efforts now is to service clients directly, either as a corollary to or entirely separate from ongoing legal work between the firm and the client. This doesn't necessarily line up with a mission to streamline legal work, but it should absolutely fall within the ambit of what a legal innovation team is set up to do.

In his book, *Start With Why*,[2] Simon Sinek outlines the reasons certain companies are more successful than others, and pins it down to what he calls The Golden Circle. Figure 3 depicts the Golden Circle, which helps humans or organizations understand why we do what we do.

The Golden Circle

WHAT
Every organization on the planet knows WHAT they do. These are products they sell or the services they offer.

HOW
Some organizations know HOW they do it. These are the things that make them special or set them apart from their competition.

WHY
Very few organizations know WHY they do what they do. WHY is not about making money. That's a result. WHY is a purpose, cause or belief. It's the very reason your organization exists.

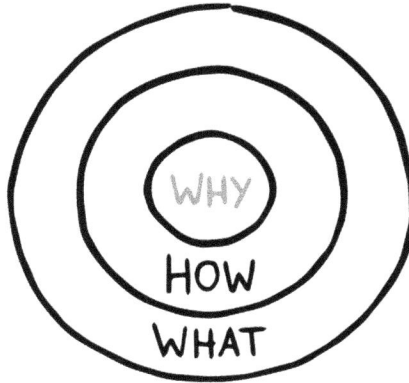

WHY
HOW
WHAT

Figure 3: Simon Sinek's Golden Circle.[3] Source: www.simonsinek.com.

Sinek says that companies that put the "Why" of their organization before the "How" and the "What" are simply more likely to succeed than other companies – because they are able to inspire people. The ability to inspire through putting "Why" at the core of a company's ethos is the reason people are so loyal to certain companies, even going so far as to tattoo company logos (like Harley Davidson) on their bodies.[4] He suggests that all of us can achieve more by reminding ourselves to start everything by first asking why.[5] By extension, he suggests that all companies will be more successful by organizing themselves in this way.

Apple is an example of a company that successfully puts its Why at the core. Sinek asks us to think about what the impact would be if Apple's core message was:

"We make great computers. They're beautifully designed, simple to use, and user-friendly. Wanna buy one?"[6]

This is a great mission statement for a company that always wants to produce only computers. What happens when Apple then rolls out the iPod? The iPhone? Sinek's point is that this type of mission, tied to external factors, is how most companies sell. It's also how most of us sell our efforts internally within our firms and organizations. By contrast, consider the power of the true message Apple puts out to market:

"Everything we do, we believe in challenging the status quo. We believe in thinking differently. The way we challenge the status quo is by making our products beautifully designed, simple to use and user-friendly."[7]

This message is not tied to any specific external factor or product, and yet it captures perfectly the ethos of Apple, Inc. It allows Apple to evolve as cultural context and technology evolves, because it doesn't tie the organization to one type of product. It also means that people know what they're buying when they buy Apple, regardless of the product they acquire – they are buying into a philosophy.

If you want to lead your team and drive innovation in a way that will truly inspire culture change in your organization, you need to understand the "Why" of your function, make it the focal point of all that you do, and communicate it to your team – and to the organization.

Crafting your vision

Only you – and perhaps the senior leaders of the organization who hired you – can know what your team's mission is, unless you successfully communicate it. For what it's worth, the "Why" for teams that I lead is transformation – both at the specific firm and in the legal industry at large. The purpose I have outlined for my function in the past is:

"We help transform the practice of law to make it better – for clients, for consumers of legal services, and for those who work in the industry."

This core mission allowed us to develop strategies and initiatives that could evolve with the times. It allowed us to undertake projects that were not specifically geared towards efficiency or costs savings or profit, because they advanced positive change in the industry and thus supported our purpose of transformation. As a result of this focus, we undertook some really interesting projects that might not have fit had we focused our efforts on external factors. For example, we partnered with universities and provided entry points for students to alternative career paths in law. We helped a client design an investor-onboarding solution as a value-add to the firm's legal services. We supported the firm's pro bono efforts. We developed revenue-generating, client-facing consulting services that had little to do with efficiency on the law firm side or streamlining legal work, but successfully transformed the model of client service delivery, enhanced existing client relationships, and actually brought in new work to the firm. Had we pinned our purpose to simply streamlining existing legal work within the firm, none of these initiatives would have fit.

If you don't identify your "Why" and inform your team and your organization about the purpose of your function, the result when you take on projects of broader scope might be confusion. It might also impede your ability to put forward effective business cases for projects that appear to management to fall outside of the core purpose of your function. If you are in the position of building a new innovation function, consider your team's "Why" before developing your strategy. If you already have a team, think about whether you have made clear to them what their purpose is. Make sure your "Why" is clearly enunciated, distinct from external factors, and focused enough to allow for the clear development and evolution of your team's function over time.

Checklist: Setting a vision

☐ Speak to law firm management and a selection of invested partners to understand why the firm believes an innovation function is important.

☐ As an innovation leader, consider what your purpose is for your team (consider also: is it to drive internal innovation only, or also external innovation?).

☐ Speak to your team about what drives them in their work – is there a common thread around their sense of purpose that is tied to what the team does? (Get your team involved in defining the vision.)

☐ Crystallize the purpose for your team based on the three elements above, and put it in terms of the "why" for your team.

☐ Make sure your "why" is not limiting, in other words that it is not tied to particular tactical goals.

☐ Push your "why" a step further: What is your BHAG? (Write it down.)

☐ Take your written BHAG and run it past your team. Is it clear enough? Is it audacious enough? Tweak your BHAG until it resonates with everyone who sees it.

☐ Promote your team internally and externally by making your "why" vision clear. Motivate your team by getting them excited about achieving the BHAG.

References
1   Rovner, Jeff. 2020. *Concept Companion: Discover the Power of Conceptual Thinking.*

2 Sinek, Simon. *Start With Why: How Great Leaders Inspire Everyone to Take Action*. UK, Penguin Random House, 2009.

3 Sinek, p.37.

4 Sinek, p.38.

5 Sinek, p.38.

6 Sinek, p.40.

7 Sinek, p.41.

Chapter 3:
Innovation strategies for culture change

Developing a strategy

One of the easiest mistakes to make upon taking up a role leading innovation in a law firm or a legal department is to omit the step of creating a strategy. Having a strategy in place is important for a variety of reasons:

- A strategy provides a path forward, allowing you to focus efforts around strategic drivers that are – ideally – also connected to the broader strategic goals of the organization.

- Your strategy will help you prioritize projects and develop mechanisms and focal points for managing a portfolio of resources and tools, growing and managing a team, and identifying the right methodologies to execute on strategic drivers.

- It enables you to justify the work your team is doing to senior leadership in a tangible manner.

- Equally important, it enables you to clarify for senior leadership the reasons why you are *not* undertaking certain work.

- It provides a yardstick against which to measure progress, and enables you to identify the metrics that will be worth tracking as your team develops and initiatives are launched.

- Your strategy, if it's a good one, will serve multiple purposes – it might be an innovation strategy but also serve as an adoption strategy, a culture change strategy, or a change management and communications strategy.

Just as upon starting a new job you will take time to learn about the politics and culture of an organization before beginning to implement initiatives or change the status quo, so you should spend the energy necessary to understand the overall strategic vision of an organization, the relative position of your department in relation to others, and your mandate along with that of your team before setting down a strategy. A strategy that is not context-specific will not serve you or your organization well. The strategies and approaches outlined in this book should be taken and adopted to fit the values, vision, and goals of your organization, and tweaked to take into account the power and influence structures of your firm in a way that will optimize their effectiveness in your specific environment.

Sample strategies

Since strategies are innately context-specific and thus not frequently publicized outside of a particular environment, and because many innovation professionals jump right in to developing lists of initiatives and priorities without first considering an over-arching strategy, there are not many publicly available sample strategies geared specifically towards legal innovation.

In this chapter, I will outline some of the methods and approaches that other industry leaders have developed and made known. I will also share the strategy that I have developed, which I have seen working and that I believe can be adopted and customized to work effectively in essentially any legal environment where culture change is part of the mandate of innovation professionals.

The 3-4-5 Method of Innovation for lawyers

One of the best-known strategies for legal innovation was developed by Michele DeStefano and outlined in her excellent book *Legal Upheaval*.[1] Generally speaking, this is not a strategy I would recommend for most law firm innovation teams, for reasons I outline below. However, it's worth understanding the methodology because elements of DeStefano's approach can be taken and used as part of any effective innovation strategy.

DeStefano outlines many of the problems facing the legal profession today, including the traditional, kneejerk way that many lawyers persist in delivering client services, and the fact that most of today's lawyers have not learned the skills they need in order to serve clients in the way that is now expected. After speaking to GCs across many industries, and to innovation professionals in AmLaw 200 firms, DeStefano concludes that the current educational framework in legal is not adequate in preparing new lawyers to respond to client expectations and deliver the highest quality legal services. She sets out a "Lawyer Skills Delta" (see Figure 4) that details the skills she argues are now required to provide the full, strategic experience that clients want. In this model, the core skills that have traditionally been assumed to prepare lawyers for practice – what DeStefano calls "Lawyering and Legal Expertise" – make up only the very base of the four-level pyramid forming the Lawyer Skills Delta. The provision of this base level expertise, DeStefano argues, in the absence of additional skills, is no longer sufficient to make clients happy. Legal expertise is the necessary baseline of lawyering, but in order to deliver the strategic services clients now demand, or to go the extra mile and actively delight clients, additional skills are required. These skills include C.O.S.T. proficiency (concrete, organizational, service, technology), whereby a lawyer becomes familiar with project management, technology, leadership, and has knowledge of the industry, of the client's industry or market, as well as business and marketing acumen.[2] They also include collaborative problem-solving skills (empathy, humility, cultural competency, a growth mindset) at level three of the pyramid, and innovation skills (including a focus on client centricity and service delivery) at the peak of the pyramid, or level four.[3]

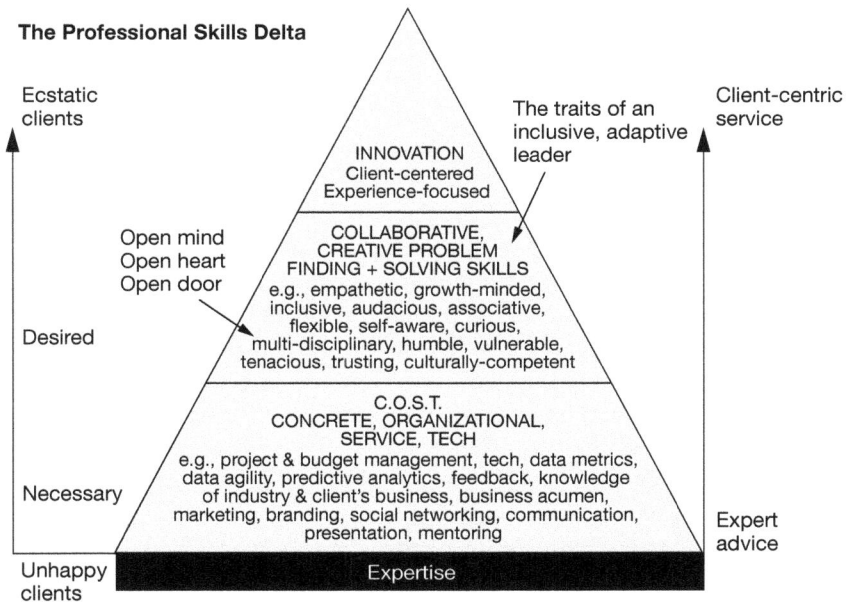

The Professional Skills Delta

Ecstatic clients — Client-centric service

The traits of an inclusive, adaptive leader

INNOVATION
Client-centered
Experience-focused

Open mind
Open heart
Open door

COLLABORATIVE,
CREATIVE PROBLEM
FINDING + SOLVING SKILLS
e.g., empathetic, growth-minded,
inclusive, audacious, associative,
flexible, self-aware, curious,
multi-disciplinary, humble, vulnerable,
tenacious, trusting, culturally-competent

Desired

C.O.S.T.
CONCRETE, ORGANIZATIONAL,
SERVICE, TECH
e.g., project & budget management, tech, data metrics,
data agility, predictive analytics, feedback, knowledge
of industry & client's business, business acumen,
marketing, branding, social networking, communication,
presentation, mentoring

Necessary — Expert advice

Unhappy clients — Expertise

Figure 4: DeStefano's Lawyer Skills Delta.[4]

DeStefano outlines in her book many of the reasons why there is such a gap between client expectations and the skills that lawyers develop, either through the legal educational system or through practice. She then offers a method that she has developed to help generate an innovation mindset and build the skills she says are frequently missing from the Delta. DeStefano calls this method the 3-4-5 Method of Innovation for Lawyers (see Figure 5), and it is an approach she has tweaked and perfected over the many years of her Law Without Walls (LWOW) program, run out of the University of Miami. LWOW is an experiential course in which law students from all over the world are able to enrol. Over the course of a semester, participants are allocated to teams comprising a mix of three to four students, mentors from the legal and business world, sponsors who might be law firm or in-house counsel, and one LWOW alumni adviser who is deeply familiar with the process from previous experience and can help keep the team on track. These diverse teams, with varying levels of experience and varied backgrounds, come together over a period of several months to solve a real-world legal problem that is assigned either by DeStefano herself, or by one of the sponsor organizations. Essentially, the course serves as an innovation sprint that follows the 3-4-5 Method and teaches students – as well as other participants – the skills that DeStefano has identified as essential in the new legal market.[5]

The 3-4-5 Method is divided into three phases over four months and involves five iterative steps (hence 3-4-5).[6] In addition to building the Lawyer Delta skills, the 3-4-5 method is also designed to foster a climate and culture for innovation, not just within one organization, but across verticals in legal. Within an organization, DeStefano says the method has the power to connect people across teams, deepen relationships with clients (assuming both law firm and client-side people become involved) and genuinely solve problems. In the first phase of the methodology, the KickOff signals the beginning of the project and gets each group thinking as a team, introduces the problem statement, sets the tone for the project, provides tools and sets expectations for what is to come. In phase two, the project develops, the team deeply explores the problem, and conducts interviews to understand end user needs. Phase 2 is also characterized during the LWOW course by regular webinars and team meetings that help to introduce new skills to participants as and when they need them. As the teams move towards brainstorming and developing a solution to the problem, they also receive coaching through which they refine the solution and develop a pitch for their "Project of Worth". The final phase of the project is represented by the Conposium, during which each team pitches the solution to their problem, along with a business case.

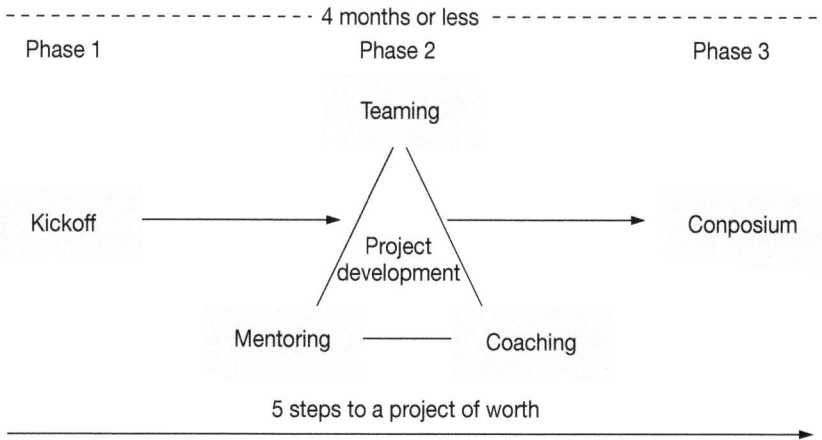

Figure 5: The 3-4-5 Method for Legal Innovation.[7]

Although DeStefano developed the 3-4-5 Method for, and continues to practice it through, the LWOW course and related events, her book suggests that law firms and other organizations can use this framework internally to build the missing Delta skills, enhance team collaboration, and solve problems. I have acted as a mentor in LWOW since 2019, and sponsored a team in 2021, including proposing the problem to be solved by that team. I feel privileged and honoured to be a part of the LWOW family, which now constitutes an extraordinary network of diverse legal professionals across six continents of the globe. I have watched students develop and grow through their involvement in the course and have seen with my own eyes that the 3-4-5 Method really does work to build new skills and get young lawyers and law students thinking in novel ways. Many of the students who take the LWOW course as part of their education go on to pursue interesting careers in law, somewhere between straight legal practice, the business of law, and legal technology. I highly recommend that those of you reading this who have not yet heard of LWOW get involved and encourage your organizations to sponsor a team.

When I think of the 3-4-5 Method in the context of legal practice, however, it's hard to imagine scaling it. Any commercial legal environment is subject to constraints that cannot be easily accommodated in a 3-4-5 format. The 3-4-5 Method requires many months of dedicated time from lawyers, and few commercial legal environments are set up to allow for this prolonged dedication to a non-billable effort. As most readers of this book will know, lawyers in practice are Busy, with a capital B. I remember a director in IT once asking me whether four clicks was really too many for a lawyer to get where they needed to go on one of our internal systems. My response? Of course. (I would argue four clicks is too many for almost anyone to get where they need to on an essential system, but that is particularly true for people who are under constant pressure to bill hours.) The level of pressure that practising lawyers are under – in both private practice and in-house – means that taking four months out from practice to undertake the ideation and prototyping phase of any project is virtually impossible. Legal work must be turned around much faster than that, and under timelines that are controlled by external forces – clients, opposing counsel, courts. And business-of-law projects that are conducted in real world legal environments are almost always spread across multiple departments, with varied stakeholders and pressure from many sides. In a real business environment, the 3-4-5 Method is therefore unlikely to find a place unless innovation is so well established that leadership will accept the effective part-time secondment of personnel to an innovation workshop that will last several months. If your senior leadership supports that kind of commitment from practising lawyers, you may have little need for a book about culture change!

The 3-4-5 Method should not be discounted as a viable – and proven – model for teaching lawyers or prospective lawyers how to think creatively. It is best showcased, however, and most effective, outside of the context of the commercial practice of law. The 3-4-5 method is also an ideal addendum to law school education for students who want to understand the benefits of practising smarter and innovating the practice of law. As a method of culture change and skilling up in a legal organization, there are aspects of the 3-4-5 Method that might work – but in most instances they would have to be abbreviated. I could envisage, for example, a mini 3-4-5 project that takes place over the course of a summer associateship program, or that forms part of a trainee program in UK law firms for first year associates. Bringing clients and partners into the program would be of particular value, but it would be tangential to legal work, forming part of the professional development of junior lawyers. The notion of teaching or skilling up legal professionals during the course of a project, as set out in phase 2 of the 3-4-5 approach is also appealing. It's easy to see how potentially effective it could be to take this element of DeStefano's methodology and apply it by introducing relevant innovation-related educational sessions for lawyers in the context of their practice or over the course of a particular deal.

The utility of the 3-4-5 Method as an approach stems from the fact that it can be broken down into parts and applied as part of another strategy. In this way, it is similar to some of the other methodologies outlined later in this book – design thinking, for example, and hackathons (although these also have other attributes that can be used more broadly, as discussed in chapter 11). It's a way of teaching a philosophy of problem-solving to lawyers and helping them to learn new skills. As an overarching strategy for culture change in a legal organization, however, it is unlikely to work. Any such strategy has to have the capability of making an impact at scale, across the whole organization, while the organization continues to operate its core business.

Strategizing for culture change

Often, firms will decide on a practical innovation strategy first, setting out:

- The technologies with which they wish to gain traction;
- The pilots they will run over the next few years; and
- In which areas of the firm will they focus their efforts.

Any conscious strategies around adoption are usually secondary to these tactical goals, acting as addenda (almost an after-thought), individualized and re-developed as necessary for each project or pilot launch.

Unfortunately, putting adoption second doesn't work. Nor does the assumption that culture change will simply happen as a result of your tactical innovation strategy and your team's iterative implementation of practice technology projects. A sample innovation strategy of the traditional kind might be:

"We will focus our efforts on getting traction with AI, and accordingly we will run pilots with X and Y tools this year, and as A practice is under particular pressure and B is having realization problems, we will make addressing pain-points in those practices a priority."

Although some strategic decisions have been made here – the decision to focus on AI, for example, and the decision to concentrate on certain practices – this statement is more tactical than it is strategic. It's effectively a business plan, setting out what your team will do rather than describing how your team will achieve it, or how you will achieve the culture change in your organization that will be necessary in order to get lawyers in the A and B practices on board with your team's efforts. Moreover, it's limited in scope. Focusing on certain practices absolutely makes sense – but if your team's efforts are limited in this way, you run the risk that most lawyers across the firm will remain ignorant of what is happening in terms of innovation and change – not just in your firm, but in the legal market at large.

Focusing in on tactical initiatives also means that your team is not tasked to think more broadly about how they can achieve the greatest internal impact and drive change, or why they are doing this. Instead, they are merely focused on execution. The way this type of strategy is drafted means that:

Success = roll-out and implementation

As all of us working in innovation know, however, rolling something out – a new process or a new technology, for example – makes no difference at all unless your lawyers and timekeepers use it. Success should not be defined as implementation or roll-out. If your innovation team gets to the end of the year and they have run the pilots that were planned, implemented the technology you wanted to roll out, and mapped out a more efficient workflow in a practice group that was under pressure – great. If none of the lawyers are using that new workflow, though, and the new technology is not being broadly adopted, then I'm afraid your team has not been successful. And yet, they may have hit all of the targets outlined in your innovation strategy. Approaching innovation in this way, setting annual targets and calling it a strategy, means that your team will almost inevitably be involved in "innovation theatre". You can show your firm's leadership that you are kicking goals, you can tell the industry that you are "doing" things – but the impact you are having internally across your lawyer population will remain minimal.

Instituting instead an overarching strategy that puts the team's focus squarely on adoption, culture change, and the way that work is executed, means that success will always have a different, more impactful definition. The specific initiatives you wish to execute upon should still be itemized, and will fall under this strategy, as the tactical manoeuvres through which you seek, annually, to advance your broad culture change strategy. At the end of a year, when you look at what has been achieved, it won't matter as much if one of your pilots failed, or if you ended up unexpectedly solving pain-points for a different practice than planned because lawyers in that practice reached out needing more help than anticipated. What you and your team will instead be evaluating is: Did we push the needle on change? How many people reached out to us, how many people are using the new processes/tools we put in place? It means that your team will deeply understand that:

Success = Adoption

The Three Es is an example of such a strategy. It will help you focus your team's efforts in the right place, setting the stage for broad, systemic change in your organization.

The Three Es

Over my years working in the industry, I have developed a strategy that is simple and flexible, and proven to work at scale in high-paced commercial settings. It has the power to genuinely change organizational culture and to help innovation teams move initiatives forward. I call it the "Three Es", (see Figure 6) and it works both as a strategy for culture change and for driving adoption. Unlike other innovation strategies, it does not outline the specific actions or initiatives to be taken by the innovation team. Instead, it operates as an overarching philosophy that will shape the way each of those initiatives are run. It turns the traditional strategic structure on its head.

The Three Es stand for Education, Engagement, and Execution. Each phase of the strategy is ongoing and continuous. The impact of every cycle is amplified with each revolution, and because every project that runs under the high-level strategy kicks off another cycle of the Three Es, they form concentric cycles that gradually grow in power and effectiveness. The cycles can and should be driven through different delivery mechanisms at your organization, which will operate simultaneously and iteratively. The innovation cycles will overlap, with the effect of driving forward an openness to innovation on many levels across the firm. Deceptively simple, this is a strategy that you can therefore apply broadly, but also to each individual project you run in your organization.

Education

Education builds a sense of urgency to persuade people that change is necessary.

Engagement takes this a step further and helps build a coalition of people in support of change, who are supportive because they are part of the initiative.

Engagement

Execution creates small or quick wins that build on momentum.

These forces work together as iterative cycles that are amplified each time they revolve.

Execution

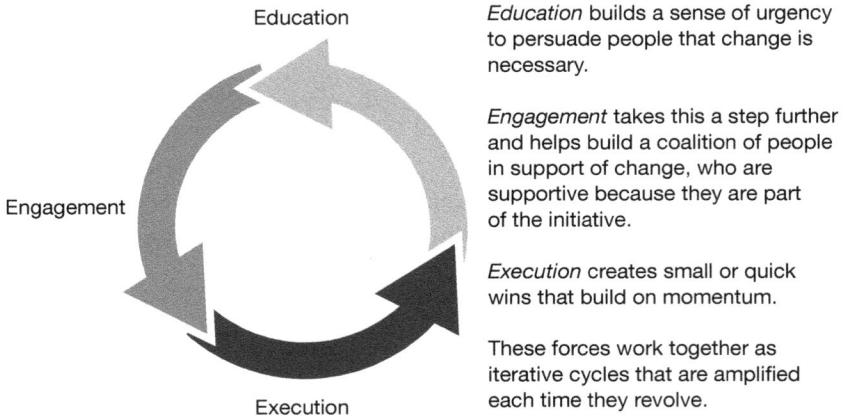

Figure 6: The Three Es Strategy for Legal Innovation.

Education

Education is the critical first step to the Three Es method. No one will be compelled to change or adopt new ways of working unless they understand the need to do so. In change management terms, the educational component of this strategy might be analogous to establishing an awareness of a "burning platform", a reason to change the status quo – except that rather than instilling fear, it:

- Explains to the lawyers and other timekeepers in your organization why they should be motivated to try new ways of doing things;
- Contextualizes the work that your team is doing within a broader narrative of change in the industry;
- Provides them with information about ongoing innovation initiatives and lets them know how they can get involved; and
- Conveys success stories that build credibility, instill pride in the lawyers who were involved in the successful projects, and drive adoption of those initiatives.

Since you are reading this book, it will seem obvious to you that the legal industry is undergoing change and that lawyers will need new skills as that change occurs. For most working lawyers, however, their lives likely look and feel the same way they always have. They communicate with their clients, take on legal work, and then strive to get it done – sometimes in teams, but most often by sitting in a room alone and pushing through one task after another. They bill their time and think about where new work will come from. Although we might know that email was once considered a radical way of communicating, and that eDiscovery represents the successful entrenchment of serious change to a once-manual process, lawyers conducting their daily work regard these as par-for-the-course, the usual mechanisms by which they get their work done. This nonchalance represents a success – it means the new processes and technologies that were once innovative are now part of the status quo, which is exactly how change is supposed to happen.

The reality is that if lawyers don't feel there is a reason to change the way they work, they simply won't do so. If you are working in a jurisdiction with a large, sound legal market, partners in top tier law firms are likely taking home millions of dollars each year. Although clients may be expressing their desire for change, they are not (yet) walking away *en masse* from firms that don't hear that message. Either that, or the vague responses often provided in answer to questions on RFPs around technology use and innovation are hitting the right note and persuading clients that firms really are undergoing transformative change. Most of them, however, are not.

Without clients walking away, in a market where annual rate increases are accepted with little push-back and associates can still be charged out at close to a thousand dollars an hour, where brand new associates with no experience are paid over $200K in their first year, and work continues to be billed predominantly by the hour – why should lawyers feel any immediate need to change the way they work? The motivation for change is low, and understandably so. None of us should feel surprised that there is resistance to change. The fundamental business model of law is still working for many firms, and the vast majority of lawyers see no immediate need to alter it.

This means that part of our job as innovation professionals is to educate lawyers about both the external and internal forces in the industry that make change necessary – not at some point in the future, but right now. Most innovation professionals and law firms dramatically underestimate the importance of education and training in altering the culture of a firm and gaining traction with innovation initiatives. We train timekeepers on individual tools, we educate people as we release new technology – but we don't think enough about the context or framework in which we provide that narrow training. For years there has been an assumption that openness to innovation is somehow related to age – that the most senior partners are naturally the most resistant to change, and that junior associates entering the profession will be on board with change because they've been using technology in their personal lives almost since birth. In my experience, neither of these assumptions is true. Age may be somewhat influential, but there are senior partners who absolutely understand the value of innovation, just as there are young partners who adhere rigidly to the way things have always been done. As for incoming associates – unless they have learned at law school about the changing nature of legal practice, they will walk in the door with the same expectations as every previous class of associates. In fact, the ubiquity of technology in their personal lives can have a stultifying effect on their interest and ability to pick up new tools in the workplace – they are used to innate, intuitive technology like iPhones and Apple watches that require zero adjustment time. Legal technology is unfortunately not as advanced and almost always requires some training before it can be used within practice. This barrier to entry may ironically prove to be more daunting to young lawyers than to older practitioners.

If your innovation function is going to have an impact, you need to get your lawyers on board with change at a broader, institutional level before you even begin to introduce new tools and processes. Then, when you later introduce narrower training programs to launch your initiatives, they will occur within the context of an overarching narrative that your practitioners understand. This makes it far more likely that the individual launches will be successful and your set of tools will be adopted.

In order to develop the first prong of your strategy, therefore, think about what ongoing, broad educational mechanisms you can put into place that will have the greatest impact in your environment. Consider:

- The variety of timekeeper personas that you have at your organization and whether you will need different programming for each of them.

- What tools you have available in your organization that your team could use in order to carry out this programming. I encourage you to use multiple types of delivery mechanisms, so that your lawyers are exposed to this messaging in different ways (not just in writing, but also through in-person or virtual sessions, learning apps, workshops, social media posts, and so on).

- What resources you have available to develop the programming. If you don't have the expertise on your team to develop a curriculum and programming that puts your innovation initiatives in the context of industry change, and keeps your lawyers updated on developments in the market, consider outsourcing some of this work.

In addition to your strategic approach to broader educational initiatives, you may also want to set out in your strategy the approaches your team will use for more focused educational or training initiatives as they become necessary. You don't need to set out the specifics of your educational planning in your strategy document but having a sense of the major programming mechanisms you will undertake over the next three to five years will help to inform the rest of your strategic vision. These should be tied, where possible, to the values and broader roadmap for your organization, and must make sense for the way that your organization operates.

As far as impact is concerned, once you have kicked off your educational programming, you should start to see results relatively quickly. At Paul Hastings, when we instituted a firm-wide newsletter outlining market changes that were affecting our clients and pointing out our ongoing initiatives at the firm that addressed these changes or reflected trends in the industry, we immediately received feedback from lawyers – not just once, but every time we sent it. A regular consequence of any of our educational sessions was lawyers reaching out to us and asking to participate in pilots or to be notified about new technologies. This dramatically changed the scale at which we were able to operate – rather than constantly going to lawyers and asking them to use our tools, we now also had lawyers coming to us and requesting to use them. In short – our educational programming was highly effective.

Examples of broad educational programming

- Firm-wide innovation newsletter:
  - In developing a newsletter that goes out broadly, think about the tone, and why the content would matter to the recipients.
  - Consider sending out different newsletters to different persona groups, so that you can tailor the "what's in it for me" messaging accordingly.
  - Consider covering not just industry trends but what your organization's competitors are doing by way of innovation – there is no more surefire way of getting a partner to read a newsletter than highlighting the successes of their competitors.
  - If there are trends that are relevant to both the practice of law and the business of law, these are worth highlighting. For example, every time a new state adopts the ABA's "Tech Competence"

amendment to Model Rule 1.1, we published it. This served the dual purpose of informing lawyers about changes to the legal Rules of Professional Conduct, and also impressed upon our lawyers that they had an obligation to be familiar with legal technology.

○ Choose key pilots and initiatives and showcase them in your newsletter – even better if these align with what competitors are doing, or the market trends you have also highlighted.

○ Note that while I have called this a "newsletter", it could be a regular post on an internal networking app, or a podcast. Use the format that will work best in your environment.

- Summer/fall associates program:

  ○ Get your professional development team on board with educational programming for incoming associates on the business of law, and include topics on legal innovation and the use of technology in practice.

  ○ This type of program is an ideal opportunity to use experiential learning. Provide access to no-code or chatbot technology, and run a hackathon or design thinking session while associates are fresh and eager to learn.

  ○ Make sure all sessions in the program are geared towards what will matter to the associates in practice – they will stay focused if you are telling them how their own careers are likely to be affected by market change.

  ○ If you can stagger the program, make the second phase (for fall associates/articling students/trainees) more practical, providing hands-on training related to actual tools the associates will have access to as they practice.

- CLE series with client legal ops:

  ○ In any educational programming, using client voices is highly effective.

  ○ Consider a panel or an ongoing series where legal operations or compliance personnel from key clients talk about initiatives on their side of the relationship. Law firm practitioners don't necessarily know about legal operations or connect the dots on the fact that this team on the client side is in many ways the equivalent of an innovation team on the law firm side.

o Have clients highlight the ways in which new things now matter to them in panel selection, get them talking about innovation or process improvement processes they are running in-house – the idea is to generate lightbulb moments for your lawyers, getting them to realize that they need to keep up with their clients in these respects.

o Pull in stakeholders across the organization by pointing out that this type of series will give lawyers insight into alternative career paths at client organizations.

o If you are on the client side, reach out and ask your law firms to come and showcase their innovation efforts, and find ways you can collaborate for value-added services.

• How to speak to your clients about…

o Partners and mid- to senior-level associates who interface with clients regularly rarely know how to speak to them about legal technology or legal innovation. Make it easy for them to do so by providing easily digestible resources that they can grab as and when they need them. Topics can include, for example, What is AI? How is it being used in law?

o Develop one-pagers on the technology tools that are available to lawyers. Distribute these regularly and make them centrally accessible so that it's easy to pick up succinct reference materials that explain through an "elevator pitch" exactly what each tool does.

o Consider lifecycle graphics that show lawyers when they should be using which resource during their common matter workflows. Helping them understand where technology fits into their regular practice will help them pick up the tools they need at precisely the moment they need them.

Engagement
The best way to get lawyers to adopt new technology or processes is to involve them in developing, configuring, and implementing those solutions. Their involvement in the ideation or execution of a new tool or process will make them feel a degree of ownership, which generally means they will be motivated not only to use the new solution but also to help you spread the word about it. One of the key aspects of your high-level strategy should therefore be a focus on engaging lawyers and other timekeepers in your innovation initiatives.

When thinking of your team's strategy over the next three to five years, consider how you can ensure that end user needs are the focal point of every project, and that your timekeepers are involved at every stage of those projects. We will delve deeper into adoption strategies in chapter 14, but it's important to note here that engagement really sits at the core of the adoption problem in legal organizations. Too often, for example, decisions are made about bringing on new technology in the absence of validation by the people for whom the investment is being made. You may believe that a new tool on the market is "cool", even ground-breaking, and you might assume that it will hold value for your lawyers – but without validating your hypothesis, you will be effectively gambling with your organization's resources if you license that tool. In his book on *Successful Innovation Outcomes in Law*, Dennis Kennedy quotes Professor Dan Linna from NorthWestern's Pritzker School of Law as saying that many innovation and process improvement techniques are just the scientific method in action.[8] Kennedy distils the steps of the scientific process down to observation, hypothesis, prediction, experiment, and conclusion.[9] It's interesting how closely these steps align with the processes involved in creative problem-solving techniques such as design thinking, which innovation teams are increasingly using in law firms.

I would argue that the proven best practices of software development are a better analogous framework for innovation techniques than the scientific method, but it's true that we start off with an observation and a hypothesis, and that without experimentation and validation, no conclusion can or should be reached about the viability of any solution to address a particular problem. Your assumptions, no matter how well informed, if they are made in the absence of speaking to end users, will not provide a solid foundation to move towards a solution. The fact that a shiny new tool is getting press in the market does not mean that it will appeal to your lawyers, fit into their workflow, or that it will be intuitive enough or integrate well enough into their core technology stack that they should take the time out of practice to learn how to use it. Deciding to invest in practice technology without engaging your lawyers in the decision-making process is a sure-fire way to end up with a graveyard of unused tools within your organization – and to promptly reduce your team's credibility.

Errors around engagement are also frequently made during the development of proprietary solutions. Teams supporting lawyers often feel that they should wait to show end users what is in development until it is essentially finished. There is a fear that if something isn't perfect, timekeepers will be put off and won't use it. Certainly it's true that if you launch a platform to end users that is not ready for use or has been poorly designed, you may never get your lawyers using it. However, that's different from sharing a platform that is in development with end users in order to get continuous feedback. In service design, as in agile methodology, the rule of thumb is to "share early, share often".[10] Rather than holding off until development is complete to show end users, service designers advocate involving end users in all phases of development. This iterative development ensures that every time the solution is tweaked or refined, it becomes even more responsive to user needs. This ongoing engagement by end users also means that the end solution won't come as a surprise, but will instead represent an expected, anticipated result of collaborative effort.

As you set down your strategy, think about how you will ensure that your team keeps end users engaged. How will you identify use cases and understand your user needs? How will your team go about involving end users in the various phases of projects? What processes can you put in place to encourage that engagement? If you don't already have best practices around engagement, consider whether it would be beneficial to work with your team to develop these. Involving your team in a brainstorming session and setting down ideas for additional engagement opportunities is a great way to collaborate across your function. Developing a list of substantial methods for engaging the lawyers in your organization will help to maintain momentum on innovation initiatives and can add an element of gamification. Some of these methods will be outlined over the course of this book, and might include running a series of design workshops, developing an ideas or innovation challenge, or launching a hackathon to motivate associates to propose their own innovation ideas.

Another consideration (that will likely require executive support) is whether there are incentives you can – and should – put in place in your organization to ensure that lawyers spend the requisite time on projects that will allow your team to execute them. Billable hours credit is one such incentive. Other examples include baking a concrete requirement to contribute to innovation efforts into the performance review cycle for associates or providing internal "certifications" for hitting innovation milestones. The more institutional structures you can put in place to support this type of engagement, the more successful your team is likely to be, and the more enthusiastic and active your lawyers will be as they participate in your initiatives.

Sample engagement best practices:

- Involve end users in ideation exercises. For example, run a series of design thinking workshops focusing on specific problems or pain-points that have been raised.

- "Listen" to end users before moving to develop or buy any solution, to understand better what their needs are in relation to the problem that has been identified, and to let them know that they have been heard.

- Involve end users during demos of new practice technology tools so that they have a say in which product is preferred.

- Wherever possible, run a pilot or a POC with new practice technology before implementation, to validate with end users that the solution does indeed address their needs. A pilot is not a pilot if it doesn't involve the end users (your lawyers).

- When configuring or developing a solution, share early and share often with end users, and use their feedback to tweak the product before release.

- Develop institutionalized incentives to promote timekeeper engagement in innovation projects.

- Engage end users in change management and communication efforts – use the lawyers and other timekeepers who were involved in project development to promote it to other timekeepers when it is launched.

Execution

No matter how grand the idea is, an innovative concept cannot have any impact until it is actually executed. In lay person's terms, the execution stage of an innovation strategy is the point at which you are "Getting S*** Done" (GSD). It might seem strange to plan for GSD, but it's important

– execution means different things in different contexts, and your team will need to have a roadmap for execution.

As discussed earlier, effective execution does not constitute simply completing the implementation of a technology platform or finishing the mapping of a process. To properly execute on an initiative, you need to:

- Roll it out successfully;
- Target and reach the right people with your communications;
- Develop and implement an effective change management plan;
- Architect and communicate any necessary information governance policies driven or affected by the roll out;
- Identify the right metrics with which to measure ongoing success;
- Create maintenance and renewal procedures where necessary;
- Lock the new way of doing things into existing systems; and
- Achieve adoption of the new workflow within legal practice.

Phew! That is a significant list of necessary precursors to effective execution, and it may not be exhaustive, depending on the context and size of your initiative. Many people underestimate the layered complexity involved in GSD. The difficulty inherent in executing successfully is why it's so important when you recruit people that you make sure you have not just ideas people and collaborators, but also people who have proven that they are able to GSD.

In order to strategize for successful execution, think about how you can make sure that your team has the necessary resources and expertise to deliver on key initiatives. You may need to provide for skilling up certain members of your team, make available change management and communications training, and plan for collaboration with stakeholders outside of your department who will help your team get things across the line.

The reason execution forms the third prong of the Three Es strategy is because it is almost impossible for any innovation team to gain credibility and buy-in for future projects unless they can first prove they are able to GSD. Planning for execution includes making sure that your three-to-five-year strategy takes into account the growth in resources and headcount you will need to execute on key initiatives. If you are setting up or leading a new team, you may also wish to set out a strategy that deliberately focuses first on smaller initiatives that nevertheless deliver value. Executing on some projects of the low-hanging-fruit variety will enable you to begin your next cycle of the Three Es by communicating these successes to relevant practices, and even across the organization. As you use your educational programming to circulate news of successfully executed projects, the impact these have will be magnified and news of your team's GSD successes will hit new pockets of the firm, opening up new opportunities. In this way, the Three Es build upon one another, gaining momentum and influence. This iterative, cyclical model is able to drive culture change and develop an openness for innovation across an organization faster than any other model or strategy I have seen.

Sample strategic plan

To build out a strategy that allows you to GSD as an innovation leader, lead with your vision, set out beneath it the key mechanisms through which you intend to achieve that vision, and outline annual projects beneath each of those mechanisms. As you move from strategy into business planning you will also need to allocate responsibilities in your team for each project, assess the resource lift necessary, and identify the relevant stakeholder groups who will need to be involved. Identifying upfront the resources necessary (both in your team and across the firm) to drive the selected projects forwards will help you determine whether your plan is realistic – do you have the resources necessary to execute on the initiatives you seek to undertake? Setting quarterly timelines for these projects will further enable you to plan. Business planning will be discussed in more detail in chapter six. Figure 7 shows what a sample strategy might look like at a high level.

Why? (Vision)	We seek to transform the practice and delivery of legal services to improve the quality and speed of client service		
How? (Mechanisms)	Education	Engagement	Execution
What? (Projects)	Initiatives	Initiatives	Initiatives
Who? (Resources)	Team lead Project manager Project team Stakeholders	Team lead Project manager Project team Stakeholders	Team lead Project manager Project team Stakeholders

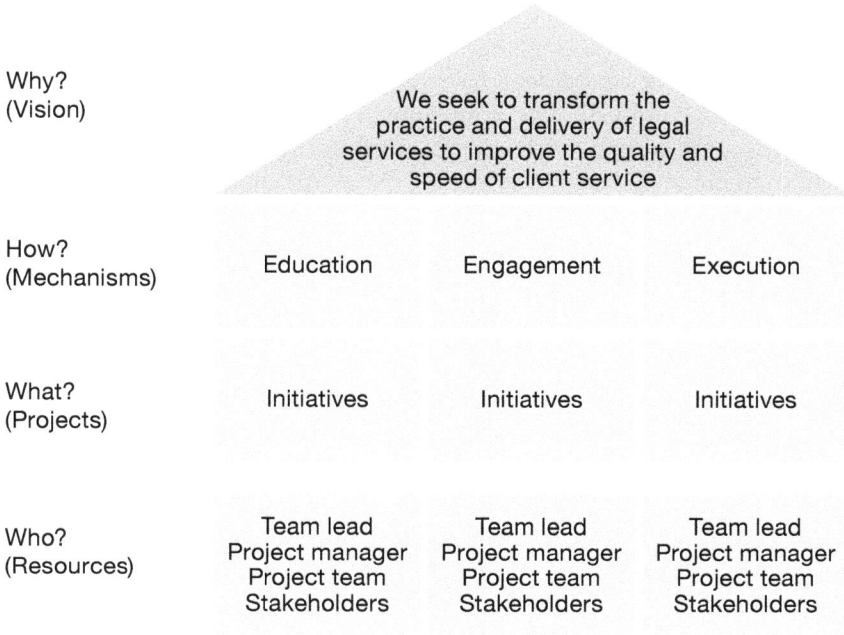

Figure 7: A sample strategy.

Checklist: Establishing a strategy

☐ Engage in the discussions and discovery work that allows you to understand the firm or organization's strategic goals and priorities.

☐ Consider what strategic approaches your team could take that would best align with the culture of your organization. In particular, consider:

- Are the lawyers in the firm already educated and knowledgeable about the need for change in the practice of law, or will you need to shift the cultural perception of the lawyers?

- How much buy-in and support do you have from firm leadership? Will you be able to build structural incentives into your program or will you need to develop support from the ground up first?

- What kinds of engagement and incentive programs currently exist, and how much leeway do you have to further develop these?

- Do you have the support to plan for advanced innovation efforts such as revenue-generating client-facing initiatives, broadscale digital transformation and the creation of a low-cost center, captive ALSP, or subsidiary?

- How much freedom have you been given within your role to develop new processes that exist outside of the traditional law firm business model – for example, will you be supported in charging out the work of business professionals, would you be empowered to create a system for opening client accounts in respect of legal adjacent work?

☐ For what timeframe are you developing a strategy? Are you looking towards the next year, the next three to five years, or the next ten years? (Have regard to the Three Horizons Theory, discussed in the next chapter.)

☐ Given your strategic goals, outlined as a result of the above discovery process, and in light of your overarching vision, how will you seek to execute on these?

☐ Record your strategy in a way that makes it clear to both firm leadership and your team that there are clear guidelines around the way that you will achieve success for the firm in carrying out your team's purpose.

☐ Seek formal approval for the strategy. This strategy will then become a tool you can go back to and rely upon when inevitable political tensions arise or when hurdles are established that make it difficult for your team to execute on its goals.

References

1 DeStefano, Michelle. *Legal Upheaval: A Guide to Creativity, Collaboration, and Innovation in Law.* Chicago, American Bar Association, 2018.

2 DeStefano, p.41.

3 DeStefano, p.43.

4 DeStefano, Michelle. *Legal Upheaval: A Guide to Creativity, Collaboration, and Innovation*, Ankerwycke Publishing, (2018) – updated version included herein at the permission of the author.

5 *Ibid.*

6 DeStefano, p.156.

7 Reprinted with permission from http://lawwithoutwalls.org/lwow-original.

8 Kennedy, Dennis. 2019. *Successful Innovation Outcomes in Law: A Practical Guide for Law Firms, Law Departments and Other Legal Organizations.* Printed by the author.

9 Kennedy, p.86.

10 Mottaz, Andrew, 2011. "Share Early, Share Often," Protoshare: http://community. protoshare.com/2011/08/share-early-and-often-collaborative-prototyping

Chapter 4:
Planning for the future

Simply put, innovation is growth. Efforts to innovate are almost always tied to the strategic goal of keeping a business moving forwards and, overwhelmingly, successful innovation also leads to economic growth.[1]

An essential consideration when developing a strategy and defining the core focus for your department or team is whether you are planning for what is considered innovative now, or what may be considered to be innovative (and competitive) in the future. Another is whether the innovation you intend to focus on is iterative and occurs within the existing business model of your organization, or whether it represents a break away from the existing business model into brand new territory. In response to both of these questions, the most innovative organizations will answer "both".

There are practical obstacles that might stand in the way of pursuing multiple streams of innovation at once, however. The budget and headcount necessary to address immediate projects may prevent you from running concurrent business plans. The strategic direction of the firm may not currently allow for the notion of "disruptive innovation". You may not be mandated with and may not yet have the influence or control necessary to pursue radical initiatives.

Nevertheless, timelines for growth and considerations around innovation types should be taken into account when you are business planning. The philosophies offered in this chapter should provide some direction and inspiration as you consider the timelines and various prongs of your innovation strategy.

Three Horizons theory

In 2000, Mahrdad Bahai, Stephen Covey, and David White released a book called *The Alchemy of Growth*,[2] which laid the foundations for the Three Horizons theory, a growth strategy later adopted and popularized by McKinsey & Company. The Three Horizons theory (see Figure 8) is useful framework for planning growth over time, positing that growth or innovation strategies should allow for initiatives the results of which will manifest in three different timeframes or "horizons". Rather than defining types of innovation, the Three Horizons theory focuses on the timing of when you might see the practical results from particular innovation projects.[3] Typically represented as a series of "S" curves, the Three Horizons model also posits that the most valuable and impactful growth is that which occurs the furthest out, presumably because the innovation efforts represented in horizons one and two build upon one another to enable the success of a horizon three effort (which would not be feasible immediately).

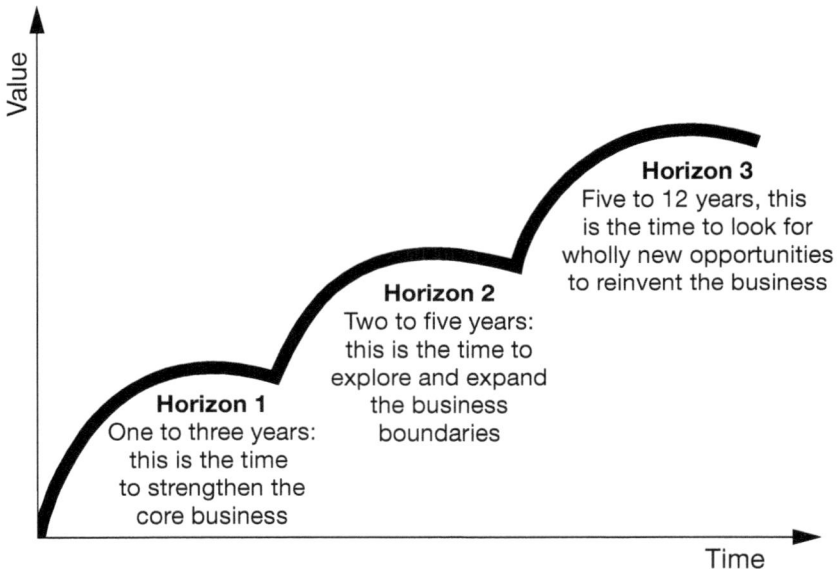

Figure 8: The Three Horizons theory.[4]

In this model, horizon one work constitutes shorter-term projects that will generate results in one to three years. This type of growth is usually represented by initiatives that are more closely linked to the current company's core business, and from which it is easiest to identify relatively immediate benefits.[5] The benefits of horizon one projects might be productivity or effectiveness, and could translate into increased profits, the minimization or eradication of obstacles to revenue generation within the existing business model, or improving the quality of output. The focus for horizon one initiatives is generally on improving performance of the current business in order to maximize its value. An example in the legal industry of a horizon one project might be the automation of suites of documents used in high-volume client work so that lawyers can draft more quickly, enabling the firm to price work differently and free up lawyer time to be spent on higher value tasks.

Horizon two initiatives, by contrast, focus on emerging opportunities. These projects are ones for which greater investment is necessary because they are related to newer ventures – still connected to the current business but representing a new direction.[6] Horizon two initiatives generally have the potential to generate substantial profits sometime in the future, usually between two to five years out, making it worthwhile to invest now in the resources necessary to build towards horizon two success.[7]

Some horizon two initiatives are inspired by advances that have been successful in adjacent markets, and are being applied for the first time in a new context or industry.[8] For example, some of these projects may involve adapting technology, processes, business models, or revenue streams to your industry because they have already worked well in other markets. Note that horizon two innovation still operates more or less within the existing business model; however, these initiatives are starting to push the boundaries of that business model. If a business model is defined by five primary domains – service, revenue, cost, operations, and performance – a horizon two initiative will change at least one of these.[9] This is an important point for innovation leaders; by planning horizon two initiatives you are leading the organization towards genuine business model transformation. An example of a horizon two initiative might be to offer entirely new services lines to client, such as practice innovation consulting, and generate an additional revenue stream as a result of these new services. The core business model is intact, but a fundamental change has occurred that puts the organization on a path to transformation. Although offering a new service line requires building and hiring new skillsets, dedicating both financial and human resources to an initiative that may not initially generate significant revenue, it's worth investing in these types of transformative projects because they:

- Are likely to become significantly more profitable over time;
- Are responsive to client demands;[10] and
- Strategically situate your organization as market leaders of the future.

Horizon three represents the growth period that is furthest down the road. While horizon one projects focus on improvement, and horizon two projects focus on transformation, horizon three projects are about disruption. These are typically longer-term, more radical innovation projects that might produce significant results in five to 12 years.[11] Seen another way, these projects set up an organization for an entirely new business model, so that as the market changes over time, they are prepared to remain competitive. Examples of horizon three approaches to innovation include product subsidiaries launched by law firms, especially those where the law firm itself has no practical control over the day-to-day running of the subsidiary and instead retains only an advisory role or an equity investment in the subsidiary. These entities are then free to adopt entirely new ways of operating, pricing work, and compensating staff.

There have been some recent criticisms of the Three Horizons model, with commentators suggesting that growth in current markets occurs so rapidly that the timeframes put forward in the original model are no longer useful.[12] Steve Blank, in an article for *Harvard Business Review*, comments that in the 21st century, disruptive horizon three projects can be delivered as quickly as horizon one initiatives within the existing business model. These critiques may hold weight in most industries, but in the legal industry change is often slow to take hold. It's also worth noting that horizon two and three initiatives carry more risk than horizon one projects. They will require different types of skills and even different management approaches than horizon one projects. Horizon three projects are likely to be entrepreneurial, and therefore require established organizations such as law firms to become comfortable with a much higher level of volatility than has been accepted before. For this reason, too, planning for all three horizons in your immediate business plan is critical – because getting the buy-in and political clout to begin to execute on horizon three initiatives may take more time than the execution itself.

Regardless of the specific time required to produce a significant result, the foundational wisdom behind the Three Horizons theory remains – in order to lead a successful enterprise-wide innovation initiative, organizations must be executing on incremental growth projects within the existing business model while simultaneously creating new capabilities and sowing the seeds for new business model growth. As you develop your project portfolio and the business plan for your department or team's next three to five to ten years of growth, it's critical to keep this in mind. Many of the projects and priorities you see as viable within the next year are likely to move the organization forward only incrementally.

In order to plan for growth that has the potential to be truly transformative, organizations including law firms should develop an innovation strategy that branches into two or even three timelines. It's therefore important that your portfolio include some projects that fall into each horizon in order to sustain and support ongoing growth in your organization.[13] If you focus your efforts and resources only on short-term, incremental innovation, you will fail to protect your organization in the long-term. If you concentrate instead on radical innovation without executing on shorter-term innovations that impact the organization now, you will increase the vulnerability of your organization to competition in the near- and medium-term.[14] Table 1 provides a summary of the characteristics of the three horizons. As we move in chapter five to explore the mechanisms that give rise to project opportunities, keep this figure in mind. It can be used as a guide when reviewing those initiatives to determine whether your portfolio has the right balance of projects to support short-, mid-, and long-term growth.

Table 1: Three Horizons model ways of thinking.[15]

Key properties/horizon	Horizon 1: execute & incrementally improve an existing business	Horizon 2: transform & make a step-change improvement to an existing business	Horizon 3: (radically) innovate a new business model
Where	Inside the box	Inside but going beyond	Outside the box
Purpose	Exploit: making the most of what we have	Pursuing new opportunities	Breaking new ground: develop new (and possibly disruptive) business
Business Model	Known. Executing the business model.	Partially understood. Testing/validating an iterated business model.	Unknown, business model not identified. In search of a business model.
Service-, revenue-, cost-, operating-, value- & performance model	Incremental	Step-change to at least one domain (with impact on all others!)	New/radical
Way of working	Execute; incremental, sustaining	Execute/Search; upgrading, substantial	Search; transformational or radical, disruptive
Strategic intent	Cost, profit	Growth	Innovation
Competencies	Operational	Change Management	Entrepreneurial
Critical tasks	Operations, efficiency, incremental innovation	New Product/Service Development, change management, organizational change	Adaptability, new products/services breakthrough innovation
Culture	Efficiency, low risks, error prevention	Opening-up, adaptability	Risk-taking, speed, flexibility, experimentation

Innovation ambitions

Often confused or used interchangeably with the Three Horizons theory is another framework called the Innovation Ambitions Matrix (IAM).[16] Essentially, the IAM maps the three horizons or three time periods of the Three Horizons theory against different types of innovations.

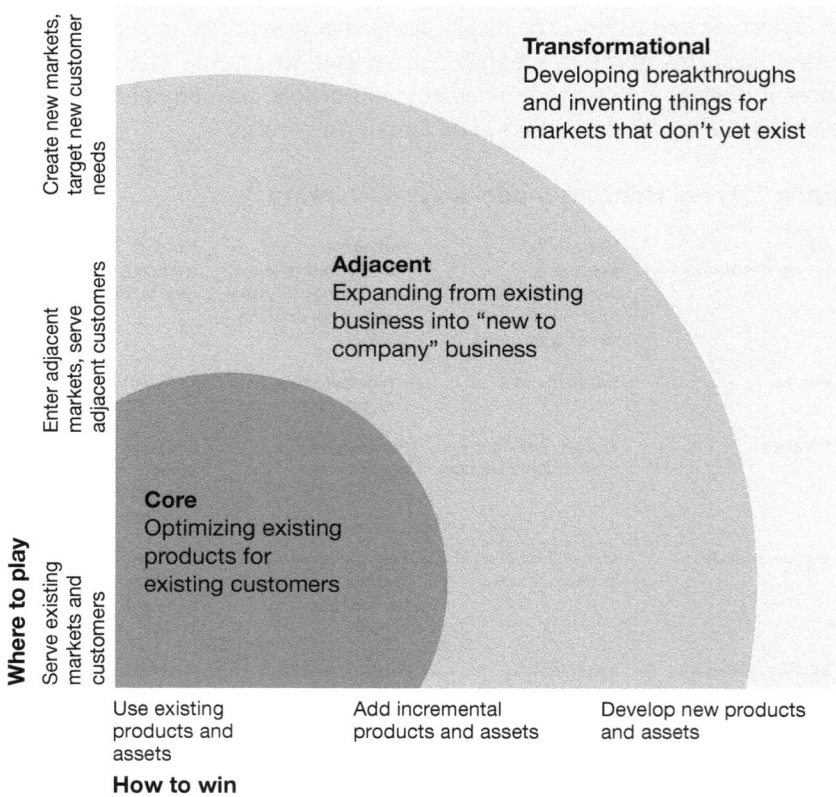

Transformational
Developing breakthroughs and inventing things for markets that don't yet exist

Adjacent
Expanding from existing business into "new to company" business

Core
Optimizing existing products for existing customers

Create new markets, target new customer needs

Enter adjacent markets, serve adjacent customers

Where to play
Serve existing markets and customers

Use existing products and assets

Add incremental products and assets

Develop new products and assets

How to win

Figure 9: Innovations Ambitions Matrix.[17]

Originally derived from a diagram created by mathematician H. Igor Ansoff, the IAM was developed into a tool for managing innovation by Bansi Nagji and Geoff Tuff in 2012 and later adopted and popularized by Deloitte.[18] The premise is similar to that discussed above with regard to the three horizons – that an organization's tactics with regard to innovation should vary depending on whether the organization is operating within its current market or targeting a new market. Figure 9 overlays three levels of distance from a company's current reality, in order to show that the originality of a company's offerings (displayed on the x axis) and of its customer markets (on the y axis) are or should be related to each other, and that they are a matter of degree.[19]

Looking at Figure 9, it's clear how this framework would intersect with the Three Horizons model, with Core IAM projects developing results in the horizon one timeframe, Adjacent projects developing results in the horizon two timeframe, and Transformational projects aligning with horizon three.

The IAM provides several key benefits to managers of innovation. First, it makes it easier to look at all of the initiatives or projects either underway or planned that are relevant to your mandate, and to categorize these. Second, it allows for an analysis of these projects by having regard to the driving ambition underlying each of them, which is more meaningful than simply referring to "innovation", which can mean many things. Defining innovation can be challenging, but the IAM provides a means to do so by referring to the intentions or goals of a growth program. If you are coming in new to an existing innovation team, reviewing initiatives in this light will give you a good sense of whether the organization's goals in relation to innovation have been skewed towards the lower left of the IAM – indicating that, in this organization, "innovation" has meant iterative improvement, or whether they have been skewed further to the right of the matrix, indicating an appetite for greater transformation.[20]

The Three Horizons theory and IAM are two ways of categorizing or thinking about the kinds of innovation efforts you want or should be planning for in relation to your organization, but they can also be used together to develop some clarity around resourcing and managing such projects. Since the IAM uses products and markets as the defining criteria rather than time periods, it provides additional guidance on where to find the relevant opportunities. For example, while horizon two is about emerging business, the equivalent adjacent innovation category in the IAM specifies that these projects involve leveraging existing capabilities to move into new markets or serve new customers.[21]

Using the two frameworks together provides a viable method for creating a strategic plan. With reference to both IAM and the Three Horizons theory, an innovation leader or indeed any leader mandated with managing growth in an organization can develop a ratio of products that represents the optimal return on investment for their organization in terms of revenue growth and competitive advantage in the relevant market.[22] This ratio can then be used as a yardstick to determine how far the organization is from its ideal portfolio, and a plan to close the gap can be developed. Table 2 provides a practical guide for reference during this exercise.

Table 2: Mapping Three Horizons to IAM.

Horizon	Innovation ambition	Impact	Timeframe
Horizon one	Operate within existing value proposition, CORE innovation	Existing market and clients	One to three years
Horizon two	ADJACENT innovation, transform value proposition	Adjacent markets and clients	Three to five years
Horizon three	Radically disrupt value proposition, TRANSFORMATIVE innovation	New markets and clients	Five to 12 years

Budgeting for future growth

As part of developing a strategic plan, innovation leaders will at some point have to negotiate a budget for innovation with senior management of the organization. In law firms and corporate legal departments, budget for innovation or legal operations might initially be considered minimal, with relevant technology investments falling under the IT or procurement budget. In large organizations, it's also standard for budgets to be set at the beginning of the financial year, in the expectation that each department or function of the organization will have an established plan for which projects are to be undertaken over the course of the year.

In practice, this kind of fixed annual budgeting is problematic for innovation teams. It is not just probable but expected that initiatives will come up during the course of the year that may carry some urgency or that for one reason or another become priorities for the business. Innovation is also fundamentally about experimentation, and any innovation budget must therefore make room for experiments, failures, and pivots. As innovation teams mature, most of them will develop some flexibility in their budgeting, setting aside amounts that are allocated to new (as-yet-unspecified) projects and resources. Holding conversations early on with senior leadership to explain how and why this kind of flexible budgeting and resourcing is necessary for an innovation effort to succeed will help you reach this kind of budgeting maturity earlier in your leadership journey.

The 70-20-10 Rule

Aside from annual budget planning, innovation leaders who are intent on supporting their organization's growth over all three horizons must also consider how to allocate resources across these types of initiatives. For most law firms and legal departments, the resources allocated for innovation of any kind are relatively scarce compared to resources dedicated to foundational technology, recruitment, office leases, and so on. As a manager leading innovation efforts and trying to guide an organization on a path towards growth that ensures it remains competitive both now and in the future, how should you plan to distribute your budget and headcount in order to support the variety of projects necessary to attain your goals? The 70-20-10 rule, which (similar to the Three Horizons theory) originated in Bahai, Covey, and White's book *The Alchemy of Growth*, and has been used effectively by organizations such as Google, provides a method to help with exactly this problem.[23]

The rule stipulates that organizations should put 70 percent of their resources into sustaining growth (aligned with horizon one or IAM core projects), 20 percent into adjacent growth (aligned with horizon two projects), and ten percent into transformational growth (aligned with horizon three projects). A study conducted in 2012 by Bagsi Nagji and Geoff Tuff concluded that companies that allocated their resources according to this rule significantly outperformed other companies, often by ten to 20 percent.[24] The effectiveness of this ratio has been proven repeatedly since then, with many major companies adopting it as the driving principle informing resource allocation.[25]

As you look at the resources your organization has dedicated to innovation, consider this rule. Sustaining innovations, or incremental improvements within the existing business model, may not seem as glamorous or impactful as more transforming initiatives – but they create the most amount of value for your organization now, in the immediate term, and should therefore be at the heart of any innovation plan.[26] Even highly innovative organizations like Apple and IBM similarly focus the majority of their resources on sustaining innovation.[27] However, as markets evolve, all businesses eventually decline or change. Automobile manufacturers that have not dedicated any resources to adjacent growth over the past 20 years will now be falling behind as their peers launch electric cars. Adjacent growth is critical for exploring markets and opportunities that are closely aligned with your organization's current business, but have the potential to expand and evolve that business to ensure it remains competitive as the industry changes.[28] Of course, these types of opportunities are riskier and the return on investment is less certain, so it doesn't make sense to devote the majority of resources here. Dedicating 20 percent of your budget to these initiatives will ensure your organization is planning for adjacent growth without betting the farm on it.

In certain markets, entire businesses or business types fail as new businesses evolve. This is particularly true of businesses focused on products rather than services, but the lifecycle of these businesses should serve as a warning even for those of us in professional service industries. No one is buying CD players anymore, for example, but imagine if Sony had dedicated ten percent of its innovation budget to disruptive initiatives and had founded Napster. Greg Satell, author of the book *Mapping Innovation*, says that his research shows that organizations that invest in "basic exploration" to find brand new paradigms almost all end up discovering something big.[29] Although there may be failures along the way, the loss of resources represented by those failures will pale in comparison to the pay-off generated by the discovery of a successful new paradigm. The only way to ensure that no such pay-off ensues is by failing to invest in disruptive innovation altogether. Nevertheless, Satell has found that it is this last ten percent of the budget that is most often neglected by innovation teams or by growth-focused organizations.[30]

What is most important when applying the 70-20-10 rule is not to do so scientifically or rigidly, but rather to use it as a rule of thumb that provides practical and strategic guidance when planning and allocating resources. Returning to the 70-20-10 rule periodically as your strategic plan unfolds will allow you to confirm that you are continuing to feed the pipeline of initiatives with the right kinds of projects to ensure you are leading your organization towards tangible growth.

Checklist: Planning for multi-horizon growth

☐ If you are new to your organization, review existing innovation projects using the Three Horizons Model and IAM to understand how the organization has previously approached or defined innovation.

☐ Generate buy-in: In your discussions with senior leadership and with your team or department, discuss the importance of multi-horizon growth and explain how you intend to plan for this.

☐ As you move towards generating a portfolio of initiatives, categorize these in line with the frameworks discussed in this chapter.

☐ Use the 70-20-10 rule to:

- Budget appropriately for the projects in your portfolio; and
- Ensure that your project pipeline is strategically balanced in line with your functional and organizational goals.

☐ If you have the wherewithal to plan for enterprise-wide allocation of resources along with other senior leadership, suggest that organization-wide resource allocation and portfolio planning be approached in a similar manner.

References

1 Forbes Insights: *Harnessing Innovation to Jumpstart Growth*. https://images.forbes.com/forbesinsights/StudyPDFs/BMOHarrisInnovation_report.pdf, p. 11.

2 Bahai, M., Covey, S. and White, D. (2000). *The Alchemy of Growth*. Boulder, CO: Perseus Books.

3 Board of Innovation. *What is the Three Horizons Model & How Can You Use It*. www.boardofinnovation.com/blog/what-is-the-3-horizons-model-how-can-you-use-it/

4 Cuofano, G. (2022). *What is the McKinsey Horizons Model and Why It Matters in Business*. https://fourweekmba.com/mckinsey-horizon-model/

5 McKinsey & Company. (2009). *Enduring Ideas: The Three Horizons of Growth*. McKinsey Quarterly, December 1, 2009. www.mckinsey.com/capabilities/strategy-and-corporate-finance/our-insights/enduring-ideas-the-three-horizons-of-growth

6 *Ibid.*

7 Board of Innovation.

8 *Ibid.*

9 Digital Leadership. *The Three Horizons of Growth Model: A Roadmap to Successful Innovation Strategy*. https://digitalleadership.com/unite-articles/three-horizons-of-growth/

10 In the Wolters Kluwer 2022 *Future Ready Lawyer Survey*, released in September 2022, 91 percent of 751 corporate clients surveyed considered it important that their panel law firms leveraged innovative technology for productivity and efficiency, and a high percentage felt it was important that their law firms be in a position to support them in selecting and implementing technology (e.g. by offering legal-adjacent services around practice innovation). www.wolterskluwer.com/en/news/new-future-ready-lawyer-survey-finds-increasing-pressures-on-legal-professionals

11 McKinsey & Company, 2009.

12 Blank, Steve. (2019). "McKinsey's Three Horizons Model Defined Innovation for Years. Here's Why It No Longer Applies." *Harvard Business Review*, 1 February 2019. https://hbr.org/2019/02/mckinseys-three-horizons-model-defined-innovation-for-years-heres-why-it-no-longer-applies

13 Acclaim Ideas. *What Are the Three Horizons of Innovation?* www.sopheon.com/products/acclaimideas/insights/three-horizons-of-innovation

14 *Ibid.*

15 Digital Leadership, (2021). The Three Horizons of Growth Model: A Roadmap to Successful Innovation Strategy. https://digitalleadership.com/unite-articles/three-horizons-of-growth/

16 www.ideatovalue.com/inno/nickskillicorn/2021/01/what-is-the-ambition-matrix-and-how-does-it-work-as-part-of-an-innovation-portfolio/

17 *Ibid.*

18 Nagji, B. and Tuff, G. (2012). "A Simple Tool You Need to Manage Innovation." *Harvard Business Review*, 9 September 2012.

19 *Ibid.*

20 Nagji and Tuff, 2012.

21 Acclaim Ideas: www.sopheon.com/products/acclaimideas/insights/three-horizons-or-innovation-ambition.

22 Nagji and Tuff, 2012.

23 Nagji and Tuff, 2012.

24 *Ibid.*

25 Satell, G. (2017). *This One Rule Will Seriously Up Your Company's Innovation Game: A Simple Principle for Managing Scare Resources.* Inc.com, www.inc.com/greg-satell/this-1-rule-can-seriously-up-your-innovation-game.html

26 *Ibid.*

27 *Ibid.*

28 *Ibid.*

29 Satell, 2017.

30 *Ibid.*

Chapter 5:
Building a portfolio of initiatives

It can be daunting to come into a legal organization, with all its many moving parts, and determine what needs to be done to move things forward. How should you decide what projects to undertake first, or identify which ones will have the most positive impact on the organization? These considerations are particularly challenging when you have a small team. The volume of requests coming your way might feel overwhelming, given the limited resources at your disposal. Alternatively, you might feel lost, unsure where to start, with few people approaching you with ideas or suggestions for projects.

Whether you are a newly appointed leader in an existing practice, have been promoted into a leadership position, or have been tasked with creating an innovation department where there was none previously, your first step will be to familiarize yourself with the firm's political structures and strategic objectives. As part of your recruitment or promotion into a leadership role, you likely had conversations with firm leadership about the roadmap and goals of the firm. Before leaping into any projects, you should dig deeper into those conversations to tease out key information about your environment that will inform part of your departmental strategy. You will need to know, for example:

- What are the core values of the firm or organization?
- What does the firm see as the most critical strategic goals for the organization over the next five years?
- Which practices are considered most important or most strategically connected to the firm's success?
- Where is the firm experiencing cost pressure, and which practices are underperforming?
- Who are the key rainmaker partners at the firm?
- Which offices are the most important to the firm's overall success?

- What firms or organizations make up your firm's "competitive set"? In other words, which other firms does leadership consider to be the core competitors for the same type of work for which clients come to your firm?

These conversations will take some time, and that's fine. As Michael D. Watkins writes in his book, *The First 90 Days*,[1] the most valuable thing you can do in your first few months of a new role is listen, learn, and begin to understand your new environment. Even if you've been at the firm for a number of years in a more junior role, it will behove you now to spend time learning about the goals of the firm. It's unlikely you will previously have had access or insight into that level of firm strategy in your previous role, so although you won't need to learn as much as someone new to the firm, there is still merit in pausing to absorb new information.

If you are new to the firm, you will need to do some additional exploration, for example by extending these initial conversations to include office and practice chairs. You will also need to spend time familiarising yourself with existing projects, technology systems, and the resources available to your team. As Watkins writes, "perhaps the biggest pitfall you face [when transitioning roles] is assuming that what has made you successful to this point will continue to do so".[2] The best thing you can do, according to Watkins, is to "climb the learning curve as fast as you can in your new organization [or role]".[3] One way to climb that learning curve and learn what you need to know quickly is by performing an audit early on in your leadership journey.

What is an audit?

A knowledge or innovation audit is effectively a detailed survey of your primary constituents, conducted in order to ascertain what infrastructure and process already exists in the areas for which you are responsible, and what shortfalls there are. It will give you a current state picture that allows you to perform gap and needs analyses and build out a project portfolio accordingly.

Conducting an audit will be valuable whether your team is called Knowledge Management (KM), Practice Innovation, or something else, and regardless of whether you are building from scratch or growing an existing function into something larger. KM audits and innovation audits will ask different questions, however, and will therefore uncover different gaps within the organization. They can be combined into one longer survey, and if you are leading both functions you will need to cover both areas to get a full current state picture. If you have an established function, an audit is still a useful tool and should not be retired once you have an initial list of priorities. In this chapter, I will discuss both the initial audit as well as examples of smaller scale surveying that can usefully be undertaken on a more regular basis.

By its nature, an audit is an organization-wide pulse-check. It's important, therefore, that it be conducted with the support of leadership, and with appropriate communications. In order to truly uncover current state in relation to KM and innovation, and generate an understanding of the most fruitful areas in which to focus new projects, an audit should be conducted across multiple persona groups at the firm – not just partners but also associates and paralegals. Ideally, you would combine a written survey with extensive interviews and conversations with key people. One-on-one conversations would be targeted towards office chairs, practice group leads, and key connectors at the firm or organization – for example, you may find that there is a senior paralegal who wields significant influence in a particular practice group. Having a longer conversation with that person will often be more productive than conversations with multiple junior associates.

For the written audit, it's important to make the questions as simple as possible to answer. Creating a Google form or a questionnaire in a tool like Survey Monkey and then distributing this widely with appropriate communications will yield best results. It may help to incentivize participation by having firm leadership send a communication first asking those surveyed to participate and letting them know it's part of strategic planning for the firm. Because the goal of an audit is to give you a good sense of what resources exist and how lawyers and adjacent personnel operate across all practices, you will need to generate a high response rate to get value out of it. Put in place a plan to follow up with people who have not responded and provide a deadline for responses.

Sample questions for an audit are set out below, both for KM and for innovation. This is by no means an exhaustive list (a real audit would be considerably longer), but instead is provided to help you get a better sense of what types of information can be surveyed through an audit. You will want to tweak these questions and add to them in order to adapt the exercise for your specific environment. Consider as well whether it may be useful to customize your questionnaire for certain practices, to get a more nuanced understanding of current state in areas of the firm where specialist tools and resources might be required. Finally, note that there are consultants in the market who can support you in developing and carrying out a full audit.

Sample knowledge audit questions

- On a scale of 1-10, how open is the firm to knowledge sharing across practices?
- Do you have access to internal precedents, checklists, and guides generated specifically for your practice group?
- Is there a central repository for storing content and knowledge such as precedents and guides? If so, how often do you use it?
- How do you find sample documents from past matters that you can use as the basis for new documents?
- Are there processes in place for collecting and organizing documents that can be re-used as precedents? If so, do you find those processes intuitive and do you regularly contribute documents for this purpose?
- Has your practice group developed a clause bank? If so, how is this organized and where is it maintained?
- Do you regularly record information about your matters so that the information is available to others?
- How do you find experts at the firm who can support your client on a niche matter?
- When pitching for new work, where do you go to locate information about past matters?

Sample innovation audit questions

- On a scale of 1-10, how open is firm culture to innovation, new technology, or working in new ways?
- Are you familiar with the concept of legal innovation and do you consider it to be important to your practice?
- Are you aware of and do you use any legal technology that specifically supports workflows in your practice?
- What repetitive tasks do you commonly perform?
- Are there areas of your practice where you undertake work manually that you feel could or should be done differently or better, for example through automation?
- Are clients able to log in to any platform that gives them access to financial information and progress on their legal matters with the firm?

- Are you aware of any technology initiatives in your practice that directly support clients or improve the way that you deliver client services?

- Have your clients ever expressed to you a desire to improve the ways they work, or to better track the way that the firm is providing its services to them?

Building a project portfolio

Once you have gathered responses to an audit, you will wish to collate these and determine what themes arise. As discussed, you will generally execute the audit after familiarizing yourself with the tools and resources that are available for lawyers in your firm. The responses to the audit should give you a good indication of whether these resources are deemed useful or sufficient, and whether lawyers are aware of the tools they have at their disposal. They should also help you determine where there may be a need for additional tools. The audit should highlight practice pain-points that might be addressed through future projects. From the responses, you should be able to isolate the following themes:

- Where there is a need for efforts that raise awareness of existing tools;

- Where there are needs for additional solutions; and

- Where there are practice pain-points or organizational problems that might be addressed by your team.

Translating these themes into a list of actual projects is a challenge that you can only address through in-person conversations and strategic discussions. Following through after conducting an audit will involve taking the themes you've uncovered and addressing them with the groups where those themes emerged. You will be seeking to validate the needs you have perceived through the audit and understand them better. This should give you a list of initiatives you can review against the strategic goals you know the firm has, in order to assess where the areas of greatest potential are for your team.

SWOT analysis

Another method for identifying opportunities in your firm or organization is conducting a SWOT analysis. SWOT stands for Strengths, Weaknesses, Opportunities, and Threats, and the methodology is widely used in other industries (less so in legal).[4]

A SWOT analysis is often depicted in a simple two-by-two grid with one dimension representing internal versus external factors, and the other representing positive versus negative impact (see Figure 10). Although a SWOT analysis can in theory be conducted in relation to an entire law firm or organization, the simple method of depicting strengths, weaknesses, opportunities, and threats makes it more effective when focused on a particular division, function, or area.[5]

Internal

Strengths
Where do we succeed, what do we do particularly well, what do we have the expertise for?

Weaknesses
Where do we fall behind, what don't we do well, where are we lacking expertise?

Positive

Negative

Opportunities
Where could our strengths give us a particular advantage?

Threats
What are we not prepared for, where are we vulnerable to competition?

External

Figure 10: SWOT analysis.

Rather than providing a method for uncovering information, the SWOT analysis is a way to categorize the information you have already discovered.

The means by which you conduct this analysis are fairly simple. For the purposes of strategic planning, you can use the information you have collected through performing an audit and holding interviews with key personnel at the organization. You can choose to perform it at the organization level or at the practice level. Assuming you approach it practice by practice, you would take the information you've gathered and consider:

- What are the strengths of this particular practice? What does this practice do better than its competitors? What are the areas in which it excels? Where is it already efficient and productive?

- What are the weaknesses of the practice? What are the pain-points for the lawyers? Where are there significant inefficiencies? What slows them down? Where is there confusion? Where is there needless repetition? Is the practice under cost pressure due to market changes?

- What are the opportunities for the practice? Are there obvious areas that would allow for automation? Is there particular information or content that could be turned into client-facing products? Is there a workflow or a particular element of practice that provides an opportunity to transform client service delivery?

- What are the threats to the practice? Do the lawyers in that practice feel the way they price their work makes it hard for them to win new business? Are they falling behind the competition in obvious ways? Have they received poor feedback from clients?

Once you have analysed the practice, you can use the information thus gained in various ways. For example, understanding the threats challenging this group will give you some ammunition when you encourage the lawyers in that practice to embrace new ways of doing things. The opportunities you've identified should give rise to project ideas that will have a real impact on the practice.

A SWOT analysis is a helpful tool to use when trying to gain buy-in from a particular practice area or function at an organization. Conducting an organization-wide SWOT analysis when you first take up your role leading innovation may also be helpful, although it's important not to get caught up in the deceptive simplicity of the SWOT matrix. As Laurence Minsky and David Aron have written for *Harvard Business Review*, a SWOT analysis, due to its format, is necessarily short and may lack insightfulness or a clear path to action, especially when conducted at a high level across an entire enterprise.[6] Instead, use the SWOT analysis as a targeted tool to help uncover opportunities and establish initiatives for practices or groups that need particular support, or that you are focusing on strategically due to their impact on the business.

Client-facing initiatives

Client-facing products and projects will be addressed in more detail in part two of this book, but it's important to also consider this aspect of innovation work when reviewing your project list. There is great disparity in the maturity of law firms when it comes to direct client-facing innovation work. Some have already realized the benefit of offering the services of multi-disciplinary professionals to clients alongside legal services, and regularly work with clients in this way. Most of the UK Magic Circle firms would fall into this category. Others have developed full subsidiaries that work directly with clients or run projects that sit between clients and internal legal teams. Some of the Amlaw 100 firms have developed this type of subsidiary and generate revenue accordingly. Still others have developed subscription products that are sold to clients – either by a subsidiary, or by the firm. The vast majority of law firms, however, are far less mature when it comes to client-facing innovation work.

If there are projects on your list that already have client buy-in, or that have client-facing potential, the value of these will be high for a number of reasons. Having a client on board will help smooth the way for any project through internal obstacles. Client involvement is also an excellent driver of adoption and usage – lawyers will understand the value of learning new processes and tools if these are being promoted by a client. Your innovation initiative will gain significant credibility and clout with each client engagement. From a prioritization perspective, initiatives that involve clients, or that are being driven by clients, should be high on your list.

If you are working in an environment where client-facing work by allied professionals is still viewed with suspicion, however, or where there are substantial hurdles to getting client work out the door, then the high value of client involvement should be weighed against your team's realistic ability to deliver. If you take on a client project and then find you are not able to give the client what they asked for or what you promised, your credibility with both the clients and the internal lawyers will take a hit. Unfair though it is (given that the hurdles standing in the way of your client project will likely be structural and outside of your control), your team is on the front line in these circumstances and is therefore likely to be subjected to the consequences of the failure. To put it plainly, you may end up with egg on your face. This is not to dissuade you from taking on client projects (I strongly recommend the opposite), but to encourage you to be strategic in your approach to them. In many cases, you will need to build up to this type of work over time, rather than embarking upon it immediately.

Listening programs

An audit is not a once-and-done event, or at least it shouldn't be. Too many firms evaluate needs at the outset of a program and then never properly check in with their lawyers again to ensure they are continuing to respond to and understand their needs. A solid innovation program must have a feedback loop built into it. One of your objectives as a leader will be to ensure your team develops the kinds of relationships with key personnel across the firm that generate regular feedback on current and future projects. If you have team members who develop these deep relationships and maintain them through regular one-on-one conversations, some of this feedback will be organic. The irregularity of organic feedback, however, means that you should not rely on it as your sole source of truth or the yardstick for how well your team is performing.

Being conscious about scheduling listening sessions with lawyers will provide you with regular feedback that you can count on. If you have a team that includes staff who work with particular practices at the organization, one of the projects they should take on periodically is the canvassing of those practices to "take the temperature" of lawyers and other professionals. Similar to an audit, your team will be surveying to find out where support is deemed sufficient, what resources are being used, which ones are not, and where there are practice pain-points that are causing frustration. In my last role, we canvassed litigation practices one year and transactional practices the next, on an ongoing basis. Listening programs take time and, given the ad hoc feedback that also comes back to the team, it's unnecessary to canvas the entire firm every year. In the same vein, it's unnecessary during a listening program for your team to meet with every single lawyer in their practices. Spending time with about 20 percent of the personnel in those practices will serve you well. However you establish the program, putting in place a schedule and expending the effort to uncover pain-points and use cases on an ongoing basis will result in a rich, productive innovation plan that evolves over time.

Checklist: Identifying strategic projects

☐ Identify the areas of strategic importance to firm leadership, keeping in mind your team's vision and the mandate set for your team by the organization.

☐ Taking into account these strategic signposts, develop an audit questionnaire that covers your area of responsibility – either KM or innovation or both.

☐ Distribute the audit by sending the questionnaire to a broad population of lawyers and other legal professionals to determine the needs they have in relation to KM and innovation.

Tips:

- Ensure you are canvassing a sample set of lawyers from every practice your team supports.

- Ensure you are capturing feedback from all levels of this population – from law clerks and paralegals to associates and partners.

- Put some thought into the means by which you will distribute the audit. Finding an intuitive surveying platform that makes it easy for people to respond will increase the rate of response.

☐ Engage leadership at all levels to communicate the importance of the audit and put in place a reminder schedule and a deadline for responses.

☐ Plan ahead for how you will review, aggregate, and analyse the responses. Remember that the audit itself is a critical aspect of your business planning, and resources should be dedicated accordingly.

☐ Use a SWOT analysis to further break down the results of the audit in practices that need special attention, either because they are facing challenges, because the lawyers in that practice are not engaged with innovation efforts and require some handling, or because the practice is particularly influential.

☐ Put in place a structure for ongoing auditing or "listening" programs across the practices that you and your team support, in order to ensure that you continue to understand the needs of those stakeholders and respond to them appropriately in your ongoing planning.

References

1 Watkins, Michael D. (2013), *The First 90 Days: Proven Strategies for Getting Up to Speed Faster and Smarter.* Boston, Massachusetts: Harvard Business Review Press.

2 Watkins, p. 10.

3 *Ibid.*

4 Minsky, L. and Aron, D. (2021). "Are You Doing the SWOT Analysis Backwards?" *Harvard Business Review*, 23 February 2021. https://hbr.org/2021/02/are-you-doing-the-swot-analysis-backwards.

5 *Ibid.*

6 Minsky and Aron, 2021.

Chapter 6:
Determining priorities

Once you have a list of the projects and initiatives that you know will be valuable to the organization's partners and leaders, it can be a daunting task to review these and decide how to allocate priorities. The projects on your list have a place on it because someone has asked for them, they are critical to firm strategy, or because you know that they are necessary precursors to other, potentially enterprise-wide initiatives. Each of them has a reason for being on your list – so how do you decide which projects are more important than others? Perhaps more critically, how do you go about communicating to partners or members of the senior leadership team that their requests or ideas are not on the immediate priority list? Taking the time to properly prioritize and set out what is realistically feasible within the next year is critical. Failing to do so will leave you with an overwhelming list of opportunities and will not allow you to build your team or allocate your resources appropriately. You may come across as a superhero if you take on all of these projects at once, but the inability of any team to execute on so many initiatives at once means that you will very quickly be stripped of superhero status when you are unable to deliver.

Categorizing projects

The first step towards prioritizing work is project categorization. The project list you have developed will include all kinds of initiatives. Some will be internal; some may be client-facing. Some will be firm-wide projects to support all practices, others might be narrow, for the benefit of lawyers in niche practices. In chapter four we have already explored various methods for categorizing projects based on timelines (Three Horizons theory), or on the markets and clients impacted by those projects (Innovation Ambition Matrix). We will re-visit these types of broad categorization in the check-list at the end of this chapter. Meanwhile, in the balance of this chapter we will examine methods for more nuanced, legally-focused project categorization that will help as you prioritize projects and consider the resources necessary to support each of them.

In an article published on the blog Legal Evolution,[1] Anusia Gillespie sets out what she calls a "Maker's Matrix", a method of classifying innovation and KM projects that regularly arise within a firm.[2] Figure 11 shows an adaptation of Gillespie's original matrix.

The Maker's Matrix	Data	Business Models	Thought Leadership
Legal Advice	1	2	3
Legal Partnership	4	5	6
Legal Services	7	8	9
Relevant Talent	Data architects, scientists, and analysts; software engineers; legal technology professionals; lawyers.	MBA-type consultants; operations professionals; legal technology professionals; project managers; graphic designers and branding resources; lawyers.	Subject matter experts; multi-disciplinary thought leaders; leadership development professionals; creative thinking experts and resources; lawyers.

Figure 11: Maker's Matrix. Source: Anusia Gillespie.

Gillespie's matrix provides a framework for examining a problem or an opportunity that has arisen in the organization and classifying it according to the aspect of legal practice that it impacts and the type of problem represented. Once you have categorized a problem or an opportunity according to this framework, it becomes easier to ascertain what the value is of a solution, and what resources will be necessary to develop the solution. Gillespie provides a flowchart to indicate how one would work through the matrix (see an adapted version in Figure 12).

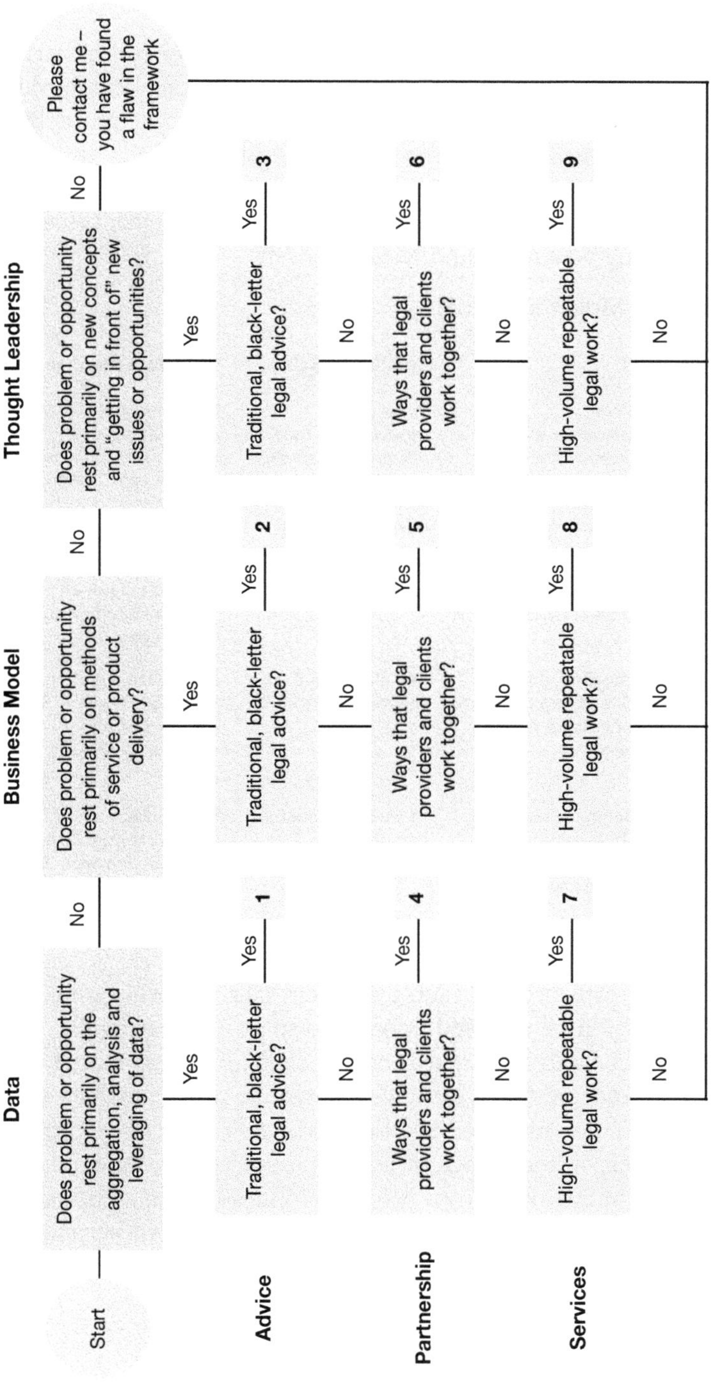

Figure 12: Working through the matrix. Source: Anusia Gillespie.

Although Gillespie's Matrix is helpful, it doesn't cater for the full spectrum of projects that now arise in law firms. Using Gillespie's excellent foundation, I have taken her Maker's Matrix and adapted it slightly, in Table 3. The new model reframes legal partnerships as legal operations and legal services as legal service delivery. It also expands the matrix to include beyond legal services,[3] to better illustrate the scope of projects that are likely to arise during your audit and needs analysis.

Table 3: Adapted Maker's Matrix.

	Data	Business Models	Thought leadership
Legal advice	Problems or opportunities that rest primarily on the aggregation, analysis and leveraging of black letter legal advice	Problems or opportunities that rest primarily on the models through which black letter legal advice is delivered	Problems or opportunities that rest primarily on new concepts and "getting in front of" new legal issues
Legal operation	Aggregation, analysis and leveraging of data to enhance legal operations	Models for organizing legal operations	New concept and "getting in front of" new issues related to legal operations
Legal service delivery	Aggregation, analysis and leveraging of data to enhance legal service delivery	Models for legal service delivery	New concept and "getting in front of" new issues around the delivery of legal services
Beyond legal services	Aggregation, analysis and leveraging of data for the pupose of providing beyond legal services	Models for organizing and delivering beyond legal services	New concept and "getting in front of" new issues around beyond legal services

Depending on the category in which a problem falls within this matrix, different resources will be required in order to solve it. For example, data projects are more likely to require technology skills; business model type projects may require technology, but will also require project management and potentially practice management skills; thought leadership projects will require research or knowledge skillsets and subject matter expertise. Figure 13 shows the breakdown of resources Gillespie has identified as being relevant depending on the type of project identified in her matrix. A similar resource analysis can be conducted using the extended Maker's Matrix.

The Maker's Matrix	Data	Business Models	Thought Leadership
Relevant Talent	Data architects, scientists, and analysts; software engineers; legal technology professionals; lawyers.	MBA-type consultants; operations professionals; legal technology professionals; project managers; graphic designers and branding resources; lawyers.	Subject matter experts; multi-disciplinary thought leaders; leadership development professionals; creative thinking experts and resources; lawyers.

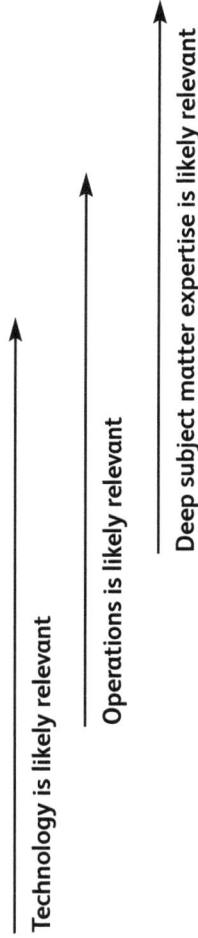

Technology is likely relevant →

Operations is likely relevant →

Deep subject matter expertise is likely relevant →

Figure 13: Resource requirements per project type. Source: Anusia Gillespie.

As you begin to categorize the opportunities that have arisen during your audit, you may find that you have many more potential projects in one area than others. It might be useful, then, to develop additional frameworks to assist with further categorization. In reviewing the many types of data projects under consideration by my team in 2021, I developed the framework shown in Table 4 to classify this category of project and understand better what resources would be necessary for each one. As you can see, spending the time to break down your project list and consider the level of

Table 4: Data project matrix.

Goal	Develop an interactive data tool on a discrete legal topic	Pool data from two or more systems to automate workflows or for the purpose of reporting	Increase flow of data across systems for intranet, enterprise search, client portal, matter management, expertise management project	Empower firm to act proactively to achieve its stategic vision based on data driven actionable insights
Project size	Medium, multi shareholder	Medium, multi shareholder	High, multi shareholder	Highest, multi shareholder
Data type	Internal data or discrete external data, narrow focus	Internal data, broader focus	Internal data, broad focus. potential for external data – enterprise-wide	Internal + external data, broadest focus, enterprise-wide
Tech requirements	• Data visualisation solution • Data extraction tool (opt) • Platform	• Workflow automation tech • RPA • Reporting/ forms tool • Data lake/ warehouse	• Core enterprise platform • Connectors/ bridges • Taxonomy management • Data lake/ warehouse	• Data lake/ warehouse • External data API • Data management system/processes
Stakeholders and project teams	• KM (lead) • SME – one PG • Data analyst • IT/innovation	• KM (lead) • Multiple departments/ PGs (ST) • Automation expert • Data analyst • IT/innovation	• KM or progam director lead • Most departments/ PGs • Consultant • IT	• KM or IT (lead) • All departments/ PG (ST) • Consultant • IT
Change/ adoption effort	Targeted workflow based PG or client-focused	Low level administrative teams	Broad, large-scale comms matrix Persona focused Workflow based	Large scale phased adoption Project focused

effort involved to move initiatives forward provides a solid basis for crafting a realistic project schedule and for understanding the skillsets required to bring a project to completion.

Having an understanding of the resources and expertise required to execute on the project will help you to determine whether it is worth undertaking sooner or later. If you don't yet have the resources to execute on a project, or if you have limited resources and these are already assigned to another, more urgent project, that knowledge will help you to schedule your project line-up and build out a strategic plan.

Value versus effort

The most useful way to evaluate projects to set priorities for your team is to compare their value to the effort and resources required to carry each of them through to completion. This will help you to see clearly whether a project should be pursued immediately or whether it can be put on the back-burner, to be addressed at a later date. There will be some initiatives that may initially seem like valuable undertakings, but after assessment reveal themselves to be distractions from more relevant, higher value, work.

The value versus effort graph, also known as the action priority matrix and shown with some customization in Figure 14, can help you determine which projects should be prioritized.[4] For each initiative on your list, consider its overall value to the organization by asking the following questions:

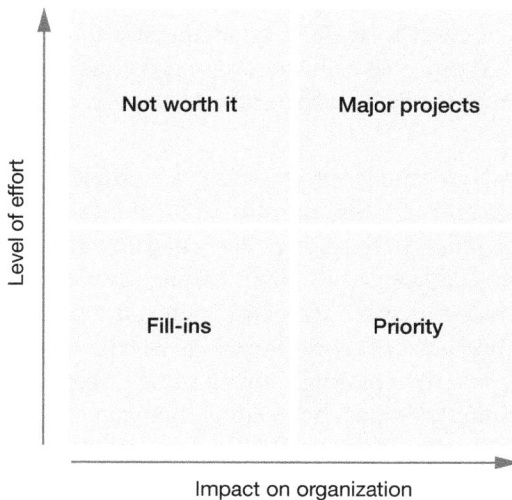

Figure 14: The action priority matrix.[5]

- How many lawyers/practices does it stand to impact?
- Are those practices critical to the firm – i.e. are they critical revenue-generating practices?
- Alternatively, will the project positively impact pockets of the firm with low utilization, in ways that might turn that utilization around?
- Is there a client involved who stands to gain either directly or indirectly from the project? Is the client driving the project?
- Is there a possibility the project could drive additional work to the firm?
- Alternatively, will the project generate new revenue directly?
- Is the project aligned with firm-wide strategic goals, and would it serve to further those goals?

The value of a project should then be assessed alongside the resources (both human and financial) required to carry it out, the level of effort involved, and the time such a project is likely to take.

Weighing up the impact of your projects against the level of effort should make it reasonably clear in which quarter of the chart your projects fall. Accordingly, you will have projects that can be deemed:

- *Not worth it.* The level of effort is not worth the low value these projects offer. The return on investment (ROI) equation does not make sense and it will be hard to make a business case for any resources you might need to pull these off. Indeed, expending many resources on projects that have low value is likely to harm your credibility in the organization.

- *Fill-ins.* These are smaller projects that are unlikely to serve you well because their impact is also narrow. Many of these may bring value to specific individuals or to small pockets of the firm. In a perfect world, these are projects your team might choose to take on during a quiet period as "nice-to-haves". In reality, that quiet period is unlikely to arrive. Keeping a list of these projects is worthwhile, however. There may be a benefit to exploring some of these projects to see if you can expand their initial impact by building them out to support additional practices over time. If so, and if the narrow group of stakeholders affected by these projects hold some influence in the organization, it may be worth occasionally pursuing select fill-in projects to help build credibility by executing rapidly on specific demands. Doing so and promoting that success may help you win buy-in for taking on larger initiatives.

- *Major projects.* These projects are absolutely worth doing, but you will need to scope them out and understand the necessary effort and resources before jumping in. Determine which of these projects represent a higher need at the firm, or which ones are most closely tied to the firm's overarching strategic goals. Depending on your resources, you may be able to schedule one or two of these projects a year. If they are huge projects – such as a new intranet, for example – you may need to agitate for additional external resources, such as a consultant who can help with planning, design, and implementation.

- *Priority projects.* This is where the bulk of your immediate resources should go. These are the projects that will build the reputation of your team. The high value will come from their clear strategic alignment with firm initiatives, from the degree to which they change for the better the way lawyers or clients work, from the number of lawyers or clients impacted by the initiative, or because they provide valuable support for the most critical practices or the most influential lawyers at the firm.

Project streams

Once you have categorized your projects and understood the value they will provide to the organization, as well as the resources and effort necessary to undertake them, it will be easier for you to assess these using the action priority matrix.

There are other considerations, however, that will come into play as you develop your business plan for the year or years ahead. As discussed in chapter five, you may be planning for different horizons of growth. You may be seeking to allocate resources and budget according to a ratio that allows your team to support both incremental and disruptive growth.

Other practical concerns that will also frequently be relevant include whether there is foundational work that must be undertaken at the firm before some of the more exciting growth projects can start. Examples of this include the upgrade or implementation of a document management system, a project that often involves some resources from the innovation or KM team, or the centralization and clean-up of enterprise data that must occur before more interesting, strategic data projects can be advanced.

Charting a business plan and allocating resources and budget across the timeline you are planning for can be a complex initiative, taking all of the above into account. Nevertheless, if you have leveraged the frameworks discussed here to deeply understand your team's goals, the needs of the lawyers your team supports, the value and effort involved in the initiatives that have been proposed, the horizons for which you are planning, the budget you have available, and the organizational priorities that you must work with and around, you will be in a better position to identify immediate priorities and to chart a course towards your team's BHAG.

Business planning

Law firms and organizations handle business planning in such different ways that it's difficult to provide guidance on how best to navigate this (usually) annual process. Instead, this section seeks to provide a basic methodology for developing a business plan that you can leverage yourself to provide clarity and chart a course to action over a given timespan. This goes a step further than the simple strategic plan offered in chapter three.

First, determine the period for which you are planning. Most business planning is conducted for the year ahead, although you can opt to forecast further into the future if you need to consider resourcing over a longer time period. In order to make it clear over the course of the year what your team's focus will be and when there may be a crunch on resources, set out the projects you have identified as priorities in a spreadsheet under the headings or categories in which they belong. For example, a project to create a program for incoming summer associates on the various tools and solutions that exist at a firm would fall under the category of education, while an initiative to build up precedent resources for a certain practice group would fall under knowledge management. Both of these projects would also fall within your horizon one planning. Developing a plan for and promoting client-facing consulting work would fall within horizon two planning, which you might choose to handle on a different tab of your spreadsheet.

For each project listed in your business plan, set out the resources necessary to execute on the project:

- What skills are required to support this project, and which people on the team (or from across the firm) will need to be involved.

- Is there a technology requirement for this project? Does it involve bringing in new technology or developing a solution within an existing tool?

- Has there been budget set aside for this project already?
- Will you need help for this project, e.g. from an external consultant, and has this external assistance already been approved and budgeted for?
- How long it is estimated that the project will take, from beginning to end.

Once you have set this out across all of your projects, you can break down the plan even further. I find it useful to consider the timing of each project and determine at the beginning of the year in which quarter of the year each project will kick off. If you have multiple technology projects in your annual plan and limited resources to build or implement technology solutions, you will need to decide which of those projects will begin in quarter one, and which can wait until quarter three or four. Understanding the resource list and the types of resource involved in each project gives you the necessary clarity to develop this kind of detailed planning, which will help you to actually execute on your projects over the course of the year. It will also help to see whether perhaps you're biting off more than you can chew. If your plan includes running pilots of six new technology solutions, but the resources on your team for managing and running pilots will not have the capacity to execute on this goal, you may wish to drop one or two of these projects into the following year. Unless you do this work upfront, you may find yourself in a situation where you have so many projects running concurrently that your team is burning out or simply cannot execute well on any one of those projects.

Checklist: Prioritizing strategic initiatives

☐ Create a list of the projects that fall within your team's mandate, either as a result of the audit and conversations with lawyers and leadership, or because your team is a stakeholder in a broader enterprise-wide initiative.

☐ Break these down by project type, having regard to the notion of a Maker's Matrix categorization tool.

- What are the resources that are necessary to undertake each of these projects?
    - Consider skillsets (and whether these are located in your team or will have to be leveraged from another team, e.g. the IT

department), budgetary requirements, and whether investment in new technology is necessary.

- Where else are these same resources allocated over the course of the year [or years] you are planning for?
- What is a realistic timeframe to undertake each of these projects through to execution, including change management programs, metrics tracking, and so on.

☐ If you haven't done so already, categorize the projects into your various horizon or growth streams (see chapter four). Which projects represent incremental growth and which ones are truly disruptive?

☐ Based on your Three Horizons characterization, allocate resources and budgets for your priority projects according to the 70-20-10 rule.

☐ Develop business plans for each horizon or growth stream accordingly, noting resource lift across the team and developing a realistic timeline for these projects.

References

1 www.legalevolution.org/2019/12/innovation-as-a-service-and-the-makers-matrix-128/
2 *Ibid.*
3 I use the term "beyond legal services" to refer to services that are related but not intrinsic to the legal services a law firm is expected to provide to its clients. Beyond legal services might include data-fueled dashboards providing insight on work in progress (WIP) or matter financials for clients, knowledge tools that provide regularly updated information on the laws in various jurisdictions, or innovation consulting such as helping clients select and implement automation tools.
4 The action priority matrix was first conceived of by Stephen Covey in his 1989 book, *The Seven Habits of Highly Effective People* (Covey called it the Four Quadrants). It has since been reconceived and appropriated by the product management community. See: https://airfocus.com/glossary/what-is-the-action-priority-matrix/, https://earlynode.com/action-priority-matrix/.
5 Author's own interpretation of the Ambition Priority Matrix.

Chapter 7:
Creating and growing an innovation function

Legal innovation functions look different – and have different names – depending on the organization, its culture, and the region within which it sits. In many regions, innovation functions still exist predominantly within the confines of a different department, and the team may not be defined or called out as an innovation team. In Canada and the United States, for example, KM departments over the past ten years have expanded and now frequently include the skills and roles that constitute innovation teams at other law firms. In the United States it is still relatively common for innovation to sit within IT departments, sometimes without the nomenclature of "innovation". In the UK, innovation and KM are more typically distinct from one another, with practice support lawyer (PSL) roles sitting quite separate from any innovation function and rarely taking on the responsibilities around practice technology that have become a common aspect of North American KM attorney roles. In Australia, innovation efforts are often distributed across many functions – similar to the UK, KM is usually distinct from innovation, but initiatives that drive change and digitization might sit across project management, IT, and even marketing functions.

As an industry, this inconsistency in defining the function makes it difficult to track the extent to which law firms are pursuing innovation initiatives or actively seeking to drive large-scale change – or indeed to recognize the relative success of such initiatives. In 2019, Alma Asay (currently the director of knowledge and innovation at Crowell & Moring in the US) undertook a review on LinkedIn of AmLaw 200 firms with KM or innovation roles. Alma kindly shared that work with me and I have maintained and updated it for 2022. The data shows that over 50 percent of AmLaw 100 firms have now hired KM or innovation roles that are responsible for driving cultural change and modern work practices. What is harder to see is the progress these professionals are making within their firms, or which KM professionals are more focused on traditional content-type projects compared to technology-driven initiatives. The fact that legal innovation remains a black box in many respects, and the inconsistency in naming conventions across the industry, gives rise to common misunderstandings. It is not unusual, for example, for assumptions to be made that KM professionals work solely on content and taxonomy projects, in roles that align more closely with research than innovation. In fact, many KM professionals are also innovation professionals, and may be the richest source of information within a firm on the digitization of workflows across practice groups and the adoption of legal technology at the firm. They may also play key roles in piloting new technology. Because KM and innovation roles within law firms are often obscured, there persists in the legal ecosystem a notion that firms need help identifying the right tools to help their practices. This view holds that law firms don't have the requisite expertise in-house to navigate the complex legal technology market or to match the right solutions to use cases. In fact, many law firms – most of the AmLaw 50, the Magic Circle firms in the UK, the Seven Sisters in Canada – have invested in headcount whose expertise includes precisely that understanding of, and ability to navigate, the legal technology ecosystem. They just may go by a different name.

Roles in KM and innovation
As a corollary to, and extension of, the confusion around KM and innovation departments, there is significant inconsistency in the roles and job titles available in these fields. The list of jobs identified below is by no means exhaustive but should provide some clarity on the types of roles that exist within legal innovation. I'm including a review of KM roles here, not just because the ambit of KM often includes innovation work, but also because in my view, KM and innovation are and should continue to be linked. An innovation function that is firing on all cylinders is one that is deeply connected to KM, even if it doesn't sit within the same reporting lines – more on this later.

Knowledge management
Traditionally, knowledge management is the practice of capturing, curating, disseminating, and enabling the effective use of knowledge across an organization.

In most firms, the KM department also oversees the library or research services, with the library manager or director reporting up into KM, but the two should not be mistaken for one another. The easiest way to explain the difference is that while a library function is responsible for supporting legal research questions and licensing external third party information resources, the KM function is responsible for ensuring that internal information and work product can be leveraged most effectively by the lawyers.

Information or intellectual capital is one of the most valuable assets an organization has, and without explicit KM programs it can be difficult for organizations to properly leverage their intellectual capital and derive the greatest value from it. The reasons for this are both practical and cultural. From a practical perspective, as companies grow, pockets of critical information and knowledge can become isolated so that they are unavailable to other parts of the organization when needed. Adding to this challenge is the fact that a knowledge-sharing culture has to be cultivated, and the incentive structure of many organizations obstructs the development of such a culture.

The core role of KM is to ensure that an organization is able to derive the highest value from its intellectual capital by overcoming both practical and cultural hurdles to knowledge-sharing and putting in place mechanisms that allow knowledge workers across the organization to quickly and easily access critical information as and when they need it. The remit of KM has become broader over time and, as the data landscape has evolved, now includes helping an organization supercharge its intellectual capital by pairing it effectively with external market and industry data, allowing for even broader insights and proactive strategic momentum. The means for capturing knowledge and re-surfacing it have also changed, with technological advances allowing for more intuitive mechanisms to enable all of the key processes underlying KM. KM teams have therefore necessarily become sophisticated in the use of technology, and the skillset one might need on a KM team has changed.

Below is an outline of some of the key roles you might expect to find in a current robust knowledge management team.

Chief knowledge officer

The notion of a C-level executive in charge of knowledge is one that has emerged over the past five years and is now well established. Approximately 30 percent of the AmLaw 100 firms have a chief role for KM, or a combined knowledge and innovation role at this level. In Canada, most of the Seven Sisters have a chief knowledge or knowledge and innovation officer. In these markets, firms that do not provide for chief titles in relation to roles heading up these functions may have difficulty recruiting the right candidates, as the title now carries with it some cache. The C-level title also carries weight internally, which assists with the political maneuvering that is a necessary part of leading change in a law firm. In firms where there is a chief technology officer and a chief financial officer, for example, refusing to provide an equivalent title for the head of knowledge can set that person up for failure, as it suggests that knowledge work is not considered to be as important as that of other business units. In Canada, some chief knowledge officers (CKOs) are also partners of their firms, which lends further influence and authority to the role. In the UK, the chief title is less common, with the title "head of knowledge" taking its place. In Australia, KM is still considered to be focused mainly on content strategies, and the department does not carry the same weight as it does in the United States. Accordingly, executive level positions for knowledge management are rare. At the time of writing, only one Australian firm – Gilbert + Tobin – has a chief knowledge and innovation officer.

Most often, CKOs are former lawyers who practiced for many years, then worked in knowledge management in more junior capacities until they were promoted into or successfully applied for the lead role in a department. The level of experience for this senior role is typically 15-20 years working in the legal industry. A practice background for this type of role is generally considered to be important because so much of knowledge work depends on a solid understanding of legal practice and legal content. There are some firms where the lead role does not have experience as a practicing lawyer, but it is then critical that the individual in this position has a deep understanding of the firm, the way that lawyers work, and that they garner enough respect from peers and partners that they are able to develop requisite buy-in for key projects. Pitched at a high strategic level, this executive position typically reports to the managing partner of a firm, the executive director, or the chief operating officer (COO), and often heads up multiple functions. This role spends most of its time on high-level strategic planning for the department, recruiting for senior roles, people management, departmental culture building, and in working internally to remove hurdles for the rest of the team in order to allow projects to proceed.

Director of KM

This role is tasked with leading KM strategy and initiatives, either across the entire firm and its offices or regionally. Similar to the chief knowledge role, the director of KM is generally a former lawyer who has developed experience both on the practice side of law and on the business side. Typically, a director will have five to eight years of legal practice experience combined with a minimum of five years working in increasingly senior roles in KM.

KM directors have a narrower ambit than CKOs. They will generally be tasked with managing the KM lawyers and staff and may also have over-sight of a library or research services function. It's unusual for KM directors to oversee any additional functions, as these would generally report up into the head of the department at the executive level. The exception to this, of course, is where firms do not have a C-level role in KM and the director role heads up the department. Where this is the case, the director may have oversight of more functions and will report directly to the COO of a firm – though reporting to the CTO or another chief is also common.

KM directors work closely with the chief role to set forward-looking strategies for the knowledge and research teams and take a lead role in communicating with practice group chairs and setting project priorities for the knowledge and research functions. Much of their time will be spent on people management and actively driving projects forward. For key KM projects, such as enterprise search, the KM director will play an active lead role in execution. They may also take on active roles in enterprise-wide projects where KM or research is a stakeholder. Recruitment for new roles and building out the team is another area of focus for this position.

KM lawyer

Also known in the US as a KM attorney or in the UK as a PSL, KM lawyers are the key personnel in any knowledge function. With some exceptions, KM lawyers are embedded within or assigned to a specific practice or various aligned practices (for example, the same KM lawyer might support two or three specialized litigation-based practices). Firms that do not have the luxury of the headcount required to provide practice groups with dedicated support may instead have a small number of KM lawyers with more distributed responsibilities – such as a KM lawyer supporting all transactional practices, or one or two central KM lawyers who support the firm in its entirety.

There are two main reporting models for KM lawyers in Canadian and US firms. Either the KM lawyers will report directly to the head of the practice group they support, with dotted line reports into a KM director, or the KM lawyers will report directly to the KM director with dotted line reports to the practice group lead. The danger of the former model is that it distributes KM roles and responsibilities across the firm, making it more difficult to establish consistent best practices. The direct reporting line into a practice also risks that a KM lawyer, who has subject matter expertise in the practice area they support, will get absorbed into practice and have less time to spend on knowledge work. This is particularly likely when KM lawyers are set up to bill some of their time. In circumstances where KM lawyers have some billing responsibilities, it is critical that a centralized KM group have control of the situation so that time spent on billed work versus knowledge work can be properly managed. Unless the value of knowledge work is deeply understood and respected, as in Magic Circle firms where PSLs have been established for many years, the better model generally is to keep KM lawyers out of billing work and to have a centralized department that enshrines best practices and a consistent approach to knowledge across the firm.

The role of a KM lawyer can be quite varied. Depending on the maturity of a firm's KM function, they may be involved in any number of the following:

- Developing or coordinating the development of precedent forms and templates;
- Liaising with lawyers to create "how-tos" and guides on specific aspects of practice;
- Creating and maintaining a practice group site on the firm intranet;
- Writing legal updates and client alerts to keep both internal and external lawyers updated on critical legal developments;
- Tracking matters and entering matter metadata into a central experience or matter management repository;
- Seeking content contributions to a knowledge hub (full documents or clauses, or both);
- Developing practice-specific taxonomies for use across firm systems;
- Attending practice group meetings and providing updates on new tools, resources, and legal developments; and
- Supporting the roll-out of practice technology, including promotion and basic training on relevant tools.

KM specialist / KM administrator

Well-established KM teams will generally have at least one specialist or administrator, who supports the KM lawyers by administering key KM systems. While KM lawyers support practices by working on detailed content development and coordination projects that require subject matter, KM specialists support KM lawyers by undertaking much of the repetitive, manual work that is a part of content curation. KM specialists rarely have a legal background but may have educational qualifications in information management. It's also common for KM specialists to have a research or library background. Given the increased sophistication of knowledge delivery solutions, a KM specialist might also have a technology background and experience. Tasks might include:

- Mining the document management system for relevant knowledge content and following up with lawyers to determine its appropriateness for inclusion in knowledge collections;
- Tagging content according to firm taxonomies and adding it to a knowledge base;
- Collecting data on firm matters and adding it to a matters database;
- Performing administrative functions relating to clause banks, knowledge hubs, enterprise search, and other KM tools; and
- Entering data on the firm intranet.

Knowledge engineer

In firms where the KM and innovation functions are separate, or where there is either no innovation function or a minimal function reporting up into IT or some other department, the KM team may require technical support beyond a KM specialist. Knowledge engineers are the technologists of the KM world, with a deep understanding of KM delivery systems and the ability to quickly understand and manipulate new technologies. Knowledge engineers might be responsible for setting up content libraries and importing and managing taxonomies into knowledge tools. Where the KM specialist is content-focused, the knowledge engineer is systems-focused. The knowledge engineer may also be responsible for training lawyers on the more technical aspects of resources and tools they have at their disposal, thereby supporting adoption efforts. For example, this role might help get lawyers up and running in a contract review tool so that they are able to leverage due diligence automation, or provide ongoing training to deal teams who wish to use transaction management software to facilitate client collaboration and closings.

Innovation/practice innovation/practice technology

Although innovation teams are mostly tied closely to the KM function, they are still often separate teams. Where KM functions will usually be populated by lawyers with subject matter expertise, innovation functions are more likely to have staff with technology, product management, or business analysis skills. In contrast to the KM team, whose focus is on leveraging an understanding of legal practice to support attorneys in optimizing processes related to and managing access to critical content, the innovation team is tasked with solving internal use cases, usually through technology. As will be discussed in chapter 13, a core part of that work will involve applying a build, partner, buy framework to determine whether existing technology can be used or new technology is necessary to solve a particular problem. Because legal work is fundamentally knowledge work, many of the problems and use cases addressed by the innovation team will have content and legal practice components and so most projects will end up requiring input from both innovation and KM functions (where these are separate). For example, an initiative to support co-editing of documents in a transactional practice may require new technology but will also necessitate careful processes to ensure version control is maintained during drafting. The roles below represent some of those now becoming common in innovation teams.

Chief innovation officer/chief practice innovation officer
Similar to CKO roles, C-level executive roles for innovation are becoming increasingly popular. Where this role exists, it will usually be one that heads up both KM and innovation functions – it's unusual (but not unheard of) for a firm to have both a CKO and a chief innovation or practice innovation officer. For the most part, then, the role of the chief innovation (or practice innovation) officer is the same as that of the CKO – although the strategic goals of a pure innovation officer may vary slightly from that of a CKO. The priorities of the role are strategic and political, with senior recruitment efforts and people management taking up additional time. The chief innovation officer might also chair a firm's innovation committee, which frequently includes partners, and will serve on other business-critical boards or committees.

Director of innovation
A director of innovation leads the team responsible for identifying technology solutions and guides the implementation of those solutions. The director will work with the chief innovation officer or with the head of KM to develop strategies to drive innovation across an organization, including developing models for ideating and designing solutions, running pilots and proofs of concept (POC), developing protocols around roll-out and implementation, and planning for adoption. It used to be the case that, similar to KM directors and CKOs, innovation directors were former practicing lawyers. As the industry matures, we are starting to see more

innovation directors appointed from outside of industry. At a conference recently, I met two innovation directors who had segued into their roles from completely different commercial organizations – one had previously been a strategy consultant for an engineering firm, and the other had been a director in an oil and gas company. Given that the skillset for innovation is not the same skillset as that of a lawyer – in some ways they are diametrically opposed – this is a positive development and one I hope we see more of.

Often, a director of innovation will have a skillset that includes software development and the ability to code. Although the director will not themselves be exercising these skills, having a strong understanding of technology and what it is capable of will serve them well in leading a team of technologists. Effective innovation directors will be familiar with service design methodologies and well-versed in user-focused design. Beyond setting strategy for the team, this role is likely to include the following responsibilities:

- Helping to develop best practices on running departmental projects;
- People management, including recruiting and building a multi-disciplinary team, and developing agile work practices that provide a foundation for effective solution development;
- Coordinating with innovation managers, practice technologists, KM leaders, KM lawyers, and other departmental leads to identify use cases and prioritize initiatives;
- Establishing metrics for identifying project success, tracking usage, and reporting up; and
- Liaising between project teams and lawyers within a practice, communicating on project progress and managing expectations.

Solutions architect/product manager

The role of product manager is still unusual in law firms and legal departments, but where a firm has started to develop client-facing products, it should be considered a necessary one. In some instances, the director of innovation will have a product management background and will effectively serve this role. Nevertheless, it's important that the director (who will be kept busy on strategic initiatives) be supported by another person on the team who understands how to dig into problems, understand user needs, develop requirements, and design solutions using existing or new technology capabilities. This role will be responsible for scoping out innovation projects and, along with the director of innovation, will determine the buy / partner / build decisions around new solutions.

Legal technologist/practice technologist

The title "legal technologist" is becoming more common in law firms. It is a generalist title, providing an organization with some flexibility in the skills they require. A legal technologist will always have software skills, but these will vary from role to role. Depending on project needs, some legal technologists might be required to have expertise in automation technology, others in machine learning, still others in data visualization. A basic skillset for a legal technologist will include the ability to code, familiarity with SQL databases, and an understanding of the software development process including versioning and maintenance. Strong innovation teams will have multiple legal technologists, each with slightly varying expertise, thereby creating a group that is well able to support the full stack of technology capabilities leveraged by the team.

In some firms, technologists will be assigned to specific practice groups, similar to KM lawyers. This is more likely to be the case where innovation and KM sit in separate departments, and the innovation team is unable to easily leverage the relationships generated by the firm's KM lawyers to identify technology use cases in specific practice groups. Practice technologists may have a slightly different background than legal technologists – though they will still have a strong aptitude for technology, they may not be software developers. Instead, they may be former lawyers whose job is to listen for practice problems, match solutions to use cases, and effectively act as project managers running pilots and roll-outs in particular practice areas. A common alternative title for a practice technologist is an innovation manager, although in a larger department an innovation manager may also be a middle management position with some people management skills who is not connected to any particular practice.

Data analyst/data scientist

Firms or organizations that have embarked on significant data projects will have a need for data expertise that goes beyond that of a legal technologist (whose skillset may include some data fluency but rarely deep expertise). As seen in chapter five, there is a large variability between the types of data project that may arise in a legal organization. Many of these will sit outside of legal practice and will likely be run by other departments at the firm – for example, projects leveraging financial data for the benefit of the pricing team, or to refine recruitment and HR data, are unlikely to give rise to resourcing needs on the innovation team. Enterprise-wide projects will have multiple stakeholders including KM and practice innovation functions, but may be run by IT. Many discrete data projects will, however, sit with the innovation team. These include the development of tools that provide lawyers with a view of the market based on extracted data from deal documents, or dashboards providing judicial analytics that marry internal and external data and allow for early case assessment and improved litigation strategy. The prevalence of these types of projects in a firm will make it necessary for an innovation team to bring on board highly specialized skills around data. If litigation support and responsibility for eDiscovery sits within a practice innovation department, there will be an even greater need for this type of skill.

Notes on recruiting

With any of the roles described above, the way that you post them in the market (with respect to both title and description) will matter more than it does for traditional roles. Given the slippery nature of naming alternative roles in legal, a job description should make it explicitly clear what types of skills and expertise are being sought. Titles matter less than substance in relation to these types of roles, and the positions defined above are only some of those now prevalent in legal innovation teams. Additional roles might include:

- A resource dedicated to document automation, to perform the coding of document automation questionnaires;
- An intranet content manager, with responsibility for maintaining and managing content and metadata tags on a firm's intranet;
- Legal technology project managers with experience driving multi-stakeholder projects through to completion;
- A business analyst, who designs wireframes and optimizes the operational impact of technology solutions; and
- An enterprise search manager, with responsibility for ongoing development and innovation within the firm's enterprise search system.

Multi-disciplinary teams

Law firms of the future will deliver legal services through teams of multi-disciplinary professionals, rather than lawyers alone. This is not a theory or a hypothesis, it is a fact. Already, the nature of large-scale legal matters is such that they require the support of project managers, paralegals or law clerks, and research analysts in addition to lawyers. High volume due diligence is frequently managed by lower cost alternative time-keepers who are able to leverage AI contract review technology to automate part of the review in the context of a larger matter. Data analysts and data scientists are frequently included as part of a litigation team during eDiscovery processes.

As practice technology becomes even more embedded in legal workflows, most parts of legal work will require support by a range of professionals who each bring their own expertise to the matter. Every piece of legal work will be scoped not just from a pricing perspective but also from a resourcing perspective, with law firms strategically dedicating resources from across the business to the client. In some ways, this is already happening. The big shift will come, however, when these professionals are recognized both by firms and clients as equal members of a legal team, rather than mere lackeys supporting the important work of the lawyers. Even now, clients are regularly interacting with a broader spectrum of law firm staff than they used to. Soon, clients will be paying for the team as a whole, rather than being charged exclusively for lawyer time and getting the services of related professionals as a "value-add".

As firms move to provide beyond-legal or legal-adjacent services to legal departments and legal operations teams, relationships and connections are being forged across the law firm–client divide that serve to increase the strength of the commercial bond between these entities. It makes sense for law firms to charge for this work, just as they charge for legal work. It offers high value to clients and is increasingly expected to be part of the package of services a law firm delivers. Large consultancies recognized the benefit of multi-disciplinary services many years ago. Once law firms collectively recognize that they must move in this direction in order to modernize their offerings, the compensation model for law firm professionals who are not practicing lawyers is likely to change. These professionals will be seen as integral to the success of a law firm, just as lawyers are.

As you seek to build out your team, keep these shifting tides in mind. We are well past the days where a law firm could get away with hiring lawyers or former lawyers to fill every role on a KM or innovation team. If you want a successful team that is able to build growth opportunities across your organization, you must have the requisite skills on that team to deliver quality outcomes.

Organizational structures

At the 2022 SKILLS conference hosted by Simpson Thatcher and organized by Oz Benamram, Ron Friedmann, Lucy Dillon, Tanisha Little, and Mary Abrahams, participants were surveyed regarding the functions included in their KM and innovation departments. This annual conference is by invitation only and has a carefully restricted participant list, with a deep history in KM. Invited participants are typically CKOs, or the equivalent lead KM role at a firm. Over the years, the conference has expanded to allow some innovation leads to join, but only where they also head up KM within their organization. Many of the regular attendees previously had KM titles and now have titles such as chief practice innovation officer, which folds underneath it both KM and innovation.

The survey results make for interesting reading because they show how many different functions now frequently sit within what was previously known as the KM department. Indeed, as shown in Figure 15, it's common now for such a department to include between five and seven different functions. Several respondents oversee departments with over nine different functions reporting into them. This is a far cry from the KM department of old, which is the precursor of these new giants.

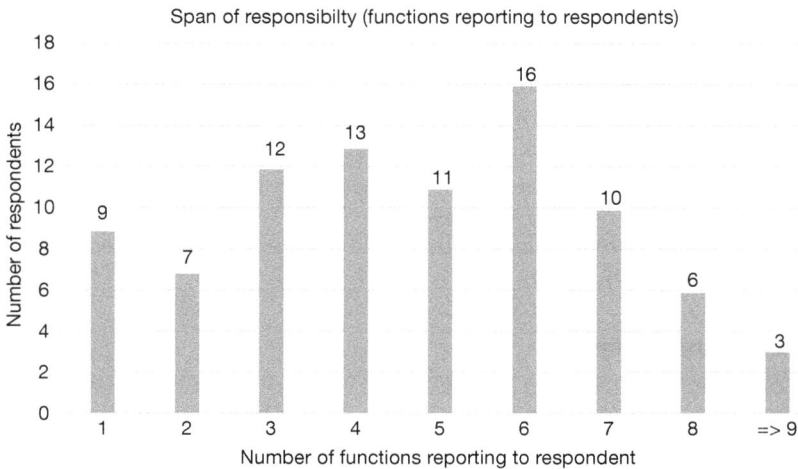

Span of responsibilty (functions reporting to respondents)

Figure 15: Span of responsibility for KM departments, courtesy of SKILLS Committee based on member survey 2022.

Figure 16 shows the variety of functions that report into innovation and knowledge departments in law firms. The range serves to illustrate the way that business of law functions have evolved. Responsibility for KM is almost always included (because that's the function out of which almost all these departments have emerged), closely followed by innovation. What is more interesting is the way that these types of departments have evolved to now include functions as diverse as record management, information governance, and new business intake. These functions have traditionally reported elsewhere, but as the graphs show, when KM departments develop credibility and prove value, it's not unusual for them to gradually absorb additional responsibilities across a firm.

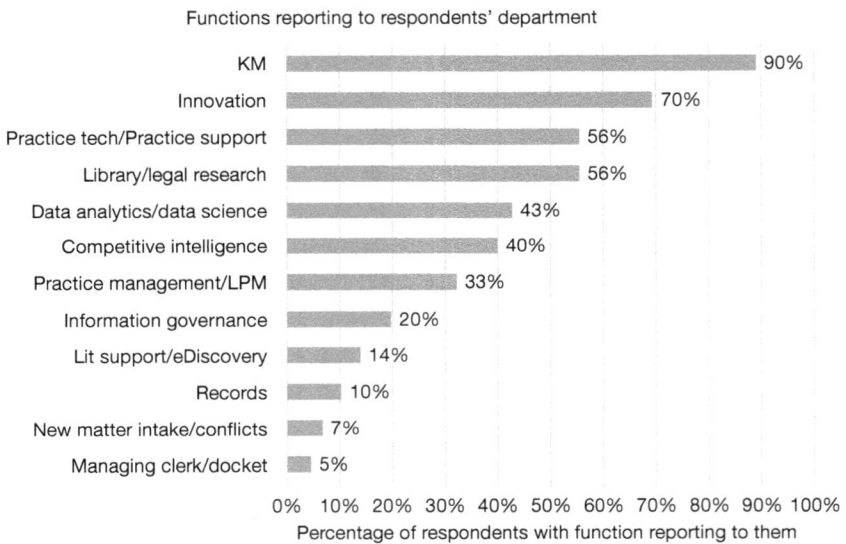

Functions reporting to respondents' department

Function	Percentage
KM	90%
Innovation	70%
Practice tech/Practice support	56%
Library/legal research	56%
Data analytics/data science	43%
Competitive intelligence	40%
Practice management/LPM	33%
Information governance	20%
Lit support/eDiscovery	14%
Records	10%
New matter intake/conflicts	7%
Managing clerk/docket	5%

Percentage of respondents with function reporting to them

Figure 16: Functions reporting to head of KM, courtesy of SKILLS Committee based on member survey 2022.

Building your team

The fact that we are seeing ever-growing KM and innovation departments in large firms should not be intimidating, nor does it mean that's what you should aspire to if you are setting out to build a new legal innovation function, or to develop an existing such function. The fact is that KM and innovation is still in its infancy in some firms – even in some of the AmLaw 100, but especially in mid-sized firms.

For firms that are starting out on this journey, headcount growth can happen in one of two ways. In rare instances, a change in leadership might give rise to a sudden desire to heavily invest in KM and innovation.

Significant firm resources will be allocated to the development of a market-leading department, a senior professional with deep expertise will be brought on board to lead it, and headcount growth can occur rapidly. Consider the example of Simpson Thacher in the United States. In 2020, the firm hired Oz Benamram from White & Case, creating an inaugural chief knowledge and innovation officer position, and dedicated very significant resources to the creation of a KM and innovation department. Within one year, the firm went from having a small KM department to having a team of more than 60 personnel spread across KM and innovation.

This kind of rapid growth is rare, however. More often, a firm will cautiously embark upon a journey to develop a legal innovation function. They may still hire someone external but are just as likely to promote someone internally. Headcount growth for these firms will be incremental, motivated by project needs, and dependent upon proof of value from initial investment in the function. This is the position in which most early leaders of KM and innovation departments find themselves – needing to prove themselves and the value they can bring to a firm that is unwilling to invest more resources to the cause until they see tangible merit in doing so.

If you are in the position of building a department and wondering who you should hire first, your best bet is to go back to your project list. You've done the work by now of determining what resources will be required to undertake the priority projects on your deck, and to ascertain how those resources should be allocated according to the 70-20-10 rule. Review the headcount needs that arise from your priority projects to ascertain what skills you'll need that you don't yet have. Consider those against the role descriptions above to understand who you need to hire first. You may have projects that are data-driven and will require data analysis skills. You may need to resource particular practices – employment, intellectual property, or tax, for example – with KM expertise before others. If your firm has not invested in KM lawyers and you are not in the position of heading up KM, you may need to bolster your innovation team with practice technologists who can develop the critical relationships you will need in order to get traction with your strategy. If, on the other hand, your department or the firm has already invested in KM and you can mine that team for use cases, you may instead require deeper technical expertise on your team.

Every environment will be different and, as a result, the way that an innovation department evolves will be different from firm to firm. Below are a series of organizational structures illustrating KM and innovation departments in various stages of maturity. These will give you an idea of how you might consider going about hiring headcount, but again, the decisions you make about what types of skills are necessary on your team are entirely dependent on your remit, your departmental vision and strategy, and the broader goals and growth plan of your firm.

Organizational structure 1: Early-stage KM and innovation

This structure represents a department in its early stages, where the lead has been tasked with both KM and innovation resourcing at the firm. This is a firm that has never previously invested in either KM or innovation, so both are in their infancy. The headcount depicted in Figure 17 indicates that the lead has seen value in building out KM support for both the corporate and litigation practices, but does not yet have buy-in for practice-specific resources. It also reveals that the director is responsible for both KM and innovation, and on the innovation side has opted to prioritize building generalist software skills in order to provide support for a number of different types of projects.

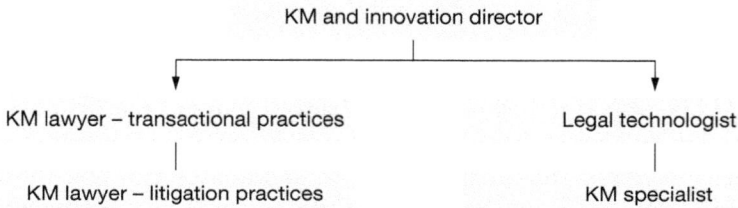

Figure 17: Early-stage KM and innovation.

Note that early-stage KM or innovation might look even more bare bones than this. You might have a director who is also a KM lawyer, and perhaps be in a position to hire just one or two additional staff. Alternatively, you could be in a lead innovation role, expected to carry out firm-wide projects in support of all lawyers, yet with the approval to hire only one or two additional staff. In both of these instances, depending of course on the projects in your pipelines, hiring staff whose skillsets complement rather than replicate yours will prove useful. If your expertise is legal and KM, perhaps you then need to hire a technical specialist with service design skills. If you have a software development background but are lacking legal expertise or the ability to support content initiatives, you may wish to hire an experienced KM lawyer or manager.

Organizational structure 2: Traditional KM

This second structure represents a traditional KM remit, where KM has had some long-term cultural support and buy-in. In this instance, the library or research function reports up into KM, as do the KM lawyers. The focus of this department is likely to be on content-related projects. In spite of the fact that this is a fairly well-staffed team, the potential for the department to undertake meaty technology-driven or custom innovation projects is low. This is where many KM departments started. Teams like this have often proven successful by partnering with a firm's IT department to take on and lead content-driven projects such as enterprise search, intranet, and matter management. The historic effectiveness of this model (depicted in Figure 18) proves that if you oversee KM and have the benefit of a solid collaborative relationship with your IT department, and the potential to have IT staff seconded to KM projects, you may not need dedicated technology personnel until your department matures.

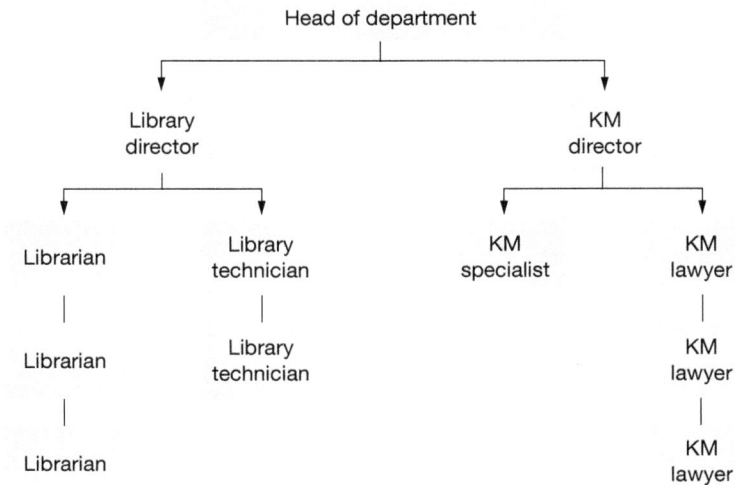

Figure 18: Traditional KM.

Organizational structure 3: KM in transition

In Figure 19, we see a KM department that has recognized the benefits of having some dedicated technology staff. This is a KM department that is on its way to becoming a practice innovation department. The addition of a business analyst role and the knowledge engineer means that the team is likely taking on more complex technology projects, including rolling out third party technology tools that serve specific practice areas. This is a team that has moved beyond pure content support and knowledge delivery systems and has started leading innovation at the firm. From the outside, it may still look like a traditional KM department but in fact this is a firm with some maturity around innovation.

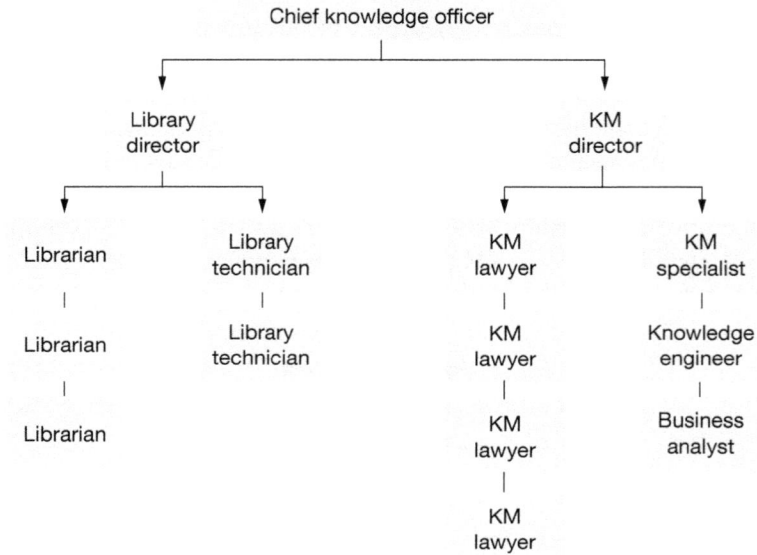

```
                        Chief knowledge officer
                                 │
         ┌───────────────────────┴───────────────────────┐
         ▼                                                ▼
     Library                                             KM
     director                                         director
         │                                                │
   ┌─────┴─────┐                              ┌────────────┴────────────┐
   ▼           ▼                              ▼                         ▼
Librarian   Library                          KM                        KM
            technician                      lawyer                   specialist
   │           │                              │                         │
Librarian   Library                          KM                     Knowledge
            technician                      lawyer                   engineer
   │                                          │                         │
Librarian                                    KM                      Business
                                           lawyer                     analyst
                                              │
                                             KM
                                           lawyer
```

Figure 19: KM in transition.

Organizational structure 4: Mature KM and innovation

In this final example (Figure 20), we see a department that has evolved beyond KM into true practice innovation. The initial technology-focused hires on the KM side have evolved into an entirely separate function under a director of innovation. This is a department well equipped to undertake a variety of projects. The data analyst roles indicate the department has begun to tackle more complex data projects. Although the ambit for this type of department may be largely focused on internal practice improvements, it has the skills necessary to begin working with clients and undertaking direct client-facing projects. Some of these personnel may already be billing some of their time to clients in respect of these projects.

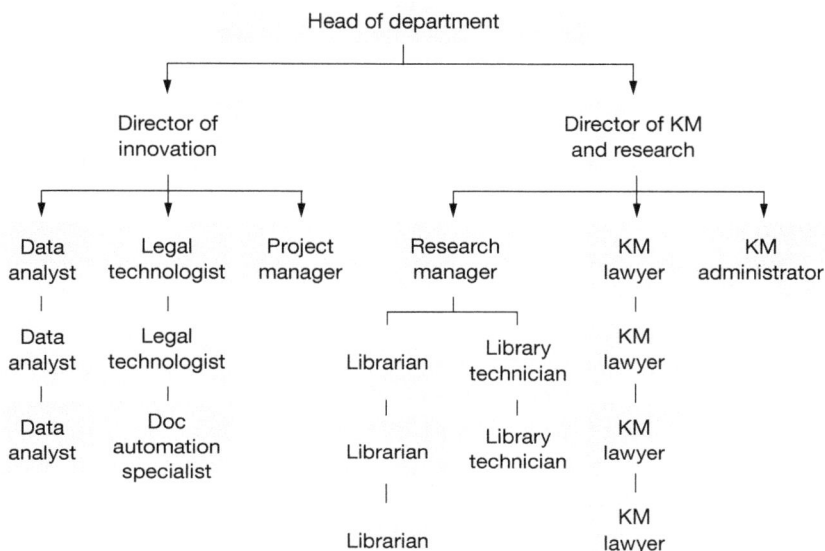

Figure 20: Mature KM and innovation.

Further development of this kind of department might see the evolution of a specific client-facing innovation arm (which could ultimately evolve into a law firm subsidiary as external projects proliferate), and the absorption of various other firm functions such as legal project management or matter management.

Creating innovation magic

There are almost as many organizational structures possible as there are law firm KM or innovation departments. As discussed above, in many firms there is no distinct innovation function. I want to stress, however, that where there is a separate innovation or practice innovation function, it is critical that this function be closely linked with knowledge management. The "magic" of law firm innovation happens in the link between KM and innovation teams. Failing to build a solid bridge between them – ideally a strategic bridge that binds the two functions – risks leaving your innovation team without adequate access to the most critical resource required to successfully drive adoption, effect culture change, and execute on innovation initiatives – your firm's lawyers.

Without the relationship to a KM department, an innovation team may find it harder to identify use cases. Without the relationship to innovation, the KM department may suffer from the absence of technical knowledge, problem-framing skills, and resources to develop solutions. This is why the most effective practice innovation departments are those that include both knowledge and innovation functions under one umbrella, or that forge close connections between these two functions and actively seek to mine those connections for the rich opportunities afforded by this critical collaboration.

If your organization does not have a robust KM function, but there are other roles with deep relationships in the practice groups – such as practice managers, for example – it would likely be possible to replicate the effectiveness of the KM–innovation link by building the bridge instead with that group. If no such team exists, your innovation team will need to be expanded to include headcount such as practice technologists, innovation managers, or innovation lawyers who themselves develop deep relationships within the practices. Without this "secret sauce" of innovation, your program will be unable to get the kind of scalable traction you need it to.

Hiring hints

Building your team according to your immediate and forecasted resourcing needs is an obvious necessity. There are also some less obvious elements to recruitment that are just as critical in creating an effective innovation team.

Innovation is not based on hard skills alone. It is fueled by several critical qualities that allow new ideas to emerge and flourish. Innovation staff who excel at their job almost always display the following key attributes:

- *Curiosity* – testing new platforms or configurations and digging into problems will come naturally to them because they like to figure out how things work;
- *Empathy* – they will have a natural inclination to seek user input on iterative releases of a solution, because they understand that the value of such a solution lies in its ability to make someone's life better; and
- *Creativity* – they are highly creative in their approach to problem-solving, brainstorming, and getting things done.

Together, these are known as the CEC attributes.

In the past, when hiring new members of my team, my approach has been to first ensure that they have the requisite skillset on paper, and then interview them to get a sense of their CEC attributes, and to determine whether they would be a good cultural fit on the team. This approach has been highly successful, ensuring that the teams I've had the privilege of leading are filled with outstanding people operating optimally. It is the opposite approach of one that is frequently taken by firms when hiring for KM lawyers, for example. Because there is a perception that lawyers in a firm won't respect a KM lawyer unless they have similar backgrounds to them, firms often prefer candidates who come from the top ranked law schools and have had many years of practice experience at equivalent firms. The difficulty with this hiring strategy is that, though this person may indeed build immediate credibility with lawyers in the practice they support, they are unlikely to exhibit the skills needed to drive innovation initiatives forward. KM lawyers play an integral role in those initiatives. They must be able to think creatively about problems and bring natural curiosity to the role in order to succeed. Another problem with this traditional hiring framework is that lawyers of this type almost always find the transition from billing practice to support role difficult. The transition gives rise to teething pains for new KM lawyers, and quite frequently sees them return to practice.

Rather than hiring for excellence in the practice of law, those recruiting for KM candidates should look for organizational skills, attention to detail, and an understanding of the importance of taxonomies, curation, and categorization in structuring information. Of course, subject matter expertise in the relevant area of practice is important, but so is the ability to listen without interjecting, and the instinct to delve deeply into problems and apply analytical frameworks. Often I find that professionals who become knowledge or innovation managers are those who instinctively started organizing and categorizing content or finding better ways to do things in a previous role. You can ask questions during an interview that tease out this information. Some of these questions include:

- How did you know you wanted to become a [role]/transition into [KM/innovation]?
- What is it that initially sparked your interest for this type of role?
- Why do you/did you think you would be good at this type of work?
- Describe some of the activities you enjoy in your spare time.

This last question is important because people's hobbies can reveal some of their "soft" strengths and skills that won't readily be apparent on a resume. In hiring for lawyers, recruiters in many law firms look for athletic successes that reveal discipline and dedication. In hiring for innovation roles, I am always interested in creative hobbies, especially ones that involve making things. In my last law firm role, I realized at some stage that almost all of the members of the innovation team were makers of some sort – they did woodwork and built cabinetry, or they knitted, or they produced ceramics. Each of these hobbies requires creativity, a curiosity into what makes one method work better than another, the ability to accept that mistakes are part of the process, and the resilience to fix those mistakes and forge a new path. Looking back, it is no accident that the team was so successful.

Both KM and innovation require the patience to recognize something is not working and the energy to pivot and try another method. This type of work also requires an acceptance of uncertainty. As someone who works in these fields, your task of improving and enhancing the way people work will never end – there will never be a moment where this is "done", like a corporate transaction, and you can move on to the next thing. Some people – especially many traditional lawyer personalities – find this uncertainty difficult to stomach.

Nathan Furr, Kyle Nel, and Thomas Zoega Ramsoy discuss the importance of becoming comfortable with uncertainty in their book, *Leading Transformation: How to Take Charge of Your Company's Future*.[1] They call this attribute "negative capability" – the ability to entertain uncertainty rather than to become anxious by it and therefore rush to resolve issues. Those who demonstrate negative capability, Furr et al. write are able to facilitate the exploration of new problem spaces and are more likely to discover adjacent opportunities:

> "*Individuals with negative capability remain curious and focused even when your project is far from the end goal. Chances are, they will even find this point of the project enthralling, rather than overwhelming, which is exactly what you want. They will also be able to suspend judgement about an end result and stay open to many possible outcomes rather than becoming fixed early on to one version of success.*"[2]

Danish politician and social worker, Uffe Elbæk, called individuals with the skillset of leading through uncertainty "chaos pilots".[3] These people have negative capability in addition to other skills such as the ability to take action and create structure within chaos.[4] Chaos pilot leaders are able to drive projects forward even as things shift and change around them.[5]

If you have put in place all of the building blocks for a successful innovation program and it's still not working, you may want to re-evaluate the skills you have on your team. Furr et al. point out that chaos pilots can be difficult to find, and difficult to keep – they care more about creating meaningful change than they do about climbing a corporate ladder or earning more money. One suggestion provided by Furr et al. for finding this type of person is to look for people who are highly prized by their organization in spite of mixed performance reviews.[6] It's likely they are getting mixed reviews because they make people around them uncomfortable as they push the status quo. However, they continue to succeed within the organization because they achieve what they set out to do.[7]

Hiring for diversity

Diversity, equity, and inclusion efforts have become centrally important to most legal organizations, especially as pressure from general counsel and clients has grown. Law firms, with a business model that has traditionally seen many more male partners than female, are under increasing scrutiny when it comes to diversity.

For those leading innovation there are other reasons beyond client pressure and general equity to focus on diversity – it has been proven that diverse teams perform better, and that diversity of thought breeds innovation. In an *HBR* article published in 2013, Sylvia Ann Hewlett, Melinda Marshall, and Laura Sherbin reviewed and presented findings of their research across a representative group of more than 1,800 professionals, which found that diversity unlocks innovation and is a key factor in driving market growth.[8] The study evaluated two types of diversity – inherent and acquired. Inherent diversity represents traits you were born with, such as gender, ethnicity, race, and sexual orientation.[9] Acquired diversity defines traits you have gained through experience, by living in other countries, for example, or working in different types of environments. In their research, Hewlett et al. defined workers with both inherent and acquired diversity as "2-D employees".[10] They found that companies with 2-D diversity both out-innovate and out-perform others. Where 2-D diversity is represented at a leadership level, it can unlock innovation by creating an environment where "outside the box" ideas are heard and welcomed.[11]

In studies conducted in 2015, 2018, and most recently in 2020, McKinsey confirmed that diverse teams and companies outperformed non-diverse teams, with a significant impact on profitability.[12] This finding has been reiterated repeatedly over the years, including by Forbes and Gartner.[13] In 2016, David Rock and Heidi Grant published findings that diverse teams were actually smarter than other teams, more likely to process facts accurately, and reach correct conclusions.[14] From an innovation perspective, diversity of thought on a team means a wider idea space during brain-storming, and a greater reach of solutions during problem-solving. Simply put – your team will be more successful if it is diverse. This is another rule to keep in mind when hiring for your team. If all of your hires look and sound exactly like you, you may want to shake things up. Ensuring that other people are involved in the interview process can help to prevent affinity bias,[15] or the tendency to hire people who are like you. Diversity in hiring should be top of mind as you set out to recruit.

Checklist: Building your team

- [ ] If you have joined an existing department, evaluate the team and skill-sets that currently reside in that department.
- [ ] Take a broader view and evaluate the types of people resources your department or function may resort to that fall outside of your immediate reporting line. For example:
  - Are there resources in the IT department that are entirely or partially assigned to supporting innovation initiatives?
  - Are there word processing or similar functions that are centralized and could be trained to support some of the more rote tasks that make up some of the projects in your plan?
  - Is there a low-cost center or a centralized paralegal or law clerk service that you might be able to draw upon?
  - Does the organization have a relationship with an alternative legal services provider providing flexible resourcing, and do you have budget to bolster your team with these types of contract workers during particularly busy periods?
- [ ] Review your strategy and list of projects against the existing skillsets in your team and determine what additional skills you'll need in order to carry out the goals of your function.
- [ ] Plan your headcount growth in line with the projects you are prioritizing, ensuring that you are equipping your team to deal with all of the types of innovation initiatives envisaged by your strategic plan.
- [ ] As you recruit and interview people, put in place processes and interview questions that will ensure you are hiring for diversity and the CEC attributes as well as core professional skills and cultural fit.
- [ ] As you plan your recruitment strategy, consider also the terminology and titles you want to use in your department. Generating support for

title changes can be a political quagmire, but setting out strategic reasons for this type of change can help. It will make it easier for you to create a consistent culture within your department, and to promote it both internally at the firm and externally to clients if you have given thought early on to the impact that role titles might have as you set out to drive change and growth.

References

1   *Leading Transformation: How to Take Charge of Your Company's Future*. Nathan Furr, Kyle Nel, and Thomas Zoega Ramsey. 2018, Harvard Business Review Press.

2   https://hbr.org/2018/11/ if-your-innovation-effort-isnt-working-look-at-whos-on-the-team

3   www.kaospilot.dk/history/

4   https://hbr.org/2018/11/ if-your-innovation-effort-isnt-working-look-at-whos-on-the-team

5   *Ibid*.

6   *Ibid*.

7   *Ibid*.

8   https://hbr.org/2013/12/how-diversity-can-drive-innovation

9   *Ibid*.

10 *Ibid*.

11 *Ibid*.

12 www.mckinsey.com/featured-insights/coronavirus-leading- through-the-crisis/charting-the-path-to-the-next-normal/ most-diverse-companies-now-more-likely-than-ever-to-outperform-financially.

13 www.forbes.com/sites/forbesinsights/2020/01/15/diversity-confirmed-to- boost-innovation-and-financial-results/?sh=301977efc4a6; www.gartner.com/ smarterwithgartner/diversity-and-inclusion-build-high-performance-teams.

14 Grant, Heidi and Rock, David. (2016). *Why Diverse Teams are Smarter*. Published by HBR. https://store.hbr.org/product/why-diverse-teams-are-smarter/H038YZ.

15 Caccavale, J. (2021). *What is Affinity Bias and How Does It Affect the Workplace?* Beapplied.com/post/what-is-affinity-bias. See also the Forbes article *Why You Mistakenly Hire People Just Like You*, by Kimberly Giles (2018) for some of the neurological reasons behind affinity bias and strategies to overcome it: forbes.com/sites/forbescoachescouncil/2018/05/01/ why-you-mistakenly-hire-people-just-like-you?/.

Part 2:
Methodologies for change

In part two, we will move away from guidance for establishing a successful legal innovation department or function and will focus instead on actual methodologies that you and your team can use to drive projects forward and inspire culture change across your organization. This part of the Handbook is intended to arm you with a set of tools for innovation, setting you up to become a more effective leader of change.

All of the approaches covered here have their origins outside of the legal industry, and many are not yet widely used within law firms. Legal organizations have been slow to adopt methodologies from other industries, even though those summarized here have been successful in many large commercial organizations. One reason law has resisted true business model change for so long is our tendency to believe that lawyers, law degrees, legal expertise, and law firms are entirely unique, different from other industries and organizations, and that we therefore can't learn from what has happened elsewhere. Lawyers are not used to thinking of their work as a business. Our regulators in many countries have prevented people with true business acumen and management expertise from running law firms, so that only lawyers have been able to own and run legal partnerships. For too long, professionals at law firms have felt the need to add the prefix "legal" to their titles, reinforcing enshrined assumptions about what is important and what matters in such organizations. Marketing professionals aren't considered to be relevant unless they are legal marketers; technology isn't viewed as useful unless it is legal technology; and innovation in law must be legal innovation.

I recognize the irony of pointing this out in a book with the words Legal Innovation in the title. One could say that words are just words and titles are just titles – except that our predilection for the "legal" prefix is a superficial indicator of currents that run deeper and have a more significant impact on the profession. As discussed in chapter seven, legal organizations have for years assumed that people hired onto KM or innovation teams in law must have a background in law or even a law degree. Even when it comes to sales, lawyers don't look at other businesses to see what works. Law firms are still appointing lawyers to sit in executive roles – chief business development, chief professional development, chief talent, chief operating, chief digital officer. In no other type of organization does this happen. The truth is that a law degree and experience as a law firm partner does not mean someone will be a successful business executive. Nor does it mean that they will have the wherewithal to innovate on a business model, especially when that business model is all they have ever known.

In order to drive true transformation in the industry, it is imperative that law firms and legal organizations move away from this presumption that anyone who works in a law firm must be a lawyer, and that the only methodologies used in firms be those that are tried and tested in the legal industry. The chapters that follow deliberately provide insights from other industries, because as someone who is tasked with leading or helping to drive change across a legal organization, it is essential that you be armed with methodologies that genuinely work.

The legal industry has proven itself to be remarkably resistant to change. The most successful approaches to change are therefore unlikely to stem from legal. Looking outside of our profession for inspiration is your best bet for disrupting legal and achieving your transformation goals.

Chapter 8:
Supercharging your strategy

Having a strategy is one thing, implementing it successfully is quite another. The work of taking a strategic plan and embarking upon the various projects and change management challenges that lie ahead is an arduous one. If you consistently approach your team and the tasks ahead of you with the notion that you are solving problems, identifying pockets of inefficiency, addressing issues from which the organization suffers, at some stage all of you will suffer from burn-out. Especially in today's hybrid reality, taking an unwaveringly negative approach to change will ultimately affect the wellbeing of your people.

There are, however, methods you can embrace to ensure your team remains upbeat. The secret lies in applying a mix of approaches and understanding when individuals on your team need a boost of optimism. The simple mindset shifts involved in the approaches outlined in this chapter can help refresh any team and bring new enthusiasm to your change effort, no matter how exhausting it once seemed.

TNT – Tiny Noticeable Things

In early 2020, I sat on a panel for the LWOW virtual webinar series with James Batham, a partner at Eversheds Sutherland in the UK. On that panel, James spoke about what he termed "TNTs", or "Tiny Noticeable Things". He said that sometimes we are so concerned about large-scale change that we forget about the very real impact small gestures can have. James had trained his team to think about the small things they could do for their lawyers that would have an impact that was out of proportion to the minimal level of effort required to do these things. The term TNT is a beautifully apt way of describing these micro-changes – in spite of their small scale, the influence they have is tantamount to an explosion.

I recently discovered that the origins of this term come from Adrian Webster, a well-known public speaker. Webster published his book, *Tiny Noticeable Things*,[1] in early 2021, and it's worth reading for all of the examples of TNTs he has collected from different people and industries. There are also some excellent videos[2] that are publicly available in which Webster discusses the power of TNTs to disrupt industries and society. As Webster says, driving large-scale change is difficult because human brains are hard-wired to resist new ways of doing things. TNTs are so small, however, that they are able to slip right past the inhibitors and resistors in the brain, and are therefore able to have a big impact faster. As Webster says, TNTs are "absolutely tiny", but they create "the biggest, longest lasting pictures in people's minds".[3]

All of us can think of times when someone did something that took minimal effort, and yet it stuck in our minds because it made a difference. One example Webster uses is when, upon staying at a hotel in Scotland, the maid not only cleaned his room and made up his bed, but also moved the novel he had left open on his bed to his bedside table, inserting a hotel-branded bookmark so he didn't lose his place. At the same hotel, every staff member Webster met remembered his name and helped him get to where he needed to be. I certainly have stories from my own life of small actions people have taken that have stayed with me and left a dispropor-tionately significant impact. The acquaintance who sent me a hand-written card of appreciation when it didn't have to be done. The consulting team who sent my family a box of Australian goodies at the beginning of the COVID-19 pandemic, because they knew we'd had to cancel a trip back home to Australia to see family. These are gestures I will never forget, and they have spread goodwill that may mean I would be more likely to choose that consultant to perform some work at a later date, or hire the acquaintance who sent me that card.

Another story Webster tells in one of his videos had particular reso-nance. He recounts the tale of a man who had worked his whole life to build up a business. During that time, he had never been able to afford a new car. He finally reached a point where the business was not only viable but successful, and his wife told him to go out and buy the new car of his dreams. Excited, the man started researching cars. He narrowed his choice down to two brands – Mercedes and Lexus. He finally decided on a Mercedes, and was thrilled when his brand new Mercedes arrived one day in his driveway. This new car represented all the hard work he had done in his life. He got in and sniffed the new car smell. It was perfect. Except – it wasn't, not quite. The cigarette lighter was missing from the front panel of the car. The man didn't even smoke, but the fact that a piece was missing from his pristine new car weighed on him. He called the Mercedes dealer and they promised to take care of it, but the sheen of that perfect new car had already been somewhat diminished.

That afternoon, while he was out buying groceries, the man got a call from the Lexus dealer he had been communicating with during his pre-purchase deliberations. He told the Lexus dealer that he had ended up going with Mercedes. During the conversation, he happened to mention that the Mercedes was delivered – without the cigarette lighter. The Lexus dealer reassured him that Mercedes customer service was excellent, he was sure the man would be taken care of, and he hoped that for his next car purchase, he would consider Lexus.

When the man got home later that day, his neighbor ran into his driveway holding a giant box.

"A courier delivered this while you were away!" he said. The man took the package into the kitchen, got out a knife and opened the box. Under layers of bubble wrap was a package made of cotton. Inside that cotton wool, the man found a brand new Mercedes cigarette lighter. And underneath this item, there was a note reading:

"Enjoy your new Mercedes. From, your Lexus dealer."

This small token – buying a tiny part and having it delivered promptly – no doubt stayed with the man forever, and I'm sure you and I share a view as to what his next car was, or which company he would recommend to any friend embarking on a new car purchase.

Imagine if we could institute a TNT approach at our legal organizations, both in the services that our teams provide internally and also in the way that the organization as a whole serves its customers. Webster says that he eventually tracked down the head of training at the hotel he stayed at in Scotland. Webster told the training manager about all of the wonderful experiences he'd had with the hotel staff. The head of training said that the hotel's ethos was to make every customer feel as though they were the most special guest at the hotel – even as though they were the only guest.

Imagine if law firms were able to consistently make clients feel this way. If every call the client made to a law firm was answered by a person who knew who that client was by name – and what the client's business was, what the status was of the client matters at the firm, maybe even what the names of the client contact's children were and what college they were at. Imagine if every client of your firm, or every customer of your corporate legal department, was made to feel like they were the most special customer of all – no matter which office of the firm or company they called. Would those clients ever be tempted to move their business elsewhere? It's certainly less likely.

There are technology platforms that could support this ethos and make it easier for firms to go above and beyond in myriad small ways that would make their clients feel this way. Even without technology, there is power in instilling a consistent philosophy that informs the way that services are provided to all clients. As an innovation leader, consider how impactful it would be if your team was trained to use TNTs regularly when interacting with lawyers at the organization – not just to respond to queries but to listen to and anticipate pain-points, to find subtle ways of solving problems that would make an immediate and notable impact. If every lawyer who interacted with your team felt special, like their needs truly mattered, it would be far easier to sell and promote bigger enterprise-wide changes. This is a powerful extension of empathy, taking it from the individual to a systems-wide level.

In your position, consider some of the small things that your team could be doing right now that would have higher value than might be expected. In one of the firms I worked at, we had an Associates' Committee on Emerging Technology. We met with the associates in this committee about ten times a year, each time presenting technology demos, giving insights on the pilots we were running, and the initiatives the firm was undertaking. In spite of the fact that we were consistently showing them cutting-edge tools and resources, the best responses we got from those meetings stemmed from the smallest things. We would get the associates themselves to share tips on what had worked for them and made a positive difference to their practice. Often something as small as an intuitive way to convert PDFs to Word from a mobile device was sure to generate more excitement than a shiny new contract review system. The most enthusiasm we ever garnered from one of those meetings was in response to a demo by one of our legal technologists of a series of macros he had built in Word that could help with the formatting of text that had been cut and pasted from another document. What could be simpler in technology terms than Word macros? And yet these small automations made a huge impact on the associates, because they knew they would be able to use them immediately to remove a frustrating element of their daily work.

Change doesn't have to be large-scale. Don't ever underestimate the power of tiny things to improve the lives of the people you support. If your team is trained to think about TNTs, and to implement them whenever possible, the success of those TNTs is likely to build up the credibility and goodwill associated with your department, which will help you get larger initiatives across the finish line when it matters. Although some commentators in our industry feel true transformation can't occur until entire end-to-end legal workflows have been changed, those of us working at the coalface know that, in most instances, end-to-end transformation will only come as we chip away gradually, transforming one small aspect of legal work at a time. After many such tiny chips in the coalface, suddenly a change will be big enough and substantial enough to be recognized as transformative from the outside.

Change happens slowly, and then all at once. Once it has happened, only those on the inside will know the secret truth – that the transformation happened in iterative spurts, one TNT layered on top of another.

Locating bright spots

Almost all change and innovation efforts begin with the identification of areas in an organization where things are not working well. Indeed, I train my teams to watch and listen for pain-points. We direct our efforts towards processes that are inefficient, areas of legal practice that are suffering from write-offs and low realization, workflows that are arduous and manual when they need not be. Although this approach can certainly be effective, it's not the only approach we can take and there are benefits to integrating a different approach alongside this relatively pessimistic model.

Starting from the point of failure is a negative strategy, which will ultimately weigh upon your innovation professionals. In order to be truly effective as an innovator, one has to be an optimist; if you don't yourself believe that things can and will improve, it will be almost impossible to pull others along with you on the change journey. Why should they believe in a better future if you don't? Most successful change agents are optimists at heart. At the beginning of COVID-19, one of my friends and colleagues in the industry, Marco Imperiale (Italy's first ever chief innovation officer, at Italian law firm LCA Studio Legale in Milan) said to me in his usual charming way that "instead of yearning for sunshine, we need to learn to dance in the rain". Dreaming of widespread transformation that may take the legal industry decades to achieve won't serve any of us as well as finding ways to progress change now, even before institutional barriers fall. That dream is what keeps many of us going, but even the heartiest of optimists will ultimately become jaded if the areas of the organization their work is consistently focused upon are those where productivity and efficiency is at its lowest ebb. Fortunately, there are alternative approaches to change that will enable you to change the timbre of your innovation efforts and help reinstate your optimism.

Bright spots

An alternative approach that I like to use in encouraging and training my team, and to rejuvenate enthusiasm for the work that we do, is to identify and focus on "bright spots". In their book *Switch*,[4] brothers Chip and Dan Heath talk about bright spots as "successful efforts worth emulating".[5] They use the example of a man named Jerry Sternin, who worked for the nonprofit Save the Children, and was tasked in 1990 with fighting malnutrition in Vietnam. It was a daunting task – Sternin himself didn't speak Vietnamese, and the institutional reasons for widespread malnutrition among babies and children seemed clear; poor sanitation, widespread poverty, a shortage of clean water, and a lack of information about good nutrition. In addition, the government of Vietnam was not universally supportive of the organization's presence in the country, and Sternin was given just six months to make a difference.

Sternin knew that addressing any of these systemic issues would be impossible in six months. Instead, he met with mothers in rural villages, divided them into teams and sent them out to weigh and measure every child in their village. When they met to analyze the results, the question Sternin asked was not about the areas that were most problematic. Instead, he asked whether there were any children living in poverty who were nevertheless bigger and healthier than the typical Vietnamese child. Sure enough, there were instances in various villages where poor families had well-nourished children. Sternin set out to investigate these instances, in order to find out what these families were doing differently. If it was possible for these children to be healthy in spite of all of their disadvantages, it meant that malnutrition was not inevitable, even in the midst of the current systemic conditions.

Sternin and his team ended up discovering exactly what it was that these "bright spot" families were doing differently – a combination of the types of foods the families were feeding their children (they were using greens from sweet potato plants and unusual sources of protein), the quantity of food, the style of eating, and the number of times each day the children were fed. Once these specifics were understood, Sternin could work to educate the mothers in villages across Vietnam and replicate the behaviors that allowed children to flourish. The Heath brothers report that six months after Sternin arrived in Vietnam, an astonishing 65 percent of children were better nourished than when he had arrived – and, moreover, they stayed that way.

There are a number of things we can take away from Sternin's story and apply to our roles as legal innovators. First, finding the bright spots is a positive approach to change. Unlike our ingrained instinct to search out problems, reorienting your team to look instead for areas where processes are working well allows for emotional rejuvenation – it's exciting to find these pockets of success! Also, as we have seen from Sternin's efforts, focusing on bright spots within a broader system allows for change to occur from within, because it replicates positive achievements that have been able to flourish in the midst of – and in the context of – whatever systemic obstacles exist in the organization. Replicating these efforts therefore allows you to push constructive change without needing to first eliminate bigger hurdles that will take years to budge.

Another benefit of the bright spots approach is that, as the Heath brothers write, it evades the "not invented here" problem. Many of you reading this book will have had the experience of bringing an idea back to your organization that you heard was working well at another firm or department, only to be confronted with skepticism. You have likely heard comments along the lines of, "I don't care if X firm is doing that, it won't work here, because Y". The "Y" in this equation can be any number of things – the culture of the firm, the structures in place, the way the firm views its client work as being more bespoke than that of other firms where novel ideas are gaining traction. Identifying something that is already working within your actual environment takes the potency out of this objection. This isn't something that is having an impact elsewhere – it's working right here, right now, in this environment.

In 2018, our team piloted a new solution with our employment practice. The solution promised to solve a tedious pain-point around drafting discovery requests and responses to those requests. Over the duration of our pilot, which we always ran with end users to validate a solution and its ability to address a particular use case, we found that the software – though ground-breaking and powerful – did not solve the problem for the type of employment matter our firm undertook. Our firm's employment practice tended to take on large multi-party matters, often class actions, but the solution was geared towards simpler disputes between two parties. We provided this feedback to the vendor and decided to move on without investing in the new technology. As we will explore later in this book, the ability to pivot and accept that a project (in spite of best efforts) has failed is essential to any successful innovation approach.

In fact, something great emerged from the ashes of that pilot. In the course of the many discussions that were had with employment lawyers as our team worked with them on the initiative, one of our KM attorneys discovered an associate who had established a much more efficient process to collate discovery responses than the other associates in his group. Instead of cutting and pasting disparate responses and tweaking them, generating a response gradually and painstakingly through repetitive manual work, he had discovered that by assigning a number to each of the feasible response answers, he could then put together a document that simply cited the relevant response numbers at the right sections of the document. The associate turned these response formulas and the draft response document over to the firm's document processing service, and they were able to produce a complete response document in far less time than it would have taken to write out each response himself. Not only was the whole process more efficient, it also utilized low-cost timekeepers during the part of the workflow that was purely administrative, thereby further reducing costs.

Once we became aware of this bright spot in the employment practice, it enabled us to sit with the associate and map out his entire end-to-end process. We discovered that there were other ways we could improve the process, too, and worked with the associate to sanity-check these and record a better overall process. We then developed a map or flowchart that provided guidelines and a checklist that could be used by every associate in the group to cut down on the manual time and the burdensome nature of this workflow. The result was the amplification of this bright spot to the entire practice group, improving their efficiency and reducing an internal pain point – all without investing in shiny new technology. In mapping out the improved process, we also set the group up for a potential phase two of the project that would likely involve automation of the new process using one of our existing tools.

One of the interesting aspects of this project was the emotional impact it had on the people involved. Having been disappointed by a failed pilot, the KM attorney who identified the bright spot was rejuvenated to see that she could make a difference without new technology. The associate with whom we worked to map out a better process was initially skeptical of our approach, and somewhat irritated by the time required to walk us through his process. As the mapping session evolved, however, he became animated and enthusiastic when he realized the impact that it would have on his broader practice if everyone was using a more efficient means to conduct the work. I'm sure he also felt some pride that his way of doing things was considered to be a "bright spot" in the organization.

If you are ever facing a team or a member of your team who is feeling particularly jaded, consider setting them a task of going out to find a bright spot. And then, as the Heath brothers say, your job – your mission – is to clone those bright spots wherever you find them. By doing so, you will leverage improved processes more broadly without having to first break through systemic hurdles that may feel impossible to overcome.

Appreciative inquiry

If bright spots are what you want to find, appreciative inquiry is the method for finding them. We were fortunate to uncover the bright spot described above without having gone out specifically to find it. Appreciative inquiry provides a methodology for actively and consciously evaluating your firm or organization specifically for the purpose of uncovering areas of high performance. Similar to the Heath brothers' reasoning around bright spots, proponents of the appreciative inquiry methodology (which is confusingly abbreviated to "AI" in the related literature) believe in focusing on the positive. The methodology brings a strengths-based approach to organizational change, which can be used to identify best practices, shift culture, and generate forward momentum on enterprise-wide projects.[6] It has been used successfully in other industries, including, for example, to improve customer service at British Airways and to optimize value creation at Wal-Mart,[7] but it is not a methodology spoken of in legal.

Similar to the bright spots approach, appreciative inquiry distinguishes itself from other change models by focusing on the pockets of an organization where processes are working best and using this insight as a model to develop future plans. Appreciative inquiry brings a broader approach to positive change and establishes a framework for enterprise-wide projects. In order to undertake an appreciative inquiry engagement, an innovation leader would leverage resources on the team to explore the strengths and successes that already exist across an organization, both for internal processes and client-facing processes.[8] Using appreciative inquiry can help to create a common vision and direction for your team and the organization, promote innovation and learning, building a positive culture and inspiring collective action.

There are four stages to the appreciative inquiry process, which has come to be known as the "4-D cycle" – discovery, dream, design, and destiny (see Figure 21).[9]

The 4-D cycle can be undertaken at scale, by a large team, but it could also be leveraged as an individual methodology by someone on your team. For example, if a KM lawyer is looking for a new way to add value to their practice groups, undertaking a 4-D cycle with lawyers and other constituents in that practice is a highly effective way to do that.

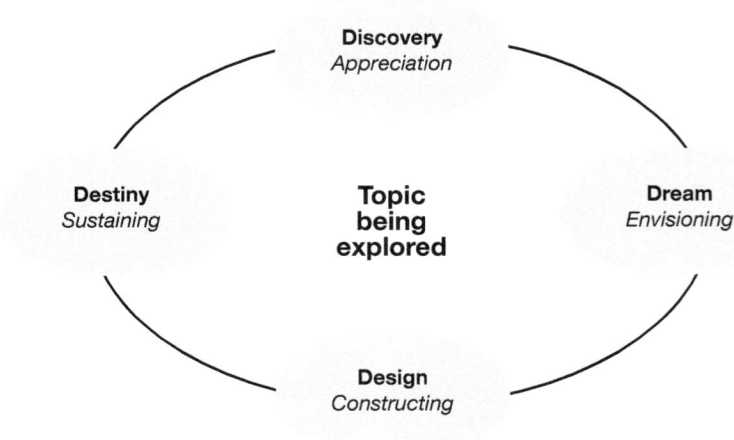

Figure 21: The 4-D Cycle of Appreciative Inquiry.[10]

Discovery

In the discovery phase, participants will spend time identifying the strengths and best practices of the organization (or the pocket of the organization targeted by this appreciative inquiry engagement).[11] Sources of peak performance will be examined. In a legal organization, one way to focus discovery might be to examine the financial performance and utilization rates of partners within a practice, and spend time undertaking discovery with those partners and their teams. Appreciative inquiry proponents call this the practice of exploring "the best of what is". After having multiple conversations with high-performing partners you might start to see common themes that reveal how high-performing teams in your organization are operating and why that leads to greater success.

Dream

The next stage of the 4-D cycle is the "dream" phase – a word that isn't widely used at law firms. In order to make it more palatable for your organization, this phase could just as easily be called Envisioning, Goal-setting, or Planning.[12] During the dream phase, participants in the engagement envision the future they want for the organization. What would the organization – or the practice group – look like if it was succeeding to its full potential around core values and strategic goals?

During this phase, participants in the engagement think in concrete terms about what the organization or practice would ideally look like in the future. In a corporate legal department, you could look at the department itself and consider, based on feedback during the discovery phase, how the team would be operating and how it would be regarded in the context of the broader organization if the "best of what is" was distributed more broadly. How would the behavior of leaders change? What resources would be necessary? How would organizational processes need to change? Would there be a requirement for changes in physical space? The vision created by the end of the dream phase should serve as inspiration to those involved in the project.

Design

In the third phase of the 4-D cycle, the project participants leverage the information gained during the discovery phase and the vision of the future they have created in order to design high-impact strategies that will move the organization effectively in the right direction.[13] Look at where you want to get to, and where you are now. Consider what steps are needed today in order to reach the vision.

The design phase will be more effective the more granular participants get in developing plans. Looking at the themes that emerged in your evaluation of "the best of what is", spend time creating models and prototypes of the various elements of the vision. This is where it makes sense to map out the processes that are working and build out the steps that would have to be taken in order to implement these processes in other areas of the organization. Record the resources that will be necessary in order to undertake those steps, and think about the support you will need in order to move things forward.

Destiny

Like Dream, Destiny is likely to be a word that does not resonate in a legal organization. The fourth and final stage of the 4-D cycle is also sometimes called Deploy[14] – a word that is more likely to engender support for your team's undertaking. In this phase, you are taking the strategies and roadmaps that have been developed during the Design phase and putting them into action.[15]

As the project evolves, some of the plans that have been designed may need to be tweaked or revised. Depending on how long the overall engagement takes, unexpected events such as departures from the core project team may occur. The deploy stage of an appreciative inquiry engagement should remain flexible enough to allow for alterations to project plans so that there is forward momentum towards the vision, regardless of what happens.[16] The end point of the Deploy phase is reached when the vision is realized.

Similar to TNTs, bright spots, and listening programs, appreciative inquiry should have a place in your toolkit as a practical method by which to drive culture change in your organization and implement your over-arching strategy. An effective innovation leader will use creativity and a variety of methods to inspire change – taking the same approach time and again is antithetical to the concept of innovation. Having a number of different approaches in your arsenal will help you frame problems in new ways and use a variety of communication tactics to overcome roadblocks and internal hurdles.

A note on mental health

Unfortunately, law is a profession particularly vulnerable to mental health issues. Compared to the general population, lawyers are signifi-cantly more likely to suffer from depression, addiction, and other mental health problems.

Innovative approaches to reducing manual and repetitive work and increasing productivity can have a real impact on the wellbeing of lawyers at work.

As someone leading change within the environments that give rise to these statistics, it's important to remember that your colleagues and team may be subject to unhealthy pressures. Ensuring that your team and the staff around you are able to maintain a healthy perspective on both work and life is critical. Implementing positive change approaches alongside negative ones will help you provide a more enriching working environment for your team.

Checklist: Optimistic change approaches

☐ Consider educating your team on the notion of TNTs, encouraging them to seek out small ways to improve client service delivery, both internal and external.

☐ As you embark on project work with your team, check in with them regularly. In order to be an effective innovation, legal ops, or transforma-tion worker, you need to have energy and optimism. And yet, as discussed in part one, the traditional organizational structures and business models that often characterize commercial legal environments can make it difficult to maintain that positivity. It's important to make sure that everyone on the team is getting the support that they need, and that they're able to take breaks from time to time to prevent burn-out.

☐ Mix up your approach to innovation. Focusing entirely on problems and pain-points may ultimately have a negative impact on your personnel – and on you. Taking the same approach to everything is the opposite of innovation; it's likely to cause stagnation. Having a few different approaches up your sleeve will allow you to mix it up when you need to. As a leader, remain open and flexible to trying new things, or to approaching existing initiatives from a new angle. Expanding your toolkit will make you (and your team) more effective.

References

1   Webster, Adrian. *Tiny Noticeable Things: The Secret Weapon to Making a Difference in Business*. Chichester, West Sussex: John Wiley & Sons Ltd, 2021.

2   See, for example, www.youtube.com/watch?v=1O1xQ6kPJYg.

3   Webster, p.21.

4   Heath, Chip, and Heath, Dan. *Switch: How to Change Things When Change is Hard*. New York: Currency, 2010.

5   Heath and Heath, p.28.

6   Benedictine University: *What is Appreciative Inquiry? A Short Guide to the Appreciative Inquiry Model and Process*. www.Cvdl.en.edu.

7   *Ibid.*

8   *Ibid.*

9   *Ibid.*

10 Adapted from AgileCoffee.com, https://agilecoffee.com/toolkit/appreciative-inquiry/.

11 Benedictine University: *What is Appreciative Inquiry? A Short Guide to the Appreciative Inquiry Model and Process*. www.Cvdl.en.edu.

12 *Ibid.*

13 *Ibid.*

14 *Ibid.*

15 *Ibid.*

16 *Ibid.*

Chapter 9:
Change management

Legal organizations are novices at change management. Law firms, for example, often approach change management as if it constitutes no more than the communications and training offered around the launch of a new solution. Sometimes project management is mistaken for or regarded as synonymous with change management. Mostly, however, change management is approached as an afterthought, or as the last piece in the implementation puzzle, rather than as the cushion in which every element of a project must be enveloped from beginning to end. In some firms, not only has change management come to be defined in terms of training, but the team conducting such training may be called the change management team. Approaching adoption at the end of a project does not address even the basic initial steps of change management philosophy, and calling a team that conducts training or issues launch communications a change management team is an extraordinary misnomer. Change management philosophy provides helpful guidance for every stage of a project, and the most successful projects run by your department will be those that are informed by change management practices from beginning to end.

Change is hard, and it's unlikely to happen organically – unless there is a significant push or "burning platform", like COVID-19, which required organizations to suddenly work in a completely different way. Generally speaking, people (and organizations) need to be supported through change or they won't successfully adapt to it or adopt new ways of doing things. In over 70 percent of projects involving major change, organizations are not successful in achieving their goals because of failure to manage the "human" reaction to change.[1] Change takes time and effort and requires a change management strategy and a deliberate plan to be successful.

One of the biggest pitfalls of innovation teams in law firms is the absence of change management expertise on the team. For years, leaders in KM and innovation teams have been making a bizarre hiring decision. They are put in the position of leading change across an organization in order to ensure that modern, digital practices are put in place. Such leadership is necessary because it is understood that legal organizations and lawyers themselves are highly resistant to change. In building support for that change effort, those leaders then hire lawyers onto their teams – the very people they know to be resistant to change. Although the diversity of talent now being hired onto innovation teams has increased, it's still rare for these teams to hire dedicated change managers. Given that you will be expecting your team to successfully drive change projects in your organization, it is therefore incumbent upon you to ensure they are equipped with the requisite tools. In my last role, after myself becoming certified in change management, I produced a 12-week change management course that became mandatory for everyone in the department. It fundamentally altered the way in which the individuals in the department planned communications around pilots, launches, roll-outs, and ongoing promotion of tools and resources, and we saw more engagement from our lawyers as a result.

I highly recommend either hiring specific change management experts onto your team or educating your team on change management principles if your collective role includes driving innovation across an organization. It will better empower them to lead change and will therefore help you reach your own goals. The information in this chapter should prove valuable to you and to everyone on your team. By providing an overview of change management philosophies and tactics, it will give all of you the tools you need to gain momentum on change efforts within your organization.

What is change management?

Change management is a broad area of study that has developed and evolved over many years. The strategies examined in chapter eight are discrete methodologies that represent modern approaches to organizational change. Traditionally, however, change management constitutes a series of practical steps and tools that provide a roadmap for pushing change through an organization, based on a philosophy most famously set down by John Kotter (the godfather of change management). It is this holistic approach to complex change projects that we will explore in this chapter.

Broadly speaking, change management for a particular project will involve:

- A plan or strategy outlining the objectives and approach to change management for a particular project;
- A change and communications plan, outlining the key stakeholders, messages, media, and frequency of communications (this aspect of change will be addressed further in chapter ten); and

- Controls to make change stick, lock in the new with the old, and alter organizational structures to support the change (this aspect will be addressed further in chapter 14).

Change management is not just about changing systems and processes, however. It is also about supporting people through change. In any change project, there will be resistance. The job of an innovation team is to move people through resistance to acceptance.

The change curve

There are four critical principles of change that it is important to understand.

- *Principle 1:* Change is registered in the prefrontal cortex, the same place in the brain as pain.[2] It is energy intensive to process new information. The perceived differences between expectations and a new reality (change) are detected by the brain as errors. The errors trigger the fear circuitry of the amygdala, which registers in the prefrontal cortex as actual pain.[3] Understanding this can help us to experience empathy for what people are going through when they experience change.

- *Principle 2:* When your brain expects something, you shape your imagined reality in response to that expectation.[4] This is how the placebo effect works. When someone knows a change is coming, they create an anticipated reality in their brain for how that change will look. In considering this, you can see that there will be implications for how you go about creating a vision of change and communicating that to the lawyers in your practice – to make sure that the imagined reality they create in response to the communication is as close as possible to the actual reality created by the change.

- *Principle 3:* The greater the difference between your expectations and what you perceive to be reality, the greater the stress you will experience in response to change.[5] In other words, if there is a disconnect between the expectations you have shaped in your brain, and the reality that ensues, you will experience a high level of stress in response to change. As legal innovators, we sometimes talk about how lawyers expect technology to be magic – a frustrating expectation that is difficult to dislodge. Lawyers have likely set expectations in their brain that if they use this particular technology tool, it will perform perfectly. Their irritation when it doesn't is a result of the stress they are experiencing when those expectations are not borne out in reality. It's why it is so important for innovation professionals to manage expectations around performance of a new tool at the outset of a project. People feel they have lost control when their expectations are out of sync with reality, especially when it comes to major change. The typical lawyer personality feels they need to be in control. Managing expectations can alleviate the stress of change.

- *Principle 4:* Change is a process. It's a process with very distinct stages, and it is best described as a curve.

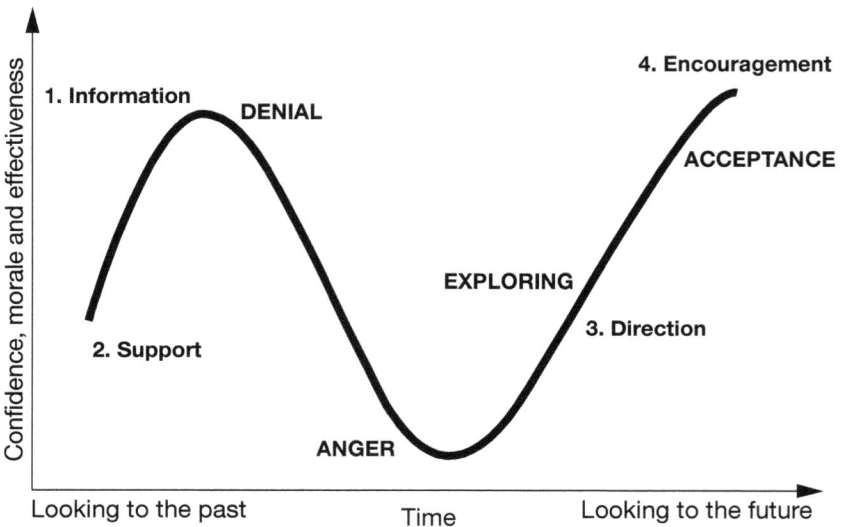

Figure 22: The change curve, adapted from John Kotter.

Figure 22 depicts John Kotter's change curve. Kotter was the first to posit that people go through a predictable set of emotions when confronted by change.[6] This model shows those emotions in line with the type of assistance we can provide to deal with each of those emotions.

At stage one, people are in denial of the change that is coming. That is when they need to be provided with information about it. They will benefit from resources that explain:

- What is coming?
- Why is the firm making this change?
- What will this mean for me?

In stage two, as they move into anger at the disruption of their status quo, people experience resistance to the change. They may even be depressed in the face of it. Here, they need support and reassurance from you, messages such as:

- "It's going to be better than it was before."
- "Once you get used to it, you'll love it and you'll never want to go back."

As recipients of the change gradually move into the exploration phase, they will need you to provide them with direction. This is where it becomes beneficial to offer training:

- Here's how you use the tool.
- Here's how it fits into your practice.
- Here's when to use it.

It's a good idea to offer training upon launching a tool or a resource to a practice group, even if the product you are launching seems so intuitive that it requires no training. The people to whom you are launching the tool still require direction in order to be motivated to pick it up.

Finally, as people move through the curve and arrive at acceptance, your role is to provide them with encouragement. This is when you can use methodologies like celebrating and promoting quick wins:

- This person started using [TOOL] and they love it!
- This metric has improved by X amount since Y percent of people started using it.
- These clients have noticed a change and are happy.

Variations of the change curve

Elisabeth Kübler-Ross, a Swiss-American psychiatrist and a pioneer in near-death studies, wrote the renowned book *On Death and Dying*, in which she first discussed her theory of the five stages of grief, also known as the "Kübler-Ross model". The Kübler-Ross model is now frequently depicted as a change curve (see Figure 23).[7]

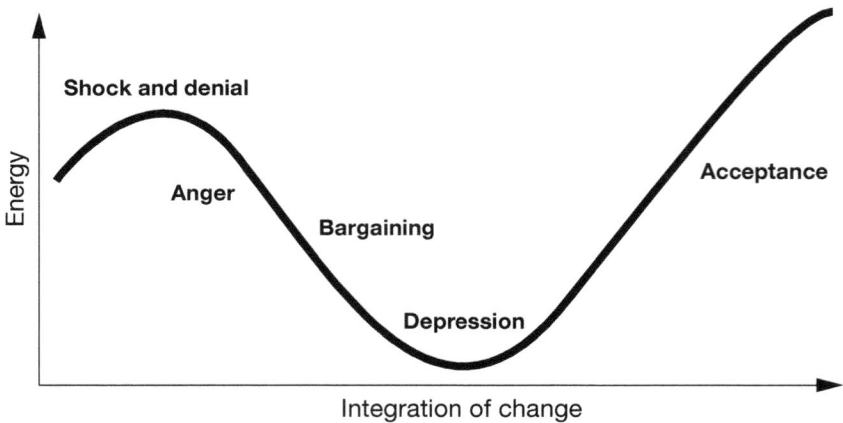

Figure 23: The change curve depicting the five stages of grief, adapted from Kübler-Ross.

Kübler-Ross proposed that a terminally ill patient would progress through five stages of grief when informed of their illness. She further proposed that this model could be applied to any dramatic life-changing situation.[8] By the 1980s, the change curve adopting Kübler-Ross's grief model had become a firm fixture in change management circles. This is another way to look at the change model – it gives us even more insight into the emotional responses people feel to change, and, hopefully, greater empathy to help us guide them through those responses.

Organizations such as the Acuity Institute have overlayed the Kübler-Ross grief stages with Kotter's change curve to propose a model of organizational change in business (see Figure 24).

This model further illustrates the fact that different types of information or reassurance are effective at each stage of the change curve. Before denial, or before hearing about the imminent change, people are neutral. They have no knowledge of the change that is coming. In order to kick off the change process, you have to communicate with the people affected by the change and give them insight of your vision of the future or they won't be able to initiate their journey through the change curve. Once people start hearing about the upcoming change, some people will actually feel some initial excitement, which should be encouraged. Then comes the denial, often caused by a jaded attitude that is skeptical of your ability to genuinely help them. "It won't really change anything. Why would this be any different?" During this stage, you will need to reinforce the vision and share inspirational stories, such as how this change has had the desired impact in other organizations. Next, the plunge into the Valley of Despair:

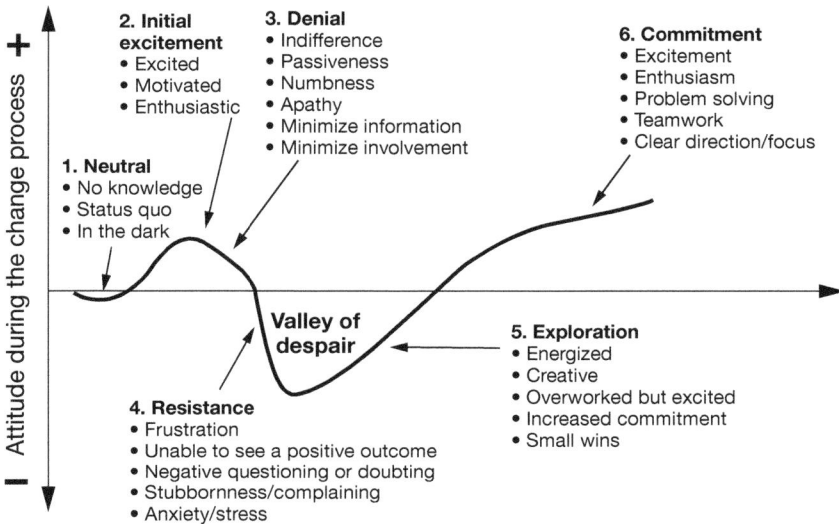

2. Initial excitement
- Excited
- Motivated
- Enthusiastic

3. Denial
- Indifference
- Passiveness
- Numbness
- Apathy
- Minimize information
- Minimize involvement

6. Commitment
- Excitement
- Enthusiasm
- Problem solving
- Teamwork
- Clear direction/focus

1. Neutral
- No knowledge
- Status quo
- In the dark

Valley of despair

5. Exploration
- Energized
- Creative
- Overworked but excited
- Increased commitment
- Small wins

4. Resistance
- Frustration
- Unable to see a positive outcome
- Negative questioning or doubting
- Stubbornness/complaining
- Anxiety/stress

Attitude during the change process

Figure 24: The change curve in business.[9] Used with permission from Acuity Institute, 2023.

> *"I don't have time to learn a new way of doing things! I don't want to. Can't I just keep doing things the way I've always done them?"*

This is the most difficult stage to overcome. People will need to be shepherded through it with more hands-on training and education. Once they get through the depth of resistance, there is the exploration phase. "Ok, I can see that maybe this looks a little better. Can you show me how to use it?" Here, sharing quick wins and early success stories will have a big impact.

Finally, commitment. "This is so much better. Everyone should be using this. It makes such a big difference." At this stage, the change has been successfully made.

Ultimately, if you have shepherded your people through these mental swings and roundabouts, the change you're driving will become the new normal. This is what has happened time and again as technology capabilities have evolved and matured. In 1996, when Richard Susskind proclaimed in his book *The Future of Law*[10] that email would become the dominant form of communication between lawyers and their clients, the resistance even from the Law Society of England and Wales was so vigorous that he was accused of bringing the profession into disrepute.[11] Now law firms complain about their lawyers' over-reliance on emails and email management is a challenge many legal technology companies have tried to address. eDiscovery followed a similar pattern, with initial resistance giving way to total adoption. In both cases, the technology has become not just an acceptable mode for doing something but a basic requirement of modern lawyers, with judges penalizing those that lag behind.[12] Once a particular way of doing things becomes the new status quo, it's easy to forget that there was resistance that first had to be overcome.

What should be abundantly clear from these various iterations of the change curve is that any "change" program or roll-out that stops before it is properly entrenched is unlikely to succeed. This is why such a high percentage of projects in major organizations fail.[13] Most launch and roll-out programs don't guide people through the emotional journey they will inevitably undergo as they learn about and try to adopt the new tool, and so users who are still stuck in the "valley of despair" or even in the early exploratory stage will slip back into the way they have always done things. Adoption requires ongoing promotion and carefully managed change programs that address users with the right messaging at each stage of the change curve.

Change planning

Kotter's work on change is foundational not just because he defined the change curve, but also because he developed an eight-stage process for successfully navigating change (see Figure 25).

Step 1: Increase urgency

Step 2: Build guiding team

Step 3: Develop a vision

Step 4: Communicate to get buy-in

Step 5: Empower action

Step 6: Create short-term wins

Step 7: Don't give up

Step 8: Make the change permanent

Figure 25: Eight-stage process for creating major change. Adapted from John Kotter.

Change management professionals have since transformed this eight-stage process into planning templates and roadmaps that can be adapted for all kinds of change projects.

Every project or initiative you undertake should include active change planning. Although communications planning is a part of change planning, having a communications plan in place is not enough to ensure that you are leveraging all of the principles of change management to adequately move your project to success.

Instead, consider creating a change management template that you review with the project team in relation to each of your projects. An example of such a roadmap document is shown in Figure 26 on the next page.

Using a template such as this will help you to define how you intend to address each critical aspect of change management as you move through the phases of your project. The change activities related to each project will involve:

- Setting out clearly the future state vision for your project;
- Understanding the change and the impact of that change on the organization;
- Developing a communications plan with messaging for each persona group that helps chart the course through the change curve;
- Identifying the project sponsor, the change team, and the network of change agents you will draw upon in order to garner support for the project;
- Setting out roles and responsibilities of the change team, establishing the actions that will be taken by the various roles on that team, and prescribing a schedule for those actions to occur;
- Identifying stakeholders and analyzing their potential influence on the project outcome;
- Planning and providing for the types of training you will need to offer in order to be confident that each persona group can learn how to adopt the change;
- Laying out an ongoing schedule for post-launch promotions and activities to manage pockets of resistance and drive further adoption;
- Establishing metrics and locking in the change; and
- Conducting an after-action review to understand what went well, what went poorly, and how to improve the change plan for the next project.

Creating a climate for change

Communicating change, implementing change

Training, adoption evaluation

Business case, "The Vision"

Why do we want the new system/process?
- Requirements incl. metrics
- Benefits / ROI
- Value

How will it change status quo?

Analyze impact on lawyer workflows, client service delivery, organization, business model.

Understanding future state

Where will the changes have an impact, what does new service / process look like?

Communications

Who needs to know what, how and when?
- Identify your stakeholders.
- Agree communication channels.
- Schedule key communications.

Chart course from current state to future state, design integration of new process with existing workflows

Implementing change, training

Who needs to be trained and when? What types of training? Resources required for training?

After action review, locking it in

- Remove old ways of doing things
- Track key metrics
- Review successes and obstacles
- Schedule ongoing promotion

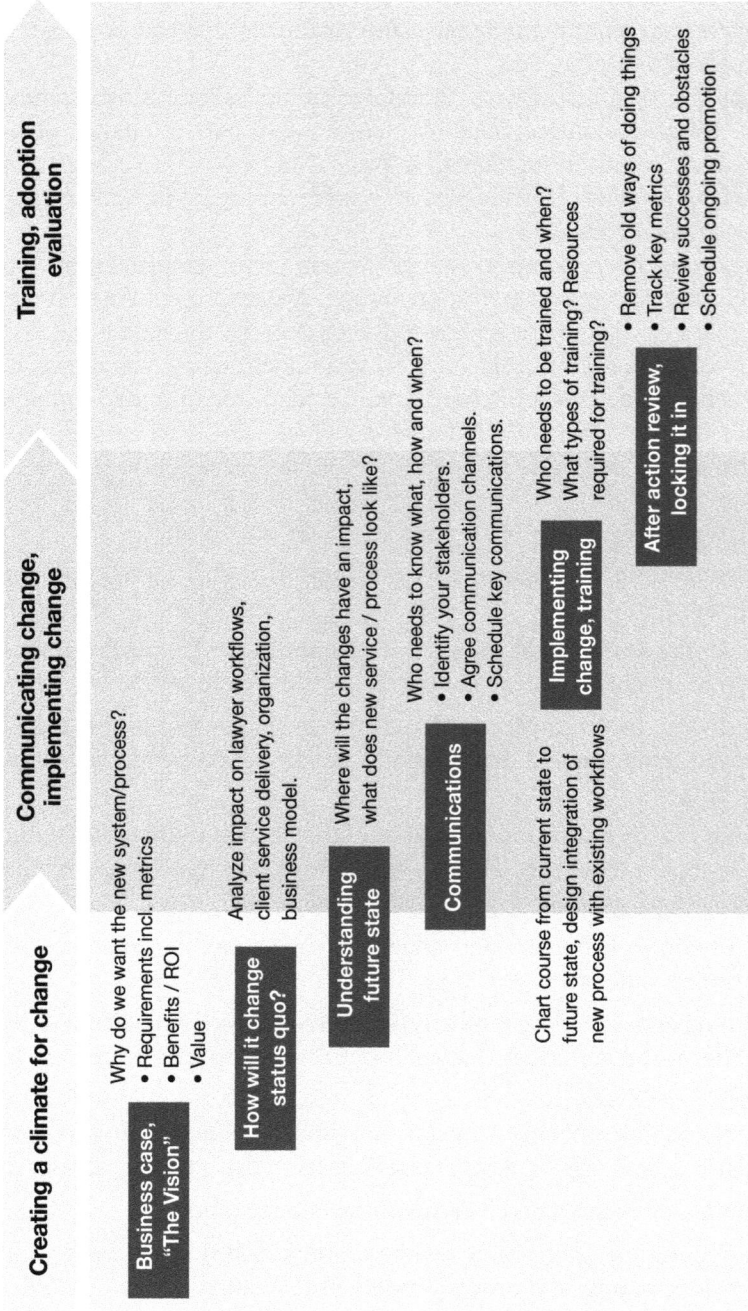

Figure 26: The Change Management Roadmap.[14]

This may seem like a lot of steps to add to a project that is likely already complex. However, there is no point in expending the effort and resources necessary to undertake a major project unless you're willing to also do the work that is required to ensure the project is successful and the change takes hold.

Communications planning, including persona analysis, will be addressed in chapter ten, as will ongoing promotion around a project. Some of the other key aspects of your change roadmap are addressed below.

Creating a clear vision

Just as it's important to set a clear vision for the role of your team in your organization, so it's important to set – and communicate – a vision for the desired outcome of any change project. Our job as change agents is to support people through change, to move them through the various emotional responses they will have as a change progresses through our firm or organization. None of that is possible without communication, which is the one constant through every stage of the change process.

Change of any kind is a disruption. If there is no dissatisfaction with the status quo, why should people endure the disruption? It's where the adage "If it ain't broke, why fix it?" comes from. It's hard to create a sense of urgency in an environment where people are feeling complacent. In Figure 27, John Kotter sets out common sources for complacency in a business setting.

Kotter points out that we tend to assume that people are generally smart and that, as a result, all we have to do is give them facts about low productivity or efficiency, or sliding financial results, and they will understand and change their behavior accordingly.[16] In legal organizations, we know for a fact that the people we are dealing with are intelligent people, so this assumption is likely even easier to make. Kotter says the problem with this is that it represents an underestimation of the power of the systemic forces that exist in almost all organizations. He is quoted as saying, *"Never underestimate the magnitude of the forces that reinforce complacency and that help maintain the status quo"*.[17]

In law firms that are not yet experiencing churn from clients who expect lower fees or automated processes, complacency is likely to be particularly high. Even in the aftermath of a global pandemic, many law firms have posted their highest ever financial results. These circumstances make it difficult to persuade lawyers that change is necessary. In order to do so, you will need to consider things from their perspective – what would inspire them to make this change? How would their life be positively impacted if

Figure 27: Common sources of complacency. Adapted from John Kotter.[15]

they adopted this new way of doing things? Why should it matter to them? The answers to these context-specific questions should be considered in relation to the communications issued around any project undertaken by your team. They will inform the clear vision you need to paint for them of what the future would look like when the change is made. The messaging around that vision may sound different than it would have before, considering the change in those terms. A communication aimed at lawyers to "improve efficiency" by using a particular tool may not resonate; but one that instead says "make your client happier" might.

Kotter describes the importance of using bold actions to increase urgency around a change vision. Some of the types of bold actions he suggests – manipulating numbers on a balance sheet in order to show a dramatic loss, for example – are not tenable in legal environments, but some are. He suggests having people speak to unhappy customers,[18] for example, which in your organization might mean bringing client feedback into your messaging. Kotter also suggests using outside consultants to reinforce your messaging, understanding that the "voice of an expert" from the outside might carry more weight.[19] Using data to paint a picture, and "bombarding" people with information about the opportunities that lie ahead if the vision is realized, are other ways to increase urgency around your vision.[20]

See-Feel-Change

Change experts including Kotter, as well as the Heath brothers, have observed that while most people believe that change happens in the order: Analyze-Think-Change, in fact the sequence of events for successful change efforts tends to look more like: See-Feel-Change.[21] We intrinsically underestimate the power of emotion in change efforts, a pattern that is likely reinforced by the culture of legal organizations where emotions are not meant to have a place and analysis is king. The Heath brothers have studied the importance of analysis, concluding that it holds surprisingly little sway as a justification for change:

> *"…Trying to fight inertia and indifference with analytical arguments is like tossing a fire extinguisher to someone who's drowning; the solution doesn't match the problem."*[22]

Instead, you need to find a way of making your vision vividly clear, painting a picture of it that people can see, so that they have an emotional response towards it that will instigate change behavior. In chapter ten, we'll explore some concrete methods for communicating a vision that creates an emotional response. For now, the take-away is to recognize that every successful change plan must include time spent on crafting communications so that the vision of project success resonates emotionally with the people whose behavior you are seeking to change.

Understanding the impact of the change

No two change projects will have the same impact on an organization. Projects that have a narrow focus and a smaller change footprint will require different change management approaches than those that are broad and have sweeping organizational impact. It's therefore important to understand at the outset of any project how significant its effect will be.

In order to assess the impact of your current project, you will need to spend the time to define it more concretely. In change management terms, this is often referred to as understanding the dimensions of the change.[23] Change dimensions generally include:

- *Breadth:* How many people are affected by the change?
- *Depth:* How profound is the change for the way people work?
- *Impact:* How many existing systems and processes does the change affect?
- *Criticality:* How vital is the change to the organization?[24]

The dimensions of change are represented in Figure 28, which demonstrates how to evaluate each of these aspects of a change project.

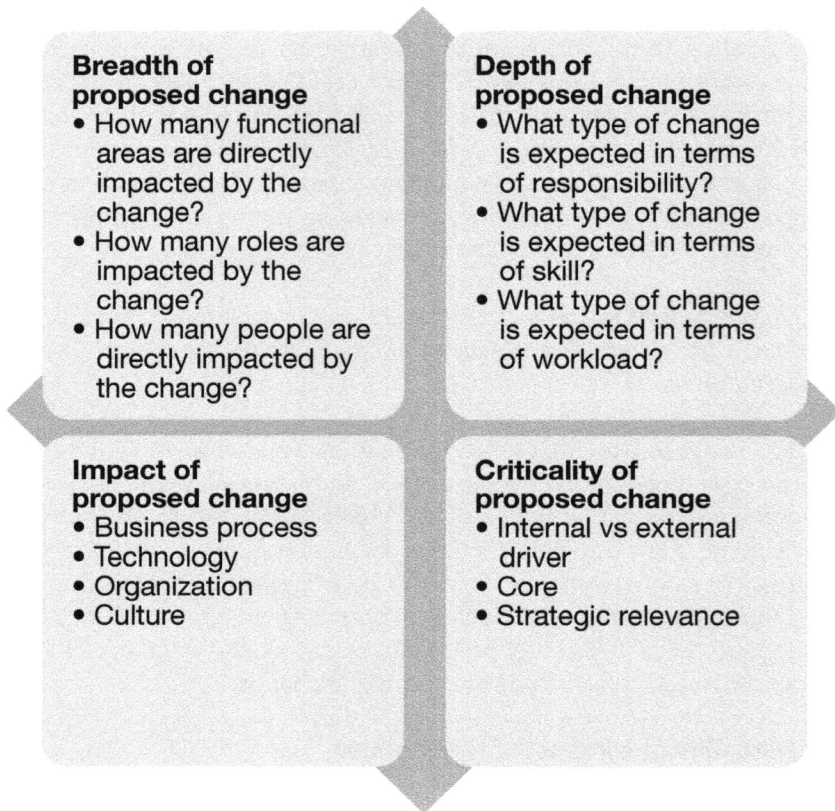

Breadth of proposed change
- How many functional areas are directly impacted by the change?
- How many roles are impacted by the change?
- How many people are directly impacted by the change?

Depth of proposed change
- What type of change is expected in terms of responsibility?
- What type of change is expected in terms of skill?
- What type of change is expected in terms of workload?

Impact of proposed change
- Business process
- Technology
- Organization
- Culture

Criticality of proposed change
- Internal vs external driver
- Core
- Strategic relevance

Figure 28: Dimensions of change.[25]

Applying this analytical model to legal projects, there are a number of questions you should ask about a project you are embarking on, including:

- Is this an enterprise-wide project or does it only affect part of the organization?
- Is it a lawyer-facing project or a business of law project?
- If lawyer-facing, how many practice groups does it affect? How many people within those practices / that practice does it affect?
- If it's a business of law project, how many departments or functions does it affect?

- Will it change underlying technology?
- Will it change the way people work?
- Does it affect the whole process or only part of it?
- Will people need to learn new skills in order to adopt the change?
- Is the project tied to key strategic goals of the organization?

The answers to these questions and the characteristics of the project across the four dimensions of change will help you assess how much risk and complexity is involved. Does the project represent incremental change in one area of the organization, or transformational change across a number of areas? If the project scores high on multiple dimensions, then it should be considered a large or complex change project, which means that if it fails it carries significant risk both for the organization and for your team. These types of projects warrant a full change team and careful management. In communications terms, they will likely require a "Big Bang" approach, with broad messaging sent out to multiple persona groups and a full change program. If the project scores low on most dimensions, or high on only one, it is likely lower risk and you may be able to take a lighter touch, both to the management of the project and to the communications around it.

Stakeholder analysis

A stakeholder analysis is usually done towards the beginning of a project, to help you understand not just who has an interest in the project, but why.[26] Understanding the stakeholder groups will help you manage change and communications effectively throughout the project.

In larger projects, a stakeholder analysis might involve interviews with each stakeholder to understand how they work, what their processes are, and exactly how the change outcome from the project will affect them. For narrower projects and in smaller organizations, you may understand enough about the stakeholders at the outset to be able to undertake the analysis without a huge amount of discovery work.

The most relevant characteristics of each stakeholder in relation to the project will be (1) the degree to which they are impacted by the project, (2) their interest in the project or project outcome, and (3) how much power or influence they wield in the organization.[27] Based on these assessments, you can then use the power-interest grid (see Figure 29) to map the project stakeholders and to assess how frequently to meet with them or communicate with them throughout the project.

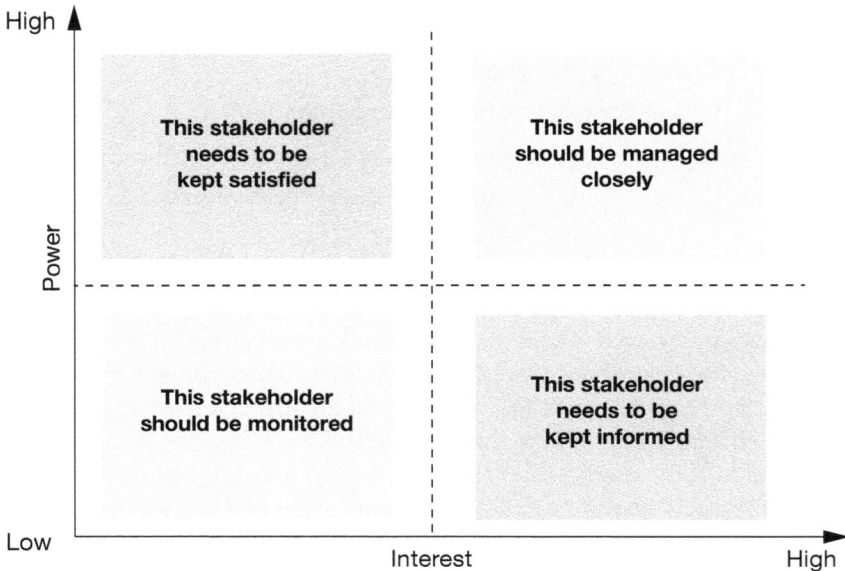

Figure 29: Stakeholder analysis – power-interest grid.[28]

The power-interest grid is a useful tool for understanding where resistance or challenge may come from in the organization if communications are not well managed. Highly influential stakeholders who have great interest in the project, or who stand to be impacted significantly by its outcome, may quickly turn on the project and project team if they are not kept abreast of progress. If that happens, their influence in the organization means their dissatisfaction can spread easily and the entire project may be put at risk. These stakeholders therefore require more careful management, compared to, for example, stakeholders who are only marginally interested in the project outcome and have low influence in the organization. Mapping out your stakeholders in this way, and managing them accordingly, will help ensure project success.

Building your change team

No one can push change through an organization on their own. As John Kotter puts it:

> *"No one individual, even a monarch-like CEO, is ever able to develop the right vision, communicate it to large numbers of people, eliminate all the key obstacles, generate short-term wins, lead and manage dozens of change projects, and anchor new approaches deep in the organization's culture."[29]*

Instead, it requires a full network of support to successfully push through a change initiative, especially one that is large-scale. Before attempting to start any change effort, it's a good idea to pause and consider whose support you can count on and how you will strategically use that support in your change plan. In Kotter's eight-stage model for change, this translates into building your "coalition" for change.

A full change team for a large project should traditionally include the following roles.

Project sponsor

The project sponsor is a high-level person in the organization, or in the relevant practice group, who champions the change.[30] For example, this could be the chair of a practice group or another influential, senior partner who agrees to send an initial change communication on your behalf. In a firm-wide initiative, it might be the chair of the firm or the managing partner, or in the case of projects on the business side it might be the firm's executive director and the relevant departmental chief.

A sponsor's role is important – it shows buy-in from the top, which will be persuasive to others in the group. But it's easy for sponsors to get their job wrong. So before you approach your sponsor for help, consider that change efforts can fail when sponsors:

- Have not bought into the change;
- Do not understand the importance of you getting buy-in, and assume that people will just naturally cooperate;
- Don't appreciate that people throughout the firm will have different reactions to change;
- Treat change as a single event (for example, the sending of that initial email), rather than as a mental, physical, and emotional process; or
- Do not initiate the change with enough urgency.[31]

You can help your sponsor to overcome these pitfalls. Instead of sending your sponsor a draft email and asking them to distribute it for you, go and speak with them about how you anticipate their ongoing support will help, what the change means, when you will need their support, and why it's important to the organization. Make sure you really have buy-in before you leave, and then check back in with your sponsor during the change journey. Not only will this interaction help get your sponsor properly on board, it will also provide you with an additional opportunity to build and consolidate an important relationship, which will help with subsequent change efforts.

Change leader

Where a sponsor's position and influence in the firm is most important, it is the skillset of a change leader that matters most. An effective change leader is able to plan, lead, and organize a change using analytical and communication skills, combined with their credibility within the organization.[32] Change leaders need to be excellent relationship builders.

A project manager is often designated as the change leader, but not all projects will be large enough to warrant a designated project manager, and not all project managers are expert change managers. For smaller-scale change efforts, individuals in a KM or innovation team who do not have project management or change management expertise might nevertheless themselves find themselves in the position of the change leader. Ideally, legal organizations would invest in headcount with specific change management skills, and a change leader would work alongside the project manager and run the change team on any large scale project. Most law firms and legal departments have not yet seen the value in hiring specific change experts, however, and so the role often falls to someone else who may have to skill up in order to lead change effectively. This is one reason why it's important to make sure that your team is equipped with sufficient understanding of change management principles and communications that they are able to lead change effectively.

Change agents

Every change leader needs a team of change agents. These are people who will be important advocates for you and the change you are pushing, and who will play a role in influencing others to adopt the change.[33] Change agents may be key associates in a relevant practice group, people who have piloted a tool and are in favor of licensing it, or paralegals and other staff who can support you in driving adoption. Similar to relationship-building, building a network of change agents in advance of a change effort is hugely valuable. Develop activities and engagement opportunities and get to know who the change agents are across your organization, so that when the time comes and you need your champions "on the ground", you know who to go to.

It should go without saying, but everyone on your team can – and should – serve as a change agent. One of the benefits of having a team is the way you can leverage each other's support and work together to bring the full range of individual skillsets to every change effort. The characteristics of change agents are explored later in this chapter, but it's important to note that, regardless of the size of the change, building relationships in your firm and identifying ahead of time who your change agents are will help you in any transformation efforts you seek to lead.

Assembling the members of your change team

On large-scale projects, it's important to assemble a change team consisting of team members who work formally together to implement the change plans. The size and make-up of the change team will look different depending on the type of project. If your project is large, you will likely need a significant change team. If it is small, you may only need a few change agents to support you. In a project to roll out a specialized tool for a particular practice, for example, the core change team might include the chair of the practice group (as sponsor), the director of innovation, the KM lawyer supporting the practice, a few associates who have been identified as change agents, and a legal technologist. On a project such as the new implementation of an enterprise search platform, the change sponsor might be the firm's COO. The change team will likely include members of the IT department, a senior project manager, the CKO or the director of KM, all of the firm's KM lawyers, the head of training or learning at the firm, and a selection of change agent partners and associates.

The core change team – other than the sponsor – will meet regularly throughout the project to review progress against the change plan, address pockets of resistance, and develop strategies for dealing with unexpected hurdles. The ongoing work of the change team allows for the early identification and neutralization of saboteurs. It also means that the change program on any initiative is a living, breathing thing, able to be tweaked and amended as needed over the course of the project.

Overcoming resistance

Even with a solid change plan and armed with strategic approaches to manage change, you will inevitably encounter resistance during most projects. Although it doesn't feel like it, resistance to change is normal and represents an expected and natural stage of the change process. In some ways, resistance should be viewed as a good thing – it means you are successfully disrupting the status quo. It's also a sure sign that people are hearing you, and your messaging is getting through. People who haven't heard that change is coming can't react to it, so this is an indication that your change communications are working.

Knowing that resistance is normal should help to alter your response to it. Instead of pushing against it as though resistance is a problem, acknowledge it and work towards identifying the causes of resistance. This information will arm you with the tools necessary to overcome it and will enable you to shepherd people in your organization towards exploration and, ultimately, acceptance of the change.

Building trust

One of the most powerful things that you as a legal innovator can do before even introducing a change is to build relationships across your organization. Developing deep relationships with key people across the firm or organization allows you to breed trust where it matters most, even before you need to call on that trust.

Dale Carnegie, in his classic book *How to Win Friends and Influence People*,[34] provides helpful guidance for developing positive, trusting relationships across an organization. Much of his advice is based on empathy. Carnegie suggests that criticizing people puts them on the defensive, forcing them to justify themselves. It's more effective to praise people, providing sincere, honest appreciation.[35] Try to understand things from the other person's viewpoint and show genuine interest in them. Basic actions like smiling, remembering names, and listening actively go a long way. During conversations with key stakeholders, ask open questions and allow the other person to do most of the talking.

Carnegie points out that feeling valued is a basic human need, so making the other person in a conversation feel important is key.[36] If you're wrong – say so right away. Rather than decrease your own credibility, this shows that you're willing to come to the table with humility and honesty.

Most important of all, it's critical to change efforts later and that you put in place the structure of these trusted relationships now. Building relationships across your organization and encouraging all members of your team to do the same is one of the most powerful things you can do to improve the efficacy of change communications when it matters.

Quick wins

As your team charts progress through a project, one of the most valuable things you can do is to identify small wins along the way. A small win may include the successful completion of a technology proof of concept, or it could mean getting the first pilot group on board. It might be the first time someone uses the new process or system in the way it was intended and obtains a good result. It could be the first piece of positive feedback that comes back to your team from one of the people impacted by the project, either internal or external.

Whatever these look like, ensure that your team has a mechanism in place to collect and record quick wins in order to develop messaging and communications that amplify the positive feedback and generate goodwill around the project. Getting the word out when there is something to celebrate will have a much greater impact than you think, and will increase the credibility of your team.

Recognizing change agents and saboteurs

Any organization will be populated by a variety of personalities, some of whom will be change agents, and others (hopefully fewer of them) who may be true saboteurs of your change efforts. As mentioned above, doing the work of recognizing these individuals early will save you a lot of stress later. Here are some characteristics of change agents:

- Positive, energetic attitude;
- Ideally, well known at the firm or organization;
- Liked by peers (not just by superiors);
- Comfortable with change and interested in trying new things;
- Keen to be engaged in firm projects; and
- Happy to take on the role of influencer.[37]

Change agents are essential, so it's helpful to keep a list of them. If you have a team that supports many or all practices at a firm, ensure that everyone on the team knows how to recognize change agents and that there is a process in place for centrally recording the identities of these individuals. In part one of this book, we discussed the importance of engaging your end users or lawyers in projects, and of generating opportunities for that engagement, such as through working groups or committees of lawyers who have an interest in emerging technology or legal innovation. If you have developed these kinds of initiatives, you likely have a strong network of change agents across your organization who can be relied upon to help spread the word about a new process or system, and who will act as your cheerleaders at critical stages in the project. Make sure you account for these people in your communications planning and share key messaging with them so that they know how to speak about the project in a way that supports your goals.

In stark contrast to a change agent, a saboteur is likely to exhibit some or all of the following characteristics:

- Negative attitude;
- Unfortunately, likely to be well known at the firm or organization;
- Respected by peers, or well entrenched enough at the firm to carry weight;
- Extremely uncomfortable with change;
- Provides consistently negative feedback; and
- Alternatively, may be entirely silent on topics of change.[38]

Saboteurs are worse than neutral bystanders. They are people in your organization who may actively try to stand in the way of change. It's therefore important to identify them early in order to minimize the impact they may have on projects you are driving. Some of the behaviors saboteurs might use for this purpose include finding (and loudly vocalizing) reasons why things can't be done in the new way, or by the new technology, and deliberately doing things poorly or very late to undermine change efforts. Where your change team is busy locating quick wins to communicate across the organization, saboteurs may be identifying any small failures associated with the project in order to communicate these more broadly. Containing and restricting communications emanating from saboteurs is therefore of critical importance to the success of any project.

It's important to recognize, however, that the success of a change effort is not dependent on getting every person in the organization on board. There will be a few people who simply won't adopt new ways of doing things, regardless of how sophisticated a change program you run. In some instances, therefore, an effective way of dealing with saboteurs is simply to ignore them and ensure that their negative messaging does not spread more widely across the organization. Even more powerful is when you are able to get a saboteur, or someone who is consistently negative about change, on board with a change effort. Some tips for dealing with this type of behavior and changing people's minds include:

- Begin with praise and honest appreciation of things they do well;
- Call attention to their mistakes only indirectly;
- Ask questions instead of giving direct instructions or corrections;

- Let the other person save face, especially in front of others;
- Praise every improvement, even slight ones;
- Play to ego – suggest that the person has a reputation to live up to;
- Use encouragement and make errors seem easy to correct;
- Find a way to make the person feel happy about doing the things you suggest;
- Make it seem like it was their idea to operate this way in the first place; and
- Appeal to nobler motives, so that by engaging with the new way of working the person feels like they are doing something good.

Ultimately, if a saboteur senses that their reputation and position in the organization will be improved by getting on board with the change, it's likely they will cease resisting. They may never become an active proponent of your initiative, but they may stop exerting effort to deliberately stand in the way of it.

Causes of resistance

In order to move people through resistance on the change curve, you need to understand what is causing their resistance. Understanding this will allow you to develop specific strategies to overcome it. Many leaders of change in firms worry that, if the resistance is coming from people more senior to them, they may not have the level of power and authority necessary to deal with that resistance. The assumption here is that, in order for change to be successful, it must be mandated from on high. However, there are many ways that individuals who do not sit in positions of authority can exert sufficient influence to help people at all levels of an organization move through resistance to adoption. The key is to understand which tactics to employ in order to deal with their specific source of resistance.

In principle, there are four main causes of resistance to change – Personality, Perception, Power, and Program. See Figure 30.

Personality	Perception
Power	**Program**

Figure 30: Main causes of resistance to change.[39]

Personality

The personalities that are more likely to resist change are those that are dominant, reluctant, or anxious – see Table 5.[40] A dominant personality is someone who likes being in control and does not like to be told what to do.[41] A reluctant personality is one that is set in their ways and averse to change.[42] An anxious personality is one that constantly worries things will go wrong.[43] For each of these types of personalities, change will at first be unwelcome, but can be overcome at the interpersonal level, by listening and reassuring them that the change will not threaten their way of being.

Table 5: Overcoming resistance at the personality level.[44]

Personality type	Tactic
Dominant	White glove training, reassurance they are still in control
Reluctant	Focus on benefits of change, reassure them not everything is changing
Anxious	One-to-one extensive training, regular check-ins

For example, for a dominant person, it will be important to provide them with the one-on-one training that will help them feel that even while operating in the new way or in the new tool, they will remain in control.[45] For the reluctant personality, you will want to reassure them that the change is not as significant as they think, and that it won't disrupt their whole way of working – just a portion of it.[46] In law firms, both dominant and reluctant personalities are common, especially among partners who have been at the firm for many years. For this type of personality, it's important to focus strongly on the benefits of the change, and to make those benefits feel as tangible as possible.

For the anxious personality, it will be more effective to introduce a thorough, customized training program that will reduce their levels of anxiety and reassure them that they won't lose work or lose their ability to respond to clients or partners and get things done.[47] Many associates will fall into the anxious category, not just because lawyers are typically risk-averse but also because the hierarchy and compensation structures of law firms create an environment where there is a significant fear of failure. In order to make sure that you are managing anxiety for associates who will be on the frontline during a change exercise, it may be useful to schedule regular check-ins with them. Regular communications and touchpoints with these individuals will help to reduce anxiety and build confidence in your ability to deliver a solution that works.

Perception

Another cause of resistance is the perception people create in their minds of the change that is being introduced. Unlike personality, this cause of resistance is not innate, and is instead able to be controlled through the messaging around a change effort.

A negative perception of the change will make people reluctant to come on board with it. Depending on the person and their status in the organization, people who have a negative perception of the change may have the power to obstruct it, or may feel that they have no choice but to change – and that they are being forced to do so under duress.

Even those with a positive view of the change, who see it as something worthwhile and necessary, may be initially resistant. Some of these understand the benefits of the change but are reluctant to expend effort themselves and will need coaching to adopt it. The desired perception of change is a positive outlook, with a commitment to doing what is necessary to get up to speed on the new way of working.[48] In order to get here, change leaders will need to develop a change program that positively influences the perception of the change across the organization, provides simple steps towards adopting the change, and creates sufficient urgency around the change in order to create commitment to the change.[49]

One of the key sources of resistance in organizations is a lack of clarity or comprehension around vision. If you sense that people in your firm have the wrong perception of the change, go back to your vision and determine whether it needs to be clarified and promoted more broadly so that people understand the benefits of the future state and are motivated to get there. This may require tweaking and adding to your communications program. Your goal is to make the change seem both appealing and approachable.

Power

Fundamentally, people don't like being changed. If your change program makes them feel like they are being forced to change without understanding why, or without themselves making the decision to do so, you will encounter resistance.[50] Unlike the intrinsic desire for control discussed above in relation to the dominant personality type, which gives rise to resistance from certain individuals regardless of how change is communicated, this is an extrinsic source of resistance that might be experienced by anyone if your change program is too heavy-handed.

In order to recognize this kind of resistance you will need your team to have an ear to the ground, reporting back any grumblings picked up during practice group meetings, lunches, or social events. Overcoming this kind of resistance requires a quick pivot. It may mean that the messaging around a project has been too strong, and the team needs to minimize communications until the negative perception of the project dies down. It likely means that you need to revisit your communications plan and develop a new tone for upcoming messages about the project. Ensure that the new messaging reminds people that there are extrinsic motivations for them to make the change, and that the choice as to whether to adopt the change is theirs to make. When they move forward towards adoption, they should feel like they are deciding to do so of their own accord – not under duress.

Program

An inadequate change plan or program is another cause of resistance. The guidance provided above should arm you with the skills necessary to develop a change program that delineates the approach your team will take to the project at each stage of it. Setting down a plan once, however, does not mean you shouldn't return to it throughout the project. You should be continuously re-visiting your change program with your team to determine whether it needs to be adjusted for the types of resistance you are encountering. Your change plan should be flexible enough that it can be tailored to accommodate the types of resistance you encounter upon launch. A well-planned training schedule that is unable to be customized to the specific needs of personas within your organization, for example, is unlikely to succeed in truly getting your attorneys working in new ways. Allowing for the fact that some people may need additional training, or specialized training on some aspects of the new resource, will get you much further down the change curve and closer to large-scale adoption.

Influencing without authority

One of the biggest challenges in driving any change is building support and momentum when you don't have significant influence or credibility. Driving organization-wide change is difficult under any circumstances, but the challenge is heightened in a hierarchical organizational structure when you sit somewhere in the middle of that hierarchy. It means you are unable to mandate change and must use more surreptitious measures.

In order to exert influence in an organization where you don't have authority, you will need to build support both from the bottom up and the top down of your organization. Develop a persuasive business case for senior management that explains to them the return on investment for the firm of a particular initiative and generates their buy-in. Adapt that messaging for particular practice groups and speak to practice group chairs and partners to get them on board. Leverage your team's relationships across the firm to build and develop a network of change agents from multiple persona groups, making sure you are including assistants, paralegals, practice coordinators, and new associates. During a change effort, build in messaging and tactics that generate support from all of these supporters, so that the word-of-mouth communications happening across the firm are coming from different groups of people and serve to reinforce formal messaging put out by the change team.

See Table 6 on the next page for a list of additional tried and true tricks for driving change without influence.

Undertaking projects within a law firm or legal department without understanding the principles of change management will make it far more challenging for you to succeed. Armed with change management methodologies, supported by a team that understands those methodologies, and with a flexible change program that accommodates and corrects for various kinds of resistance, you will be empowered to succeed in driving change across your organization.

Table 6: Driving change without influence.

Tip	Example
Have patience and be persistent	Don't expect to have immediate success; instead, create a plan that allows for a gradual building of momentum. Understand that this will involve continuous effort over a longer period of time.
Look for opportunites that have a big payoff	Use a tool or process on a matter or initiative that you know matters a lot to the people in charge of this group, so they can see first-hand how beneficial it is.
Focus on getting results that others will respect and understand	Instead of demonstrating all of the functionality of a tool, focus first on the aspect that you know will most appeal to people in this group and show them how well it works.
Involve fellow workers and share the credit	Get associates involved in roll-out and, when there is a spike in adoption, publicly credit them with that success.
Communicate success stories	Where pockets of people in the group are using a tool or process and getting great traction with it, get them to communicate that to others in the group.
Gradually build a network of supporters	Keep track of the people from whom you've heard positive comments, and come back to those people when you need to build support.
Select change efforts that will get the attention of at least one link up the chain of command	Focus business plans and roll-out communications on revenue generation, command improved realization or business development to generate the attention of partners.
Identify the most common objections/ questions that people have and find ways to overcome these obstacles	Prior to launch, think about what objections nay-sayers in this group might have, and have persuasive responses to those objections ready to go so that you are not caught out.

A note on process change

The multi-stage approaches to change outlined in this chapter are important, but what is perhaps more important is understanding how to minimize the impact of change from any project. Before jumping into a project that involves dramatically changing the way people do things, pause to reflect on whether you can or should be reducing the amount of change you are introducing. Have you properly understood the way your lawyers work, and are you introducing the new process or technology as part of an existing workflow that is already familiar to them? Is there a solution that integrates with the platforms your lawyers prefer to work in, so that learning a new process does not also mean jumping to an entirely new system? Remember who you are fundamentally doing this for, and lead with empathy. Understanding how your lawyers work and introducing change in a way that respects those processes and complements them will make it easier for you to lock in that change. It will also garner you the respect and gratitude of the people whose work lives you seek to change.

Checklist: Managing change during a complex project

☐ Either hire someone with specific change management skills for your team or educate your team on change management principles (or both). Make sure your team is well versed in managing change and understands your approach to organizational change.

☐ Build relationships across your organization and encourage everyone on your team to do so too. In everything that you do, focus on building trust with as many constituents as possible.

☐ Put in place processes to identify change agents. Record this list centrally so that your team is able to access it and add to it. Empower your team to recognize and foster change agents and develop initiatives that will have the effect of creating a network of change agents across the organization.

☐ At the beginning of every project, create a change plan alongside a project plan, including steps for:
  • Establishing and communicating a vision;
  • Assessing project impact;
  • Conducting a stakeholder analysis;

- Creating the change team;
- Developing a communications plan;
- Capturing quick wins;
- Planning for training and ongoing promotion;
- Locking in the change; and
- After-action review.

☐ Ensure you or the change leader for the project returns to the project plan regularly to tweak it as the project evolves.

☐ Train your team to manage resistance and plan for it, with strategic messaging that is intended especially for this purpose.

References

1 Ewenstein, B., Smith, W., and Sologar, A. (2015). *Changing Change Management*. McKinsey & Company Insights, www.mckinsey.com/featured-insights/leadership/changing-change-management.

2 Boschi, H. (2020). *The Neuroscience of Change: Why Changing Course is Painful for the Brain*. https://welldoing.org/article/the-neuroscience-change-why-changing-course-painful-for-brain.

3 *Ibid.*

4 *Ibid.*

6 *Ibid.*

6 Kotter, J. P. (1996). *Leading Change*. Boston: Harvard Business School.

7 Kübler-Ross, Elisabeth. (1997). *On Death and Dying*. Seattle, Washington: Scribner.

8 *Ibid.*

9 Herman, S. (2019). *Making the Change Mindset Connection. Acuity Institute*, https://acuityinstitute.com/making-the-change-mindset-connection/.

10 Susskind, R. (1996). *The Future of Law: Facing the Challenges of Information Technology*. Oxford: Clarendon Press.

11 www.vqab.se/2010/05/law-firms-and-the-internet-generation/.

12 A line of cases have confirmed this view. See, for example, *James v. Nat'l Fin. LLC*, No. CV 8931-VCL, 2014 WL 6845560 (Del. Ch. Dec. 5, 2014): "Professed technological incompetence is not an excuse for discovery misconduct."

13 Gleeson, B. (2017). *1 Reason Why Most Change Management Efforts Fail*. www.forbes.com/sites/brentgleeson/2017/07/25/1-reason-why-most-change-management-efforts-fail/?sh=2cf3604e546b, citing McKinsey & Company study revealing that 70 percent of change projects fail.

14 Adapted from McHale, B. (2019). *How to Use Change Management to Bring Your Projects Across the Line*. ProjectCentral: Best Practices. www.projectcentral.com/blog/project-change-management/.

15 Kotter, p.42.

16 Kotter, p.44.

17 *Ibid.*

18 Kotter, p.46.

19 *Ibid.*

20 *Ibid.*

21 Heath, C. and Heath, D. (2010). *Switch: How to Change Things When Change is Hard.* New York: Crown Publishing Group, p.106.

22 Heath and Heath, p.107.

23 Nelson, G. (2016). *Change Management: The Secret to a Successful SAS Implementation.* ResearchGate, www.researchgate.net/publication/318866073_ Change_Management_The_Secret_to_a_Successful_SASR_Implementation.

24 *Ibid.*

25 *Ibid.*

26 Hoory, L. and Bottorff, C. (2022). *What is a Stakeholder Analysis? Everything You Need to Know.* www.forbes.com/advisor/business/what-is-stakeholder-analysis/

27 *Ibid.*

28 *Ibid.*

29 Kotter, p.53.

30 Frahm, J. (2016). *Offering Role Clarity in Change Management.* Conversations of Change, https://conversationsofchange.com.au/1943-2/.

31 Panorama Consulting Group. (2022). *What is a Change Sponsor? (Everything You Need to Know).* https://conversationsofchange.com.au/1943-2/.

32 Frahm, 2016.

33 *Ibid.*

34 Carnegie, Dale. (1888-1955). *How to Win Friends and Influence People.* New York: Simon & Schuster, 2009.

35 Carnegie, Principle #22.

36 Carnegie, Principle #9.

37 Arinze, C. (2022). *How to Identify Change Agents in Any Organization.* https:// businessyield.com/business-strategies/change-agents/.

38 Kay, M. (2022). *Detecting a Saboteur the Ultimate Leadership Skill.* AboutLeaders, https://aboutleaders.com/detecting-a-saboteur-the-ultimate-leadership-skill/.

39 Author's own, inspired by Abbas, T. (2021). *Types of Resistance to Change.* Change Management Insight, https://changemanagementinsight. com/08_types_of_resistance_to_change/.

40 Beans, J. (2018). *Let's Change That: How Different Personalities Interpret Change.* Emergent Performance Systems, https://emergentps.com/2018/12/06/ lets-change-that-how-different-personalities-interpret-change/.

41 *Ibid.*

42 *Ibid.*

43 *Ibid.*

44 Author's own, inspired by Beans, 2018.

45 *Ibid.*

46 *Ibid.*

47 *Ibid.*

48 Herman, S. (2020). *System Factors for Managing Resistance to Change.* Acuity Institute, https://acuityinstitute.com/system-factors-for-managing-resistance-to-change/.

49 *Ibid.*

50 Beans, 2018.

Chapter 10:
Communications and storytelling

It's difficult to speak of change management without referring to communication. Ultimately it is only through communication that change planning can be conveyed to a broader audience. This chapter is therefore in some ways a companion chapter to the previous one, and the two should be read together.

Law firms are notoriously bad at internal communications, partly because, as with many other things, communicating is frequently left to lawyers, the IT department, or other professionals who have not learned how to craft or deliver impactful messages. Similarly, legal departments have rarely invested in staff with specialized communications skills. As successful change management is so reliant on effective communications, learning how to communicate in a way that causes people to both hear and remember the message can be an innovation superpower.

Developing a communications plan

A communications plan should be part of every change program and every change project. As discussed in chapter nine, communications planning is a sub-section of change planning. In larger projects, you may consider having a working group that is focused exclusively on the communications aspect of a project. For smaller projects, this may be just one or two people who plan ahead for the types of messaging and communications that will be sent throughout the project.

As you plan your communications, think about the various stages of the project. Most projects are easily broken down into phases that make planning easier. If the project is large enough to have an assigned project manager, he or she will likely define the phases. Even smaller projects with no assigned project manager will usually involve phases that are relevant to a communications plan, which may include:

- Running a proof of concept to validate functionality of the new process or system;

- Announcement of project and project vision (either to the whole organization or the relevant sub-section);
- Development milestones;
- Pilot with single practice group or sub-group;
- Pre-launch communications;
- Launch;
- Training activities; and
- Post-launch promotion.

For each of the phases of a project, the communications working group should decide:

- Whether it needs to be communicated;
- If so, to which people;
- What is the key message that needs to be communicated;
- How does that key message vary from one stakeholder group or persona group to another;
- When should the message be sent; and
- How should the message be communicated.

See Figure 31 for a sample communications template, which allows for this kind of detailed planning.

Ideally, a communications plan should actually set out the messaging for each project phase. This messaging can – and should be – revisited throughout the project and tweaked but setting it out during the planning phase will keep everyone in the loop and consistent with messaging about the project.

Approval process

Once you have your communications plan established with the stakeholder or persona groups identified, and have crafted the messages and established the timing for sending these out, consider any approval process you may need to go through for any of the communications. For example, if you would like key messages to be sent from the chair of a group, ensure you approach her in advance, and have her review the message she will be sending well ahead of time.

Change project name	
Change project owner	
Change communication approver(s)	
Last updated	

Please identify the **stakeholders** for each communication, the **reason for the communication**, and a **description** of the required communication

Phase	Communication /event	Estimated date	Status	Targeted shareholders	Reason for communication	Methods of communication	Key messaging	Communication copy
Assesment and planning	Change announcement	01-20-2021	In process	All hands				
	Stakeholder survey invitation	6-25-2021	Not started	Support team				
	Training deck		Not started					
Implement change	Updated support documentation		Not started					
	Training program invitation		Not started					
Monitor ongoing change and metrics	TBD		Not started					
	TBD		Not started					

Figure 31: Change Management Communications Plan Template.[1]

In addition to the peace of mind that comes from having approval upfront, it's easy to misinterpret communications, and having a second pair of (highly relevant) eyes review the messaging ahead of time is essential.

Feedback loop

Remember that communication can't happen in one direction – it is a two-way circuit and hasn't properly occurred unless the recipient has both heard and digested the message.

In order to ensure that your messages have gotten through in relation to a particular project, have your team introduce a feedback loop.

Identify key people as your communications guinea pigs (your change agents will work well here) and ask them to provide feedback to you as your communications are distributed. For example, you might select a well-connected and sociable associate in each of the practice groups to which the communications are being sent. Check in with these associates from time to time to find out whether they have understood the key messages, and to evaluate how those messages are being received across the group.

Schedule tasks

Take the tasks you have identified in your communications plan and add them to your overall project plan, and into your Outlook calendar – as well as the calendars of the other members in your change team. In other words, make sure that you have the tasks recorded in a place that will provide you and your team with alerts and reminders, so that your change plan unfolds on schedule.

Table 7: Tips for effective communications planning.

Make the plan readily accessible to project team members.
Make sure the project stakeholders buy into the plan.
Scale the plan to fit the complexity, duration, and size of the project.
Update the plan when significant changes occur.
Periodically ask team members if they are getting the right information at the right time.
Enter change and communications tasks in the project plan.
Be specific when assigning change and communication tasks, and list the responsible people.
Get proper approval before disseminating communication, when applicable.

It's inevitable (at least with large-scale change) that things will evolve as your plan steps into high gear. For example, the attitudes of various stakeholders may change, or other aspects of the project may shift, causing delays or a change in approach.

Before moving to launch, it's a good idea to meet with your project team and define a process for updating the communications plan when such a need arises.

Communicating the vision

The communication of the project vision will always be a critical first step in any project.

After creating a clear vision, the project team or communications sub-group should therefore spend time planning how to communicate it effectively. It's helpful to think of the vision as the "North Star" for your project. Every time you feel like you're stuck in the weeds, or when the project team is experiencing resistance or unforeseen hurdles, you can look back to your vision statement to help guide critical decisions and actions. In addition to being a guide for the project team, a vision will help your audience understand what your project is trying to achieve, and why.

Five tips for communicating your vision

Keep it simple
Vision statements, mission statement, values, purpose. It's easy to get lost in a sea of words and management fads. Your vision shouldn't be complicated: in one sentence, can you describe what things are going to look like when your project is complete?

Walk the talk
A vision can be inspiring, but it will quickly engender cynicism if it doesn't feel real. Make sure you're showing your stakeholders that you're progressing toward the vision, not just talking about it. This is particularly important if your project requires a behavior change – living the new behavior is key.

Reinforce, reinforce, reinforce
For ongoing or complex change projects, it's useful to reinforce the vision in some way with every communication. You can be completely obvious about this, for example by starting or finishing every major communication with your vision statement. Or you can be more subtle by drawing key words from the vision and weaving them into your messaging.

Jargon-free zone
Jargon can be useful to create a shared understanding, but more often than not it winds up becoming a cliché and loses all impact. Nathaniel Hawthorne said, *easy reading is damn hard writing*. Spending the extra time to keep your language simple and original will be far more impactful than relying on easy-to-hand but boring buzz words.

Make it visual
Here's a challenge. Can you find a way to communicate your vision in pictures? While it's strongly recommended to avoid creating a "brand" for your project (it's distracting and unnecessary), using arresting and relevant imagery in your vision communications can dramatically increase engagement. There are lots of great royalty-free image sites online, so there's no reason to resort to cheesy stock photos.

In their book, *Switch*,[2] the Heath brothers show the importance of vision and clear communication by telling a story about two health researchers at West Virginia University who wanted to persuade people to eat a healthier diet. They knew from past research that an edict to "eat a healthier diet" would not work. It was not a clear enough message. What foods should people stop – or start – eating? Should their behavior change at home or in restaurants? Should it change at breakfast or lunch or dinner? The two researchers eventually settled on milk. Most Americans drink milk, a good source of calcium. But milk is also the single largest source of saturated fat in the typical American's diet. Calculations remarkably showed that if Americans switched from whole milk to skim or one percent milk, the average diet would immediately attain the USDA recommended levels of saturated fat.[3] But how could they get Americans to start drinking low-fat milk? They realized that people drink what they have in the house – which means that the researchers needed to make sure that low-fact milk was in refrigerators across the country. In other words, this wasn't about changing behavior around what people drink, it was about changing *purchasing* behavior. This insight brought clarity to the intervention that was needed – get consumers to buy skim or one percent milk when they are shopping for groceries.

The researchers launched a campaign in two communities in West Virginia, running punchy, specific ads in local media. One ad compared a glass of whole milk to eating five strips of bacon. At a press conference, the researchers showed reporters a tube full of fat – the same amount found in a half-gallon of whole milk. The campaign worked. Before the campaign, the market share of low-fat milk was 18 percent. Afterwards, it was 41 percent.[4]

The story conveys the importance of finding the right message and conveying a crystal-clear vision. Kotter calls vision "an imaginable picture of the future".[5] A message conveying vision shouldn't be limited to a picture of the future, however, but should include some implicit or explicit commentary or direction on how and why people should strive to get to that future.[6] It should provide focus by stating a clear target. It should be ambitious enough to force people out of comfortable routines, and simple enough to prevent people from getting lost in analysis. Analysis appeals to the intellect but will not engage emotions in a way that stimulates people to change. For that reason, too, a vision cannot be mired in data and graphs. A vision is not a business case. A vision is compelling, has impact, and should appeal to all stakeholders engaged in the change. Consider some of the ideas in Table 8 for examples of how to communicate a clear vision for a particular project.

Table 8: Effective vision communications.

Instead of ...	Focus on ...
[X Tool] contains data on all previous cases and opposing counsel and applies analytics to those data, so we should use it to better understand the cases in front of us.	Let's win more cases and create repeat business by leveraging legal analytics.
Collecting metadata on our matters is important because you will be able to easily find representative work.	When a client calls or an urgent RFP comes in, have the information you need at your fingertips
We should upgrade to [Y Tool] so that our documents are secure and GDPR compliant and our back-end systems are stable.	Find what you need in seconds using [Y Tool].
It's important as a firm that we are seen to be innovative because our clients are asking for innovation, the market demands it, and we need to stay competitive.	By the end of [year], we will be recognized as one of the nation's most innovative law firms.

Note that in all of the examples, the information in the first column is both true and relevant. It is also the kind of information that people will analyze and consider and ponder. The visions in the second column, on the other hand, are calls to action, and focus on the needs of the person for whom the project is being implemented. These statements require less analysis and are more likely to inspire people to change.

Elevator pitches

An elevator pitch is a succinct, persuasive pitch that creates interest in a project or a concept.[7] Unlike a vision statement, an elevator pitch is usually several sentences long. These simple blurbs provide a way to distil the essence of a project and its value proposition into the simplest, clearest terms. It should explain what makes the project unique or different and generate enough curiosity to make any person hearing it want to hear more. It's called an elevator pitch because it should take no longer to deliver than the time it takes to ride an elevator to the top – in other words, no more than 30 seconds to two minutes.[8]

The concept of an elevator pitch became relevant because of the reality of unexpected encounters with key stakeholders or influential leaders. It has remained relevant, however, because being able to express a vision, project goal, or new solution in a brief, effective manner is so powerful.

Developing an elevator pitch at the outset of any project will serve you well for the remainder of the project, because it can serve many purposes. An elevator pitch forces you to think about the essence of what makes a project relevant and important. It will help you develop the core messaging that will be reused in different ways throughout the project. The elevator pitch can be tweaked and expanded upon as the project evolves. It will bring consistency to project communications if everyone in the project team knows the elevator pitch and understands that part of their responsibility is to repeat the elevator pitch whenever they are asked about the project.

Elevator pitches can – and should – be used in other communications, outside of the context of a live project. They can be particularly helpful when it comes to the ongoing promotion and adoption of technologies and processes across an organization. Any team responsible for the adoption of new solutions should develop elevator pitches for each of those solutions that can be used in multiple communications, and in a variety of situations.

Launch communications

Communications to announce the launch of a project are critical to success and adoption. Choosing how you kick off your change program is a bit like choosing how to present yourself when you're meeting someone new. First impressions count. So how do you decide on the right communications approach to launch your change? First, assess whether your change initiative is large-scale or smaller (refer to chapter nine for tips on how to evaluate the impact and size of the change).

Large-scale change

If you're initiating a large-scale change project, it requires an enormous amount of planning. From a communications perspective, this is not simply a matter of having a well-known person make a big announcement. Large-scale change communications are most effective when you have a "face of the change". This will usually be someone well-known who can launch the change in person and put their name to subsequent communications. This person will often be your project sponsor, but that is not mandatory. Whomever you choose, it's important to ensure that they're charismatic, a strong public speaker, patient, and empathetic.

When a change is likely to affect most people in an organization, or if it will have a significant impact on some people's roles, a personal approach from day one will ensure people feel like they are important to the firm. One way to do this would be to hold a town hall meeting with a presentation on the change, including what's known and what's still to be decided, with lots of reassurance and opportunities to ask questions. Of course, in a firm that operates across multiple time zones, cultures, and languages this can be challenging. Interventions you could think about include a video link-up (again with opportunities to ask questions), or separate meetings in each location – either having the "Face" fly out, or, even better, identifying a locally respected and senior person to take on this role for each office.

Constant and consistent communication is key. If you've committed to update people once a week on Fridays, update them once a week on Fridays – even if there's not much to share. Your channels will be one of the primary considerations here. How are you going to provide these updates? Picking one or two main channels and sticking with them will help ensure that there's a single source of truth that people can go to for reliable information. A project intranet or wiki page is a great idea, or you could consider a weekly newsletter, or a briefing pack provided to managers to share with their teams.

In addition to the regular updates, you should of course communicate major milestones, and for these you might use multiple channels to ensure you're reaching the widest audience possible.

Low key change

When your change is a bit smaller, you'll still need to plan and communicate regularly, but you can adopt a lighter touch approach.

For a smaller change, instead of identifying a big name to act as the face of the change, you can rely on the relationships that you've built with those who will be affected by the change. Speaking with them in person, and working with a positive individual as a change agent is an appropriate, "softly, softly" way of initiating a low-key change. That's not to say you shouldn't launch the change in person. Where possible, this will always win you more friends, build trust, and head off resistance. You could attend a team meeting or schedule small group chats to let people know about the change program, including what's going to happen, who's involved, the anticipated impact, and how long it will take.

Low-key change lends itself to low-key communication. Small updates are often better than big, infrequent messages. You could send a few lines in an email (again, on a regular schedule), or attend existing team meetings to share progress.

Whether your change is large or small, the fundamental principles for launching any change are the same:

- In-person communication builds trust and limits resistance.
- Consistent communication shows a steady hand at the tiller.

- Providing opportunities for questions and comments demonstrates care and a commitment to people.

Seven Touches

The Seven Touches, or the Rule of Seven, is an old marketing adage referring to the fact that people need to see or hear a marketing message at least seven times before they will act upon it.[9]

Although things have changed in the digital world, it remains true that a marketing effort of any kind has to be consistent and repetitive in order to land. In fact, some commentators suggest that the Rule of Seven is magnified in the digital world; that in fact you need many more touches now in order to encourage someone to act.[10] The fact is that without repetition of a compelling message, buyers of products or users of new systems and services will not be motivated to change their behavior.

Keep this in mind when launching a new system or process. Sending one or two communications and simply expecting everyone to move to the new way of doing things as a result of those communications is unrealistic. Repeated, consistent promotion should be part of every launch, training, and post-launch communications plan. The goal should be that no one goes without hearing about the launch multiple times, in a variety of ways.

One of the most important aspects of the Seven Touches rule is that repeated communications will be most effective if the format in which they are sent is varied. In marketing, this is referred to as a multi-channel approach. Your messaging should be consistent; your media should not. Lawyers are drowning in emails, so sending out your launch communications exclusively by email may mean the message is ignored. If the message is not ignored, you are likely to annoy people if you send seven or more emails on the same subject.

The better way to proceed is to consider the variety of media you have at your disposal. In a law firm, for example, you may have the following available:

- Email;
- Intranet posts or alerts;
- Slack or messaging apps;
- Promotional posters in kitchenettes and hallways;
- TV displays in public areas of the firm;
- In-person presentations at practice group meetings or lunches;

- Telephone displays;
- Launch video;
- Firm podcast;
- Elevator chat;
- Branded swag or cards that can be distributed to offices;
- Monitor displays; and
- Email signatures.

Once you start thinking about the various ways you could get a message out, you'll be surprised by what you have available to you. As you build out your communications plan, and particularly your plan around launch communications, factor in the ways you will leverage different formats to ensure that your constituents are hearing the message many times from different places. This repetition across multiple channels is far more likely to have the desired effect than sending a few emails.

WIIFM messaging

The most important way to improve the impact of your communications is to consider the person to whom you are communicating, and to adapt the communication accordingly. People are by their very nature egotistical. The "ego", according to Freud, refers to one's center of consciousness.[11] In Freudian terms, being "egotistical" is not a nasty attribute, it is simply the natural human condition of focusing mostly on the things that impact one's self.[12] In other words, it is innately human to care more about things that directly affect you than about anything else.

WIIFM, or What's-In-It-For-Me, communications are those that gear messaging specifically towards the recipient, helping that person under-stand how and why the message matters to them.[13] WIIFM messaging plays to the ego, using the natural selfishness of the recipient to amplify the impact of the communication.[14] Change represents a movement away from the past to an uncertain future. Though that uncertainty certainly causes concern for people, what they are most often worried about is the transition and what it means for them. They want to know what their contextual issues will be during the change. When people know a change is coming, they have all kinds of questions about it. They want to know what they will lose in the process, how much time it will take to learn the new thing, what the new model will look like, what the expectations are from them along this journey, how their life will be better if they go along with this. In other words, they want to know what's in it for them. And your job is to validate their journey and make them feel positive about it.

Of course, WIIFM messaging necessarily requires that considerable thought be put into individual communications and the recipients of those communications. In order to play to the ego of many people within an organization, you need to have a sense of what type of messaging would hit home for which people. That means you need to know your people and tailor your messaging accordingly, increasing the complexity of any communications strategy around a new project, and requiring that you send multiple communications to get one message across – especially if you are communicating across multiple practices or an entire organization.

The effort is worth it. It's likely that, unless you use WIIFM messaging, many recipients will gloss over your communications. It's almost certain they won't remember it. Imagine, for example, that you are communicating about the roll-out of an enterprise search system. It's probably true that using the system will make it more efficient to search for precedent documents and research memos. The project team may decide that, as this is one of the primary benefits of the new technology, these aspects should form the core message communicated to promote the platform and drive adoption. Sending that message to partners as a way to drive adoption of the system is unlikely to be successful, however. Partners rarely search for precedent documents or undertake research. Consequently, they are unlikely to care about the message; it may even cause an unexpected negative reaction, with partners wondering why they have been interrupted and their inbox clogged by messaging that doesn't apply to them. By contrast, messaging for partners that focuses in on the ability to easily find representative historical matters and closing binders might have been persuasive. Sending the same messaging to all persona groups, no matter how accurate the message or how positive it appears, is likely to backfire on you.

Personas

The above example makes it clear why it's worth spending time before your team starts communicating on a large scale to identify persona groups in your organization. In a law firm, there are some obvious divisions that allow for demarcation of personas – practice groups, for example, or titles referring to different status, education, and experience groups at the firm, such as partners, associates, or paralegals.

Given the way that legal organizations operate, and considering the various ways that communications might be received, it's natural to want to define personas according to title. The basic personas across a firm, then, would include partners, associates, senior associates, paralegals, and clerks. As most people who have worked in a firm can attest to, however, this is generally too simplistic a breakdown. Not all partners work in the same way or think the same way. Some additional characteristics to take into account when creating persona groups might include subject matter expertise and seniority. As Table 9 shows, considering these characteristics immediately adds to the complexity of your personas – and, therefore, to your communications.

Table 9: Sample Law Firms Personas.

Title	Practice area	Seniority
Partners	M&A	7-10 yrs PQE
	Litigation	10-15 yrs PQE
	Real estate	15-20 yrs PQE
Senior associates	M&A	7-10 yrs PQE
	Litigation	4-7 yrs PQE
	Real estate	4-8 yrs PQE
Associates	M&A	3-4 yrs PQE
	Litigation	2-3 yrs PQE
	Real estate	First year associates

Product management philosophy, which we will be delving into more deeply in chapter 13, takes persona-building a step further, saying that effort should be put into understanding more deeply who your people are. Depending on the context of the organization and the type of change you are driving, there are many different types of personal or professional details that you may want to capture. Some examples might include:

- Age, geographic location, and education level;
- Socioeconomic status;
- Background, ethnic and cultural identity;
- Marital status;
- Goals and dreams for their professional or personal life;
- Challenges, frustrations, and fears;

- The person's typical level of engagement with the organization; and
- How the person deals with the problem today that the change initiative intends to solve.[15]

A female partner who is a single parent with young babies at home and a long commute might have different priorities and needs than a more senior male partner who is married and whose children are at college. The former will likely prioritize efficiency and perhaps the ability to work effectively from home. The latter may be focused on leaving a legacy and might be prioritizing the quality of work output and mentoring younger lawyers. These days, whether a lawyer works remotely, in the office, or in a hybrid fashion is a characteristic worth noting when developing personas – certainly their location of work will give rise to different needs from a technology perspective, for example.

Even if you don't have the time to spend interviewing many of the people across your firm or organization, it's worthwhile to leverage the relationships your team has built and use those to highlight key individuals for communications purposes – the young partner who is very keen to be seen as innovative; the senior partner who refuses to change the way he works and will loudly protest against any new technology implementation; the paralegal who is a whiz with technology and makes an excellent pilot participant. Knowing and understanding the people in your organization so that you can tweak communications to meet them where their needs are will help you ensure that you (and your team) are heard.

The power of storytelling

Humans are much more likely to remember a story than they are a straight-laced message without context.[16] Stories resonate deeply, partly because our brains are wired to make sense of facts by creating narratives.[17] Stories help people take the complex and abstract and turn it into something digestible and memorable. In some ways, then, stories have the reverse impact of change – psychologically, where change can cause fear and pain, stories can improve feelings of wellbeing by releasing oxytocin and decreasing cortisol.[18] Using storytelling to enhance communications around a change narrative has the power to reduce the stress caused by that change.

In all messaging around a change project, and in messaging around overarching cultural change, innovation teams should be focused on developing compelling narratives. In essence, WIIFM communications are stories that take a core message and tell a story to explain to someone why that message should make them feel excited. Elevator pitches are mini-stories that can be conveyed rapidly. The Heath brothers' story about milk that was referenced above used vivid illustrations of fat content to tell a story that would help people make healthier choices.

During communications planning, think about how you can leverage narratives that tell interesting stories about the experiences of people at your firm – or even at other firms – in order to make your messaging more compelling. For example, returning to the enterprise search implementation, can you locate stories in your organization of people who missed a deadline or had to stay at the office particularly late because they couldn't find information they needed? If you can return to those people later and gather feedback about how they can now find their documents in a matter of seconds, you can pull together user success stories that could form the basis of promotional messaging to drive adoption on an ongoing basis. At a firm where I once worked, we rolled out enterprise search and heard a story from an assistant who was located in the New York office but worked for partners in London and Sydney. She was asked by the partner in Sydney to find a document urgently for a client matter, and it took her over a day to find it because the author and other metadata tags on the document were not labelled as expected. When we rolled out the new platform, she performed a search right in front of us for the document that had caused her such frustration, using the same keywords she had leveraged at the time. Lo and behold, the right document came up as the first search result on her very first search. Now that was a story we could use.

The difference between hearing and listening

Successful interpersonal communication is important for teams whose job involves understanding pain-points and driving change across an organization, and yet few innovation professionals have had communications training. Generally speaking, interpersonal communication relies on three core components – the ability to listen, the ability to effectively convey a message, and the power of persuasion.[19]

Listening is the process of absorbing things we hear and the mental processes we use to make sense of what we hear. Listening is critical in communication, and in today's diverse organizations, it is often overlooked. Hearing is different from listening. Hearing is often passive, where information is taken on board without any processing. Active listening, on the other hand, requires work from the listener. It is the most intensive form of listening and requires that full attention is paid to the speaker by focusing on the elements of the message – asking for clarification of meaning and responding in ways that enhance understanding between both the speaker and listener. Active listening is a crucial skill in organizational change as it enhances personal and professional relationships. Unfortunately, legal organizations, as with most other commercial organizations, are not in a position to teach all or even key personnel how to practice active listening, nor would this necessarily help in circumstances where messages are frequently conveyed in passive mechanisms (such as email).

As your team members interact with people across the organization to build the relationships and trust that will make them effective change agents, there are simple actions they can take to ensure they are listening effectively.[20] Becoming good active listeners will ensure that constituents are more likely to open up to members of the team or come to them with problems and pain-points. It will also pave the way for effective user discovery exercises during change projects.

Ten steps for effective communication[21]

1. *Maintain eye contact and face the speaker.* Body language is an important part of communication. Facing the speaker and looking attentive will help ease the conversation.

2. *Be attentive and eliminate distractions.* Don't let yourself be distracted by computer screens or your phone. Maintaining eye contact is a good way to ensure you are not distracted by other things in the room.

3. *Embrace open mindedness.* Don't assume you know what the speaker is going to say next, and leave your judgment at the door. You don't know what your speaker is going to say or what experiences they are drawing upon, so don't jump to conclusions.

4. *Picture what the speaker is saying as you listen to the words.* Developing mental images of the concepts being described can help your brain make sense and remember them. As the conversation ensues, remember keywords that help signpost the issues.

5. *No interrupting or solutionizing.* Allow the speaker to finish their thoughts before you speak. Interrupting sends a message that your words are more important than theirs. Try to continue to live in open-mindedness and don't jump to solving a problem that has been raised. If the speaker wants advice, they will ask for it.

6. *Wait for a pause before asking questions.* Sometimes you will need to ask a question, for example if you missed something they said or something wasn't clear when the speaker first said it. Instead of interrupting to ask the question, wait for a natural pause to do so.

7. *Ask questions only to ensure you understand what's being said.* If you ask questions that are not directly related to what is being said, it can take the speaker off course. Try to limit questions to topics that allow you to delve deeper and understand better what is being said.

8. *Try to feel what the speaker is feeling.* To experience empathy, you have to let yourself feel what someone else is feeling. As you're listening, allow yourself to feel empathy. This will shape your visible response to the message and help build a connection.

9. *Provide feedback.* Feedback doesn't have to be verbal. It can include nodding your head, making a sound that indicates you're listening and sympathizing. Effective listeners also provide verbal feedback from time to time that confirms the listener's feelings or validates them. Sometimes, repeating back the message in a different way is also useful. By doing so you are also providing proof that you are listening and that you're following their train of thought.

10. *Pay attention to body language.* Sometimes what is not said is as important as what is said. If a speaker is not expressly indicating frustration or irritation but you can tell from their body language that this is what they're feeling, it's important to note that.

Appealing to ethos, pathos, and logos

In considering your messaging, think of appealing not just to the mind of the people with whom you're communicating, but also to their emotions. In communications theory, messaging that appeals to the "ethos, pathos, and logos" – or credibility, emotion, and logic – is most effective because it resonates with people in multiple ways.[22]

Ethos aligns with your credibility.[23] Ask yourself why those listening to you should believe what you say or change their habits as a result of what you tell them. In legal organizations, ethos may stem from status, which is why it can be helpful to get senior personnel on board to actively support a change initiative or send messaging about it. For example, the general counsel will naturally have greater credibility when discussing the importance of streamlining the processes of the legal department than a paralegal. There are other ways than status to gain credibility, however. Often this will come from a professional's experience and skill in their relevant area of expertise, which is why it's important to call out the years of experience a consultant has if they're working to support a change project. Credibility or ethos is also tied to reputation.[24] People who have a reputation for integrity and good character will be able to make more impact with their messaging than others, which lends additional significance to establishing your credibility through executing on projects and showcasing successes. Some innovation teams operate mainly in the background of the firm, like the IT department has traditionally done. In order to develop the credibility in an organization that will allow for more complex change projects, however, innovation teams should be at partner retreats and practice group meetings, building relationships and developing credibility as members of the team who understand lawyers and the way they work.

Pathos means making an emotional connection with the people with whom you're communicating. Developing that authentic emotional connection might involve finding things you have in common, supporting people when they are feeling stressed, spending time speaking with them about non-work topics. Once you have an emotional connection with someone, they are more likely to listen to things you have to say professionally as well. Again, this means that rather than operate as second-hand citizens who are invisible to lawyers, members of an innovation team should have a presence in the firm and appear at social functions to build and strengthen personal connections. Messaging that draws on pathos will also appeal to the emotions of those to whom the messaging is addressed. For example, when reviewing messaging about technology solutions for a legal practice group, one of the things to ask yourself is whether that particular solution will make the lives of those use it better. Will it make your lawyers happier? Beyond efficiency, improved client service, and higher quality outputs, technology that improves the lives of your lawyers is more likely to be adopted and may increase employee engagement, reducing the likelihood and rate of employee turnover. This quality in a technology platform is something I have called the "Happiness Quotient".[25] Where you have such a solution and your team is rolling it out, appealing to emotion during the communications around roll-out will be particularly effective. There are some vendors in the market, such as Time by Ping,[26] whose messaging is already focused on how their solution makes people's lives better. Where this messaging comes ready-made from the vendor, by all means take it and run with it internally – it's likely to be an effective communications tool for driving adoption.

Instead of messaging that appeals only to reason:

"Use of [X tool] will save 20 percent of time on [Y workflow],"

Think of using also messaging that appeals to the heart:

"Spend an extra half hour with your family."

Finally, logos means logic, and it refers to a person's ability to appeal to another person's reason – in other words, to persuade.[27] Communicating ideas, especially ideas that are new in an environment filled with analytical thinkers, requires the ability to express those ideas in clear, compelling ways. Messaging about change initiatives must make it clear to constituents why they should want to make the change. Being succinct about such messages is difficult, which is why it is important to spend time upfront on developing simple, clear messages that are powerfully persuasive. When developing messaging about any change project, review it to ensure it will appeal to people for the right reasons.

Checklist: Planning for effective communications

- [ ] Spend time understanding the various user groups at your organization and developing personas that can be referred to and refined during projects.[28]
- [ ] Empower your team to be active listeners and ensure that you use tried and true methods of effective communication when you are building relationships across the organization.
- [ ] For every change project, assign responsibility for communications planning either to a sub-set of the project team or to dedicated personnel.
- [ ] Develop a communications plan for each change project that sets out:
  - The types of communications to be sent at each phase of the projects;
  - The substantive message in each communication;
  - Recipient groups for each message;
  - Who is responsible for sending each communication; and
  - What medium will be used for sending each communication.
- [ ] Plan for launch communications by understanding what approach you need for the project size. Ensure your message is consistent but that it is repeated often in multiple formats so that it gets through enough times to be effective.

☐ In any messaging developed by your team, ensure that thought goes into crafting messages for specific persona groups that highlights WIIFM, and speaks to ethos, pathos, and logos.

☐ Locate and collect stories wherever possible and use those stories in your messaging to make it more compelling. Become master storytellers.

☐ Develop a bank of elevator pitches for the solutions you are promoting across the organization, so that they can be leveraged as the consistent core of any messaging that is developed.

References

1 https://blog.getguru.com/how-to-write-change-management-plan-templates

2 Heath, Dan, and Heath, Chip. (2011). *Switch*. Random House Business Books.

3 *Ibid.*, p.16.

4 *Ibid.*

5 Kotter, p.74.

6 Kotter, p.71.

7 Tharakan, M. K. (2021). *The Ultimate Guide to Writing a Great Elevator Pitch*. StrategyPitch: https://strategypeak.com/elevator-pitch-examples.

8 *Ibid.*

9 Kaatz, J. (2021). *Marketing Rule of 7s*. Illumination Marketing: https://www.marketingillumination.com/single-post/marketing-rule-of-7s#

10 *Ibid.*

11 McLeod, S. (2021). *Freud's Id, Ego, and Superego*. Simply Psychology: https://www.simplypsychology.org/psyche.html

12 *Ibid.*

13 Duncan, R.D. ((2012). *In Times of Change, "What's In It For Me" Is the Question You Need to Answer*. FastCompany: https://www.fastcompany.com/3001250/times-change-whats-it-me-question-you-need-answer

14 *Ibid.*

15 ProductPlan. (2022). *What is a Persona?* https://bit.ly/3EtFBxG

16 The Culture Equation (2021). *Tell Your Story: Communicating Change Through Storytelling*. https://thecultureequation.com.au/change-agent/tell-your-story-communicating-change-through-storytelling/

17 *Ibid.*

18 *Ibid.*

19 Edinger, S. (2013). *Three Elements of Great Communication, According to Aristotle*. Harvard Business Review: https://hbr.org/2013/01/three-elements-of-great-communication-according.

20 Schilling, D. (2012). *10 Steps to Effective Listening.* Forbes.com: https://www.forbes.com/sites/womensmedia/2012/11/09/10-steps-to-effective-listening/?sh=62b8f0da3891

21 *Ibid.*

22 Edinger, 2013.

23 *Ibid.*

24 *Ibid.*

25 Shaver, N. (2019). *The Forgotten Requirement: Happiness.* Tower of Babel Blog: https://www.babel-law.com/blog/2tap0246ept0c60r85vld1qdlkjnar

26 See www.legaltechnologyhub.com/vendors/ping/

27 *Ibid.*

28 Consider using one of the many persona building templates that exist online in order to support your team in doing this. For example, see the Miro persona templates here: https://miro.com/templates/personas/, and another Persona Canvas www.designabetterbusiness.tools/tools/persona-canvas here.

Chapter 11:
Creative problem-solving and process improvement

Much of what innovation professionals do is problem-solving. Fundamentally, innovation in commercial legal organizations involves solving a critical problem – how will the organization continue to thrive and remain relevant to clients as the competitive forces around it change so that the core business model and original revenue streams cease to be effective? This larger problem drives the strategic approach of the organization towards innovation, and all of the projects your team takes on represent smaller problems to be solved. Many of those projects will be defined as process improvement projects, but they are still solving problems – how might we improve this process so that it is more efficient / less frustrating / less prone to human error? These types of questions give rise to what might be called "research and development efforts", and really, the innovation team in a law firm is effectively a research and development (R&D) team. In this chapter we will explore different approaches to problem-solving and process improvement.

Scientific method
Professor Dan Linna and Dennis Kennedy have both drawn comparisons between effective methodologies used in legal innovation and the scientific method.[1] Kennedy goes as far as to say that if you need to persuade someone why you're doing what you're doing or why a law firm needs what is effectively an R&D team, you should cite the scientific method.[2] It's true that, to a group of lawyers who have not been educated on the methods of innovation, "science" is likely to be a more credible source for your approach than "design thinking", which we will explore shortly, even though design thinking has been repeatedly validated as a business methodology.

The scientific method involves the following steps:

- Question or problem – you start out with a question that needs to be answered or a problem (the unknown) that needs to be solved.

- Research – undertake enough research on the question to be able to come to an educated guess as to what is happening or what the answer is.

- Hypothesis – set down your educated guess, or your defined problem, as this is the statement you will be assessing in your further research.

- Experiment – conduct experiment(s) to validate your hypothesis, and gather data from your experimenting.

- Analyze the data in light of your hypothesis.

- Conclusion – based on the data gathered during your experiments, determine whether or not your hypothesis was correct.

As various commentators have pointed out, science is rarely as neat as the scientific method implies, with some of the most important scientific discoveries having come about as the result of accidents rather than conscious experimentation.[3] Nevertheless, this framework is useful in terms of providing a basic approach to solving certain types of problems.

In a legal setting, you might set out to solve a problem such as why certain types of clients are leaving the firm for other firms, or why some types of work take longer than they should in a particular practice group. The research phase for the latter question might entail mapping out the existing process, speaking to people involved in the process, and observing the process. Your hypothesis might be that there are too many hand-offs involved during the process, and that reducing the hand-offs and introducing more clarity about who is responsible for what would improve the efficiency of the workflow. The experimentation phase might involve a series of attempts to define a new process and provide guidance and training on roles. In order to determine whether the experiments demonstrate that your hypothesis was correct, you will need to gather data such as how long the process originally took versus how long it takes after various hand-offs are eliminated from the process and those still involved are properly trained.

Understanding the scientific method and bringing a conscious framework to your innovation efforts will help you to create project plans and identify the metrics required to determine project success. Indeed, all of the methods in this chapter are focused on introducing structure to innovation and experimentation, and you will likely recognize patterns in the methodologies that mimic aspects of the scientific method.

Service design and design thinking

When I moved to New York in 2018, design thinking was still relatively unheard of in US law firms. It was considered "hoky" or "soft", full of words like empathy that send shudders of discomfort through legal professionals. In the UK, Australia, and in Canada, however, design thinking has been well established as a methodology for problem-solving in law, and as a workshop offering to clients. As I write this in 2023, the concept has been tried and tested in a few large law firms in the US but is still considered foreign in most legal organizations.

The fact that it is not widely accepted as a method for problem-solving in law is notable, given that design thinking and service design methodologies have been used with great success in almost all other industries.[4] Indeed, it has been shown again and again that businesses leveraging design principles are more successful – and more profitable – than those that do not.[5]

Design thinking, legal design, or some form of human-centred design should be considered a core methodology in your legal innovation toolkit. Service design, which is the approach out of which both design thinking and legal design emerged, was designed precisely for the purpose of solving problems in service industries.

Given that background, it might seem surprising that it has taken so long for design to take hold in law firms. When one considers that the process involves a strong focus on the human experience and their emotional needs, however, it's understandable that conservative lawyers have shied away from it.

As legal innovators supporting the optimization of client-service delivery, having an understanding of service design should be mandatory.

Service design

Historically, human-centered design has been re-defined numerous times in different regions across the world, from cooperative design to participatory design to service design.[6] The term "user-centered design" was originally coined by Don Norman in 1986, and gained prominence in the 1990s. Service design, however, has been around far longer, with academics and practitioners working to evolve its core tenets so that it has become a full discipline.

Service design essentially involves taking the same approach that companies have for years taken to the design of products and applying it to services. The global world has many clear examples of companies whose services have been designed with the user in mind. For example, every time you walk into a Starbucks, you know exactly where to line up. You know that there will be one person who takes your order, and that you will move further down the line for the next person to deliver your order to you. You even know that if you order a coffee, they will ask for your name and write it on the cup (and in modern lore, will take pains to write it the wrong way).

Think about the efficiency that this consistency brings to Starbucks as an organization. Every time a new Starbucks store opens, the requirements for lay-out are clear – the long service area is a necessity given the multi-stage line-up, order, and delivery process. When new people are hired, they are likely allotted a specific role, with training no doubt structured according to whether they will be taking orders or delivering them. McDonalds is another obvious example. When you go to a consulate to pick up a new passport, or you take your car to be washed, or you go to the doctor for a check-up, or to the ER with a child in distress, you expect that there will be processes in place that streamline the demand for the service in question and improve the efficiency with which it is offered or delivered.

Service design has become such a well-practiced and important skill that educational programs and certification courses are widely available, including from the New School, and an International Service Design Institute has emerged,[7] defining service design as:

"A non-aesthetic design practice that helps service providers offer a benefit to users. Skilled service designers fulfil service provider goals with new services or by improving existing ones. Service designers employ user-centric tools and techniques to achieve more predictable, successful outcomes for users. A successful service delivers a satisfying, desired outcome."[8]

The popularity of service design compared to previous methodologies around services and processes stemmed from its conscious focus on the human needs at the core of the service. Rather than looking at a service by regarding the individual aspects of it that might be spread across an entire (potentially large) company, service designers approach the service as a whole, identifying the problems and opportunities both for those using the service and those delivering it, and developing a whole solution by crafting an improved service.[9] Service design principles have been widely adopted as the principles that also drive user-centric digital services, through focusing on the user's journey and experience (UX). It is thus a widely accepted approach to modern technology development and digital transformation.

The general principles underlying service design include:

- Design of a service should be underpinned by a real understanding of the purpose of the service, the demand for it, and the ability of the provider to offer the service;
- Services should be designed with the user needs in mind, rather than the needs of the business, and input from the users should always be sought during the design of the service;
- Rather than looking at the individual components of a service, the service should be approached as a whole process;
- Extreme or outlier events should be accommodated in the design, and should be regarded as common events rather than unlikely;
- A prototype of the new service should be developed before the design is completed, and a minimum viable product (MVP) created and released to users for testing so that the design can be iterated upon in response to user feedback to optimize value to the user;
- Services should be developed in the context of a clear business case and within a clear business model; and
- The design of the service should involve collaboration with all relevant stakeholders.[10]

These principles scratch at the surface of the service design methodology, which has evolved over many years into the complete approach to the design of complex services that it represents today. You may recognize the fundamental philosophy behind these principles because they run through all aspects of this book. I view them as central to the process of innovating legal services. Indeed, the principles of service design are useful to anyone who solves problems and aims to increase efficiencies in a service business.

However, not everyone can be a service designer. Like product design or industrial design, this is a full professional occupation that requires genuine training. In some ways, design thinking is therefore more accessible. Nevertheless, keeping the principles of service design close at hand will serve you well in all that you do as a legal innovator. All other design methodologies we explore in this chapter are in some way derivative of service design.

Design thinking

Design thinking as a methodology has developed out of service design and alongside other human-centered design theories, but California-based design agency IDEO, specifically Tim Brown (its CEO), has been widely credited with coining the phrase and popularizing the process. Building on the statistics around service design more generally, design thinking has become very popular in all kinds of industries, with 79 percent of companies that have used it agreeing that it improves the ideation process, and 71 percent of companies having experienced a shift in work culture after adopting it.[11]

Design thinking takes the principles of service design and applies them to business processes and other "wicked problems", distilling the process into five steps – empathize, define, ideate, prototype, test. The term "wicked problem" first emerged in the 1970s (the same decade as Tim Brown established IDEO) and was used by design theorists Horst Rittel and Melvin Webber to refer to complex problems that lacked clarity in both their aims and their solutions.[12] Wicked problems, in addition to being hard to describe, are also subject to real-world constraints that increase the difficulty in solving them. Unlike problems to which logic applies and there is a definitive answer, there is no single answer to a wicked problem, nor can logic be applied to it in the same way – there is no true or false. Design thinking is a problem-solving methodology that actively welcomes the uncertainty and ambiguity of a problem and considers a problem from all sides.[13]

In the legal industry, most of the problems we seek to solve are wicked problems. Even within the confines of a law firm, a problem around how to improve the efficiency of a particular workflow and improve delivery times to the client involves significant complexity. The question of how to bill for work when the output has the same value but the mechanisms for achieving that output have been optimized so lawyers, who bill by the hour, can deliver the same quality in less time – that is a wicked problem. How to price work that is undertaken partly by machine and partly by human beings is another. Not to mention the problems inherent to access to justice, which are large-scale and amorphous; these are seriously wicked problems.

The process of design thinking is intended to address the ambiguity of wicked problems by helping to guide practitioners through a series of steps to help define the problem in terms of user needs, and only then solve the problem from the perspective of one of those users. Design thinking prevents problem-solvers from jumping to "solutioning" – trying to solve a problem before they properly understand it. Lawyers, in particular, are prone to doing this because when clients ask for something they think they need to immediately respond. Almost always, digging further into the problem in order to first understand it properly will serve you better than jumping too quickly into developing a solution. In fact, it's what we train our associates to do – stay in the partner's office and ask questions after receiving instructions, make sure you've understood what you're being asked to do before you get too far down the course of doing the work. This is the same approach that should be employed in relation to all problem-solving in your organization. Design thinking can provide the necessary discipline to train your team to wait to solve a problem until you've fully understood it.

The fact that it's "human-centered" means that design thinking puts the end-user at the heart of all decision-making. The philosophy underpinning this methodology is that through exercising consistent empathy for your customer or client, you will be able create products, services, and experiences that genuinely help people and perhaps even change their lives.

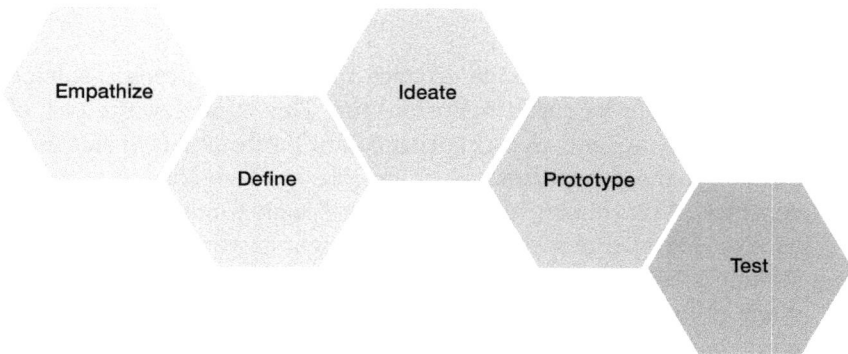

Figure 32: Design thinking process.[14] Source: IDEO.

Although in practice the process of design thinking is not always linear, the framework for undertaking a design thinking exercise is set out in a linear way (see Figure 32) and involves the following five steps:

1. *Empathize.* The first step of the process requires practitioners to actively spend time interacting with and observing the end users of the product or service, or those who experience the problem you are solving, in order to "empathize" with them – to understand exactly

how they experience that problem, how they feel about it, and what their needs are.[15] In real design thinking work, this step would be carried out through observing the end users in the current process, and interviewing them about their experiences.[16] During interviews, asking open-ended questions and listening is critical; this is not an interrogation where the interviewer is as active as the respondent. The point of the exercise is to gain as much information as possible about the end user's feelings and needs. A tool called an empathy map is often used during this stage in the process, which can help practitioners flesh out the various needs of the user.

2.   *Define*. The define stage involves bringing clarity to the problem. Although you will start out with a view and some understanding of the problem you have set out to solve, it will be rife with ambiguity until this stage in the process. At the end of the define stage, you should have a clear "problem statement", which is a way of succinctly expressing the crux of the problem you are seeking to solve. According to design agency the d.school, the problem statement "should be a guiding statement that focuses on insights and needs of a particular user, or composite character".[17] Effectively, the define mode is synonymous with sensemaking.

3.   *Ideate*. Ideation is the mode or stage that in other problem-solving exercises might be called brainstorming. This is my favorite part of design thinking, and an aspect that can be easily extracted and used outside of the design process to improve problem-solving in many contexts. What makes ideation during design thinking different is its goal – instead of seeking to find the right answer or idea, you are seeking to explore as wide of an idea space as possible, and get as many different ideas on the table as you can, from which the most promising ones can later be selected. The mindset that practitioners are encouraged to embrace at this stage is one of openness – in order to ideate you must try to be "judgment-free", including by not judging yourself or letting your inhibitions stand in the way of an idea.[18] The idea is to let yourself go wherever your mind takes you, no matter how wild, with the knowledge that you will later come back and evaluate the ideas with your rational mind. In this stage, you are bringing together what you know of user needs with the defined problem statement in order to develop ideas that might go towards solving the problem to address the specifically identified user need.

Design thinking practitioners have all kinds of exercises they use to facilitate ideation. The exercise is generally undertaken in groups, with the understanding that the best ideas are those generated by a room full of diverse people rather than by one individual. Putting people under pressure to generate ideas quickly often helps to generate a broader swathe of ideas. Techniques for doing so include bodystorming, mind-mapping, and sketching.[19] In a design thinking workshop, ideation might include writing many ideas on post-it notes during a set period of time, after which participants vote on the solutions, or combination of solutions, that they think are worth pursuing.

4. *Prototype*. During the prototyping stage, the goal is to actually begin to build low-resolution versions of some of the most promising ideas. The concept here is to build something that is easy, quick, and cheap, but comes close to being able to provide an "experience" of the solution for the end user.[20] Viability of a solution will become clearer during the prototyping stage, which allows practitioners to explore an idea or solution (or more than one) relatively quickly to ascertain whether they will work – before committing to building a whole solution. In a design thinking exercise, a prototype might be a sketch, a storyboard, a skit or role-playing activity, or anything else that enables the end user to experience an early version of the solution.

5. *Test*. In test mode, you are letting end users experience the prototype, and obtaining their feedback on it.[21] This is when you are able to gather information that will allow you to tweak or change the prototype, or move in a different direction. You will likely also gain more information during this stage about end user needs, which will help in refining the prototype and the ultimate solution.

These five stages are iterative, which means that during a real problem-solving exercise you would cycle through them multiple times in order to progress further towards a real solution that addresses end user needs and solves the problem in the right way. On its website, IDEO now sets out a process that involves six steps, likely in an effort to simplify the traditional stages for those discovering design thinking for the first time. These steps are practical and may help you if you're considering using design thinking in your firm or legal organization for the first time:

- Frame a question.
- Gather inspiration.

- Generate ideas.
- Make ideas tangible.
- Test to learn.
- Share the story.[22]

In corporate environments, if you engage a professional to solve a problem in the organization using design thinking, they may take weeks or even months to properly interview and observe end users during the empathize stage. This is not to say, however, that you can't yourself (with some training) use the methodology to address discrete problems in your organization. Months of user interviews are not necessary when the problem you're solving is smaller.

Underpinning the process of design thinking is the notion that what you are building – whether that is a product or a service – should hit at the intersection of what is desirable (and will delight the end user), what is economically viable (what you can afford to build, and – if it's a product – what users can afford to buy), and what is technically feasible to build.[23] As we will see in chapter 13, this is the same philosophy that underpins product development, especially as it pertains to establishing the product-market fit of a particular offering.

Design thinking is a collaborative method of problem-solving that draws upon the creativity of everyone involved, so it is an ideal method to use with your team. It is also characterized by processes of divergence and convergence, meaning that at various stages of the process people will work individually, and at others they will converge to work together. This flow of individual and collective work allows for both introverts and extraverts to participate equally. The mindset of openness means that people must not judge an idea or dismiss it until it has been explored, which creates a safe space for all kinds of personalities.

Later in this chapter, we will explore ways that you can use design thinking in your organization and with your team. It is an extremely useful methodology to have up your sleeve – to solve problems, and to bring about widespread culture change.[24] First, though, it's important to address the phenomenon of what is termed "legal design", and to understand whether and how it is differentiated from design thinking.

Legal design

Legal design is simply the application of design principles and methodologies to legal processes and documents.[25] The practice of applying human-centered design principles to law and legal practices was conceived of by Dr Colette R. Brunschwig in her PhD dissertation in 2001, and gained greater visibility when other academics such as Helena Haapio, Stefania Passera, and Margaret Hagan held the first legal design event in 2013.[26] In the States, Hagan, who is the executive director of the Legal Design Lab and a lecturer at Stanford Law School and the Stanford Institute of Design (the d.school), has popularized the term. While she was a fellow at the d.school in 2013-14, Hagan launched the Program for Tech and Design, experimenting with how design could make legal services more usable, useful, and engaging. The work of Hagan and other academics has spun off many legal design agencies and given rise to a generation of legal designers whose careers are focused on improving the practice of law through the application of design. Today's legal designers are generally people who have a combination of a legal background (either through studying the law or working in legal organizations) and an education in design.

Perhaps as a result of the fact that both design thinking and legal design have gained in popularity over the past few years, there has been more discussion of late about how the two are distinct from one another and whether "legal design" now has a meaning beyond its original framing by Hagan. Anusia Gillespie, senior vice president, enterprise at UnitedLex, in a piece written for the *Legal Evolution* blog in 2022, explored this question and quoted Meghann Kelley of White & Case LLP as distinguishing between the two by specifying that while design thinking encourages you to think outside of the box during ideation, legal design is "a step-change within the confines of the same solution"; in other words, ideation is confined within the box of your current environment and context.[27] Gillespie suggests that the potential consequences of applying an "outside of the box" methodology in law might involve undesirable radical change such as the elimination of legal instruments such as contracts, which is why legal design better serves the industry.

Design thinking is not applied in a vacuum, however. To assert that a design thinking exercise, when applied to a legal problem, might eliminate the law or legal instruments altogether, is to fundamentally misconstrue the central principle of design thinking. It is a methodology focused entirely on the end users, taking into account their specific context and needs. In commercial legal organizations, the needs of end-users in the circumstances of a corporate M&A transaction, for example, very much include the requirement that there be an executed contract to memorialize the deal points and to legally uphold the agreement between parties. A design thinking exercise seeking to address the problem, "How might we improve the readability of a contract in order to allow for clients to more easily digest critical terms" could not, therefore, result in the very contract being tossed out altogether.

So in spite of the valiant effort to identify a reason for the difference in terminology, legal design – like legal innovation, legal marketing, legal technology – is just another victim of the tendency we have in law to affix the prefix "legal" in order to legitimize something for use in our industry. Legal design is, as stated above, and as its originator Hagan established from the outset, an application of design thinking or design principles in the legal industry, for the purpose of addressing legal problems. Sometimes, this may indeed lead to some fairly radical departures from how things have always been done. However, by virtue of the fact that the end users of legal services have needs that are – at least partially – legal needs, the departure from tradition will not involve a departure that is too radical for lawyers or their clients to adopt.

Indeed, the fact that design thinking focuses on end user needs is precisely why it is so critical in legal. Law is, by its very nature, a service industry, focused on serving the needs of clients. If we are concerned by the notion of adopting in the legal industry *the* quintessential methodology for solving problems by putting clients' needs first, there is something broken with our approach to law. This is why I recommend design thinking as an essential process for leaders and teams who have been charged with changing the culture of a law firm or legal organization – using it with your lawyers will help them focus on what the needs of their clients might actually be, beyond the mere words spoken in an exchange. It will help lawyers understand the need to dig deeper, to better understand their clients and their clients' businesses, and will enable them to better accept processes and technologies where the purpose of these is to improve the client experience. In short, it will help lawyers put their clients first, where they should always have been.

Although there has been more talk of legal design in the past few years, it is not yet a widely established practice. There are some books on the topic, and an increasing number of legal designers and legal design agencies, but these still predominantly operate on the fringes of the industry.[28] Unlike Starbucks, legal services have never been designed. No one sat down with clients at the beginning of civilization and figured out how best to solve legal problems for them in a way that really delighted them. Instead, lawyers have bungled their way through service delivery, often considering the actual process of that delivery the least of their concerns (the legal work itself being the only really important part of the relationship). That is like Starbucks positing its success on having the best coffee, the assumption being that if they have the best coffee, people will come to drink it, regardless of how awful the service is. If the coffee is good, it doesn't matter if it takes three hours to prepare, or if it's served in coffee cups that always leak, or if it's often served cold. We all know Starbucks would not have become the behemoth it is if that was the case, but in many law firms the focus on service has been so lax they may as well be serving their coffee cold. That is where legal design has a role – to improve the practice of law and the delivery of legal services to the benefit of clients.

Some of the ways in which legal design has been applied in law include:

- As addressed above, making contracts more accessible and easier to read, sometimes by incorporating visual elements;
- Improving the methods of communication between lawyers and their clients;
- Designing improved workflows for specific legal matters; and
- Enhancing the ways lawyers collaborate in their execution of legal matters.

Given the many types of matters in law, and the multitude of workflows and service touchpoints, the opportunities for legal design to make law better are wide-ranging. Unlike the general application of service design or design thinking principles, however, for the most part applying this type of methodology to legal practice is best left to professionals – partly because you are likely to get more buy-in from lawyers if there is an expert leading the way. If you're interested in leveraging legal design to improve the way lawyers in a practice group operate or serve clients, or the way your legal department serves the business, I recommend engaging a professional legal design agency.

Systems thinking

It would seem remiss to address other variations of service design and not mention systems thinking. However, given the limited ability innovation leaders have to address systemic issues in law, I will keep it brief.

Systems thinking is the application of service design principles to complex problem-solving on a much larger scale. The concept of systems thinking arises from the belief that the mutual interaction of the various parts of a system give rise to characteristics that are not characteristic of any of the individual parts of that system – in other words, that the whole is greater than the sum of its parts.

Daniel H. Kim, in his text *An Introduction to Systems Thinking*, defines a system as any group of interacting, interrelated, or interdependent parts that form a complex and unified whole that has a specific purpose. Meadows defined it as follows:

> "A system is a set of elements or parts that is coherently organized and interconnected in a pattern or structure that produces a characteristic set of behaviors, often classified as its 'function' or 'purpose'."[29]

Systems thinkers look at an entire system – rather than any one of its composite parts – in order to understand processes, underlying dynamics, and to identify patterns amid chaos. They look at the system as a whole and focus on the interrelations between elements.[30]

One of the best-known proponents of systems thinking was Professor Kaoru Ishigawa, who provided his own technique for systems thinking. In practice, systems thinking involves examining the major factors that could be causing a particular problem, changing an element or a factor in the system, and then reviewing the consequences of that change and taking that feedback into account as to whether another factor must also be changed. Typically, systems thinkers will examine a problem from three angles – events, patterns, and structure.[31] The problem – what is seen, or the event that gave rise to awareness of a problem – is the tip of an iceberg, with the causes lying underneath and including:

- Patterns of behavior: what has been happening routinely? What are the trends?
- Structure of the system: what has influenced the patterns? (for example, politics, laws, physical structures). What are the relationships among the parts?
- Mental models: what assumptions, beliefs, and values do people hold about the system?[32]

Unlike problems that can be addressed using design thinking or service design, systems thinking is for problems that are – well – systemic.

Although a law firm has its own events, structures, interactions, and patterns of behavior, it is not big enough to be considered a "system" for the purpose of systems thinking. Some may disagree with me here, and if one was indeed tackling the entirety or a large international or a verein, and solving problems that involved many parts of it, that may well constitute systems thinking. Still, it's rare for innovation leaders to be tasked with problem-solving at that macro-level.

The legal industry, however, is certainly a system. If your goal and that of your team is to bring change more broadly across the industry or to understand the changes happening in the legal ecosystem, having some knowledge of systems thinking is important.

There are also elements of systems thinking you can take and apply to your existing environment. The notion that the problem you are seeing is only the tip of the iceberg and there are many unseen forces that have given rise to it is an important one. It's important to keep in mind the fact that there are all kinds of factors at play in any problem that comes up as a priority within your organization, and these must be explored thoroughly before it's helpful to find a resolution. Trying to do so without understanding the underlying causes may well lead to the development of a solution that doesn't actually solve the problem. This is an aspect of systems thinking that is a helpful takeaway to those of us leading change within an organization.

How to apply design principles in legal

As promised above, I want to leave you with some practical advice on how to actually leverage design principles in your work, even when you don't have the benefit of design thinking certification or a service designer on your team.

One of the most powerful takeaways from design thinking is the knowledge that you don't have to apply the entire five-step process in order to get value from it. There are limitations to the formality of the design thinking process, and hosting day-long workshops won't work in most legal environments. Even if your team has been able to get traction from more formal design sessions, I would encourage you to also consider applying the discrete principles from design thinking more broadly. Design thinking is an approach that requires a certain mindset – one of openness, infinite curiosity, and empathy. The understanding that these qualities are essential for user-focused problem-solving is useful. It is a mindset that I would encourage you to adopt in all of your legal innovation work, and one that should be encouraged in the people who work with you.

The principles of design thinking, and some of the methodologies and tools, can be used as individual components to bolster your innovation program. Examples include:

- The principle of empathizing with the end user should underpin every aspect of the work that you and your team does.

- Encouraging your team to listen rather than interject, in order to identify true user needs, is hugely valuable.

- Spending time to define the problem, rather than jumping to a solution, will always be helpful.

- In meetings or when the team is stuck, using some of the design thinking techniques for ideating, encouraging everyone to lay aside their inhibitions, and to explore a wide solution space, will ensure your team is more creative and comes up with better ideas collaboratively than they otherwise would.

- Encouraging the development of a quick prototype before committing to a solution, and requiring that end-users be exposed to that prototype, comment on it, and ensuring these comments are then taken into account during further development, will ensure that the solutions your team develops are genuinely useful.

What I am suggesting is that you take the principles of service design and design thinking and carry them through everything you do as a team. Put this philosophy at the core of everything that you do, and you will excel as a problem-solving team in a service industry. Another way of integrating design thinking into your work is by implementing design thinking workshops. These can be workshops aimed at solving a specific problem (either internally, or between a group of lawyers and select clients) or workshops that are conducted for the purpose of educating lawyers and allied professionals and advancing your culture change objective.

How to start[33]

If you seek to more formally introduce design thinking in your firm or organization, through problem-solving workshops, for example, you will need to make sure that you have the right skills to execute the initiative. There are two ways to do this: (1) either get some training yourself (and have members of your team trained up), or (2) hire someone (on a consultant basis, or as a permanent member of your team) who has real experience with service design.

In my experience, this kind of initiative works best if you do both. In order to sell design thinking internally, you will have to know something about it. You may have to demonstrate its value with small groups of people before you get budget approval for an external resource. It's worth getting some training, and attending some workshops, to ensure that the relevant people on your team understand enough to be able to communicate effectively about design thinking. There are some online courses (including an excellent series by IDEO). These provide enough insight into the principles of design thinking that you will be able to start using parts of the methodology informally – for example, by introducing ideation exercises into meetings, or running diverge-converge practices with your team. In-person training is essential if you intend to facilitate sessions yourself.

When the time comes to run a session with decision-makers at your firm, however, I recommend hiring a consultant. Having an external facilitator will add the necessary professionalism and expertise to your program.

The most concrete success you will ultimately derive from design thinking at your firm comes from utilizing the methodology as a means of effectively collaborating with clients. However, there is also significant benefit to be gained from using it internally. There is no need to immediately kick off this initiative with clients – or even with the practicing lawyers at your firm. Indeed, starting slowly behind the scenes may get you the quick wins that you need to generate the buy-in necessary to move towards external sessions.

In any firm, there are countless problems on the business side of law that could benefit enormously from user-centered design practices. In two different firms, I have had success by starting slowly and using design thinking first within my own department. This approach has value not only because it teaches your own staff about design thinking, and gradually builds support for it, but also because it can provide an early success story on the business side.

Decide on the participant group

- Your own team makes an obvious starting point, and starting here will explain to colleagues what the practice involves and why it's useful.

- Alternatively, start with one business department, or perhaps two that work closely together.

- Once you have a quick success under your belt, broaden the initiative and expand to multiple departments on the business or administrative side. There are many problems in any firm or organization that affect all departments.

- Next move to your lawyers. You can bring lawyers from across practice groups to solve a problem from different angles (this diversity will enhance the ideation process, and has the added benefit of building relationships at the firm). Alternatively, work with one practice group to solve a targeted problem.

- Once you have momentum with timekeepers, use your lawyer champions to approach clients and offer design thinking as a service, whether this starts as a listening session, or a workshop, or you jump straight into problem-solving alongside the client.

Note that as you are introducing your initiative, it may also be useful to begin each session with a brief presentation about design thinking. Although design thinking is about doing, rather than talking, part of what you are doing when building your program is educating your colleagues. Presentations are so ubiquitous in commercial settings that you will lull them into their comfort zone this way, before you shake them right out of it.

Choose the right problem

No one will want to come along to your session unless it is addressing a problem that resonates with them. For this reason, and because you want the session to be genuinely helpful, it makes sense to spend time at the outset to develop the right problem statement to draw participants.

Of course, the ideal scenario is that you are holding a design session because there is a burning issue that must be addressed, and everyone has agreed that design thinking is the best way to do that. For example, a client has asked your team to collaborate with them in solving a particular problem, and you are running a session with that client (with the relationship partner's blessing) in order to develop a solution.

Before you get to that point, however, it's likely that you will need to develop some quick wins internally at the firm, using different participant groups. In these circumstances, there may not necessarily be one obvious problem to solve – indeed, there may be many, and your job (or that of your team) is then to identify the one that will work best to engage participants, that will also give rise to useful solutions.

Develop a problem statement

The problem that is at the core of a traditional design thinking session will generally be phrased as a "how to…" or "how might we better…"

statement. Remember that the problem will be further explored, narrowed, and defined by participants within the session – so all you need is a topic and a starting point for the statement. Here are some ideas for problem statements that you may wish to use with different participant groups:

- How might we better communicate better or collaborate across departments;
- How to improve the project intake system / the business planning process/reporting to the partnership for administrative departments at the firm;
- How to reduce email traffic;
- How to improve the capture of data around the firm's matters;
- How might we better collect / access the information we have about our clients;
- How to onboard our clients more effectively;
- How to ensure we understand our clients' business;
- How to improve the training of our incoming associates; and
- How to break down silos.

When it comes time to work with clients, think about using design thinking to explore your firm's touchpoints with them. What are the processes in place for delivering legal work to the client, and how could those be improved? Ask clients what they are interested in improving around the service delivery model, and use this as the basis for a session.

Don't underestimate your lawyers

This is a statement that applies across the board with your initiatives. Many of you are likely reading this thinking that your lawyers (and your clients) will be uninterested in design thinking, or that they will scoff at the very notion of it.

At the firms where I have worked to introduce design thinking, the same trepidation and reluctance initially existed. Yet at these same firms, the lawyers quickly became fans and, at one firm, the managing partner ultimately became the biggest proponent of the methodology. Sometimes we forget, perhaps because the discourse around the "lawyer-personality" is now so entrenched, that the practice of law involves creative analysis. Without question, many lawyers will be uncomfortable in initial sessions when there is overt discussion of empathy, or if they are asked to draw a persona instead of write a description. However, in my experience it does not take long before these inhibitions are overcome in favor of the natural curiosity that lies at the core of these intellectual professionals. Certainly by the time ideation begins, most lawyers will have thrown themselves into the process. Don't let stereotypes put you off launching a design thinking initiative.

Develop buy-in

With all change projects, you need to generate top-down support as well as bottom-up interest to truly gain ground. Design thinking is no different. In order to drive such a program forward, you will need to gradually build momentum through gaining supporters across your firm or organization.

One way to do this is to invite key people, the decision-makers at your firm, to attend sessions. Ensure that you have some practice with the methodology before you do this, so that you can talk intelligently about it. If you have some wins under your belt already, partners and senior management will have heard about the program and are likely already interested in participating. Choose a problem that you know is of particular interest to them. If possible, populate part of the room with people who have previously participated in sessions and are enthusiastic. This is the right session for an external consultant – bringing in an expert will build your credibility at this stage. Make sure you follow up with your key attendees afterwards and involve them in the follow-up with other participants. Once they see the engagement of the people in the room, and the ideas that have come out of the session, they are likely to come on side. If you are able to tie client narratives into the experience, for example by referencing real RFP requests that could be answered if your firm was undertaking design thinking exercises with clients, your rate of success will skyrocket.

Deliver value

There is no point in running design thinking sessions at your law firm or in your legal department unless there is an actual outcome from them. As discussed above, one of the unique attributes of design thinking is its ability to deliver a result at the end of a session in the form of a prototype that is able to be used and tested.

It may sound obvious, but at the end of a design thinking session you should collect the prototypes and work to implement at least one of these. At the end of any such session, there will be much paper left behind. Gathering it all up and collating a list of the key themes that have emerged over the course of the session will be useful. Get back quickly to participants, to remind them of the outcomes they developed, and include them in the decision-making process about which of these to move forwards, and how. Ideally, you will engage the lawyers in following through on the solutions or improvements that were identified during the session. Similar to a business development effort, a problem-solving or process improvement effort is only as good as the follow-through afterwards. The last thing you want is for the session to stand alone in people's minds, as an isolated instance of attempted innovation that resulted in nothing.

Once your program is client-facing, design thinking sessions can provide an avenue for experimenting within the existing service delivery model with clients. Before actually changing anything, these sessions provide a forum within which both client-side and law firm-side participants can come together and think about how to improve the ways in which they interact, the services the firm provides, and the value the firm can bring to the client.

In contrast to the endless meetings that often define our days in corporate legal environments, it is a practice that can serve to get things done (for real!), to effect real change, and to properly collaborate across departments, practice groups, and with clients. Like anything of value, it will take some hard work and determination to get a design thinking initiative off the ground.

Manufacturing methodologies

Manufacturing is an industry in which, more than most, efficiency is king and risk is rife. In manufacturing, workers are exposed to risks stemming from exposure to foreign substances, bodily injury from factory accidents, equipment failures, motor vehicle incidents and more.[34] There is a powerful need for safety procedures that are followed consistently and that reduce human error. Additionally, because more product made faster often means more product sold, efficiency in manufacturing processes is directly relevant to revenue generation.

As a result of these drivers, the most impactful process improvement methodologies have stemmed from the manufacturing industry. Interestingly, many of the more influential have come specifically from Japanese manufacturing. Some of these methodologies are now considered important in the legal profession.

Kaizen

Kaizen is an approach to creating continuous improvement based on the idea that small, ongoing positive changes can reap significant improvements.[35] The methodology is focused on positive change, with a focus on preventative measures that will diminish the likelihood of mistakes and operational waste. Kaizen has its origins from Toyota, post-World War II, where quality assurance workers were focused on preventing defects. The word "Kaizen" is a composite of the words "Kai", meaning improvement, and "Zen", meaning good. The philosophy behind it is about more than productivity. It's a belief in humanizing the workplace and instituting continuous improvement in every aspect of life. It is differentiated from other process improvement methods due to a focus on enabling involvement from across the organization. In a Kaizen improvement effort, every type of employee may raise problems and ideas for improvement. Kaizen was brought to the West and popularized by Masaaki Imai via his 1986 book, *Kaizen: The Key to Japan's Competitive Success.*

Figure 33: Kaizen cycle for continuous improvement.

The aim of Kaizen is generally widespread cultural change, but the events to kick-start a Kaizen process usually focus on how a specific set of problems have evolved. As someone leading a Kaizen initiative, there are a number of ways that you can prepare. The steps involved in a Kaizen cycle are set out in Figure 33.

Educating and training the staff who will be involved is the first step. It's important that there is buy-in, not just from management but also staff. Next, you must provide the relevant employees with the ability to provide feedback in relation to the specific problem. This step is designed to get ideas flowing, so it's important to ensure that the avenues available to employees for reporting suggestions are as accessible as possible. Employees need a way to communicate their ideas effectively and document them. Kaizen boards (visual tools that help teams and organizations manage their continuous improvement effort), quality circles, and suggestion boxes are all tried and true methods in Kaizen cycles.[36]

Similar to design thinking, once employees have generated ideas for improvement, some of these will be chosen and implemented. An important Kaizen principle is measuring results, so that the effectiveness of a solution can be tested. If an idea is shown to improve a key metric (for example, safety or productivity) without negatively impacting another area of the business, it will be adopted.

Unlike most other methodologies for process improvement, Kaizen is ongoing, representing a long-term strategy, the goal of which is to develop the capabilities and confidence of workers. Kaizen works when employees at all levels of the company work together proactively to achieve regular, incremental improvements. In a sense, it combines the collective talents within a company to create a powerful engine for improvement.

In legal organizations, adopting the Kaizen philosophy could involve changes as minimal as:

- Ensuring all lawyers and business professionals understand that their voices are important when it comes to improving the way the organization at large operates;
- Making available a centralized system for the reporting of problems or issues (where no judgment or penalty is incurred by personnel reporting such problems);
- Allowing for and encouraging suggestions for continuous improvement from all workers; and
- When there is a specific problem that needs to be solved that impacts

employees, actively inviting ideas for solutions from employees across the organization.[37]

Kaizen works because it draws upon the active experience of workers who operate across an organization. As a result, management is made aware of problems as soon as they arise, no matter where in the organization they originate. Workers who intimately understand the way that a particular process works because they are the ones executing it are more likely to come up with a realistic measure to improve that process. As an added bonus, when people feel that their opinions matter in an organization, they will be more engaged in their work and more likely to stay in their roles. This makes instilling a Kaizen culture appealing to organizations like law firms, where attorney and employee retention can be difficult.

Kaizen is a long-term strategy, however. One of its goals is to develop the capabilities and confidence of workers, and doing so requires the long-term adoption of Kaizen processes so that these are built into the framework of an organization.

Lean Six Sigma

Lean Six Sigma is a methodology created from a composite of two other process improvement approaches – lean and Six Sigma. These are not simple methodologies to employ. Training courses are widely available to allow professionals to earn credentials that qualify them for working with organizations on Lean Six Sigma improvement initiatives. Similar to Karate or other martial art disciplines, qualifications to undertake Lean Six Sigma initiatives are represented by various "belt" colors, White being the easiest and Master Black the most difficult. The overview provided here does not qualify any reader to undertake a Lean Six Sigma exercise. There are plenty of training courses available, both within and beyond the legal industry, and I encourage anyone interested to seek out this education. However, some of the approaches involved in Lean Six Sigma are advantageous on their own and can be leveraged as part of your toolkit for legal innovation.

Lean

Lean methodology, like Kaizen, was established in Japan. Japanese auto-maker Toyota developed Lean in the 1940s. Its purpose was to remove non-value-adding activities from the production process to reduce the time it took from an order being placed to delivery of a car.[38] Six Sigma, on the other hand, was established in the 1980s by an engineer at US

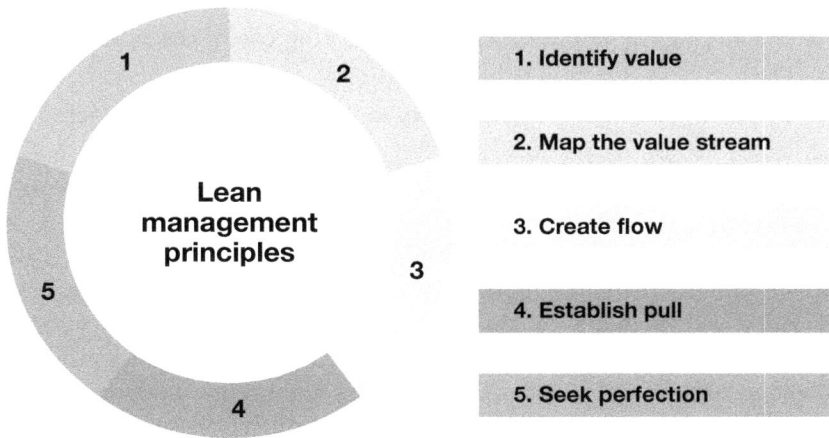

1. Identify value

2. Map the value stream

3. Create flow

4. Establish pull

5. Seek perfection

Lean management principles

Figure 34: Lean management principles.

telecommunications company Motorola, who was inspired by Japan's Kaizen model.

Lean is a systematic approach to reduce or eliminate activities that don't add value to the process (see Figure 34).[39] In Lean methodology, these types of activities are called "waste". Lean therefore emphasizes removing wasteful steps in a process and re-building processes with a renewed focus on the steps that add value. The Lean method ensures high quality outputs and customer satisfaction with minimal outlay, which is why it's an attractive proposition in the legal industry. The basic steps of a Lean improvement effort involve:

- Identifying who is impacted by a process and what they want or need from it;
- Analyzing the current state of the process (this is often done through process mapping);
- Developing a future state that:
  - Reduces the number of hand-offs in the process;
  - Standardizes the tasks involved in the process; and
  - Eliminates redundancy in the process;
- Implementing the necessary changes to the process to move it into the future state;
- Measuring the performance of the new process;

- Sustaining the improvement by monitoring use of the new process; and
- Repeating these steps if necessary to further improve the process.[40]

While the initial focus on the "end user" of the process is similar to service design or design thinking, the Lean approach does not involve ideation so much as it requires examination of an existing process in order to identify the parts of it that could be eliminated or changed so as to improve efficiency and productivity. Mapping a process and laying it out visually allows for this type of analysis. The exercise of working with a group of people to understand exactly how a process is currently undertaken can be useful in and of itself, with people realizing during these sessions that certain parts of the process are unnecessarily complicated or confusing.

Six Sigma

Six Sigma (as illustrated by Figure 35) is an approach to management that focuses on delivering customer value by emphasizing the efficiency of operational processes and quality outcomes.[41] Sound familiar? The synergies between Lean and Six Sigma are clear. Where Lean is focused on waste in a process, the goal of Six Sigma is to reduce variation and defect rates in production processes, largely through statistical analysis.[42] One of the most important aspects of a Six Sigma exercise is choosing the right process improvement project to begin with. Ideally you should identify a problem that:

- Has a known, existing process;
- Will be meaningful if it is improved, but is not overly complex;
- Has the potential for improvement – in other words, it's clear that the efficiency could be improved or that cost savings are possible; and
- Where progress is able to be measured (you can collect data about the process).[43]

Six Sigma uses various tools to reduce defects, including one that is useful even when it is applied more broadly – DMAIC, which stands for Define, Measure, Analyze, Improve, Control.[44] Lean Six Sigma is the composite approach of both Lean and Six Sigma, giving rise to a powerful toolkit of process improvement methodologies and allowing the DMAIC method to be applied to any kind of process (not just for the purpose of eliminating defects).

Figure 35: Six Sigma DMAIC method.

DMAIC is usually undertaken by a team, rather than by an individual. During the **Define** stage, the process improvement team will draft a project charter, plot a high-level map of the process, clarify the needs of the customers (or people affected by the process, and refine the project focus.[45]

In the **Measure** phase, the team gathers data that establishes how the process currently performs in order to establish a baseline against which improvement can be measured.[46] During the **Analyze** phase, the team undertakes root cause analysis of the various problematic aspects of the process in order to understand what is causing these.[47] In this stage, the team is to hypothesize and then verify potential causes before implementing solutions. In the **Improve** stage, the team looks at how the root causes might be addressed, and these countermeasures are then implemented.[48] This phase involves a structured approach to improving the baseline or current state process. Finally, in the **Control** stage, the team is focused on sustaining the improvement, continuously monitoring and updating the process.[49] A response plan is put in place in case there is a dip in performance, and monitoring continues until the new process is well established.

Lean Six Sigma in the manufacturing industry is targeted at eliminating the following eight different types of process waste:

1. Defects, or lack of quality – output is lacking in quality.

2. Overproduction – more is produced than is necessary.

3. Waiting – bottle-necks and downtime.

4. Non-utilized talent – poor use of human resources during the process.

5. Transportation – inefficient shipping methods.

6. Inventory – holding on to a surplus of product or raw material.

7. Motion – unnecessary moving of product, material, or people.

8. Extra processing – doing more work than is needed to produce the desired output.[50]

While it's possible to see how some of these types of waste could translate into the legal context (bottle-necks, for example, apply across service industries), some of them (such as motion or inventory) are not particularly applicable. It was the recognition of the fact that these manufacturing methodologies could be useful to legal environments with some tweaks that gave rise to Legal Lean Six Sigma.

Legal Lean Sigma

Like legal design in relation to design thinking, Legal Six Sigma is the application of Six Sigma principles to the legal industry. The concept of teaching these types of methodologies to legal professionals was conceived of by Catherine Alman MacDonagh, JD, a former corporate counsel and law firm executive. In 2007, she developed legal-specific White and Yellow Belt certification courses with a practitioner who had deep experience in process improvement.[51] These courses were launched in 2008, and in 2011 the Legal Lean Sigma Institute was born, to teach and certify professionals in the legal industry.[52]

In order to apply a Lean Six Sigma approach to process improvement in a commercial legal organization, you would first identify a suitable process for improvement. In legal, you are looking for pockets of inefficiency or bottle-necks, areas where there is manual work done that could be automated, workflows that are highly repetitive, and where work is often done but is then unable to be billed. The types of waste you are seeking to eliminate might include:

- Wasted time or non-billable time during particular processes;

- Inefficient use of resources – for example, using time-poor associates for all parts of a legal workflow when there are paralegals who could do the work effectively who have more time available;

- Inefficient delivery of services to clients, or delays in responding to client calls and emails;

- Too many hand-offs during particular workflows; or

- Associates needlessly performing work individually when collaborative work would be more efficient.

The DMAIC framework is a useful approach to take in relation to any legal process improvement exercise, and various legal organizations have used Lean Six Sigma (or Legal Lean Sigma) effectively. Most notably, Seyfarth Shaw became renowned in 2005 when it adopted Lean Six Sigma and developed a process improvement team to address inefficiencies in legal matters.[53] The areas of legal where Lean Six Sigma and Legal Lean Six Sigma have been most widely applied are in the realm of project management. It makes sense that these efforts remain focused here, because project management in legal organizations looks at the way in which processes are run and attempts to reduce inefficiencies and budget blow-outs during those processes. If project management is an area that falls within your remit, ensuring that you recruit project managers with some expertise or background in Lean or Six Sigma methodologies will be important. If this arena is not your remit, consider importing the philosophies of Lean Six Sigma into your team's work. In particular, the notion of mapping processes in order to identify wasteful (read: needless) hand-offs and activities will be useful.

Upstream problem-solving and problem-prevention

Almost all of the problem-solving we do in legal environments, including the problem-solving that is part of legal work itself, involves tackling a problem when it has already happened. A client often approaches a law firm because they need advice in respect of something that has occurred, such as being served with a lawsuit by a former employee or being notified of a contract dispute. It's rare for law firms to work with clients to make sure that these kinds of problems don't arise in the first place – even though market data now exists that could help them do so. As GCs become more central to the strategic leadership of a company, they are increasingly turning to their outside counsel for strategic support and the best lawyers will be those who think ahead to understand and ward off potential risks for their clients.

Dan Heath, an author I have referenced in previous chapters, published a book in 2020 called *Upstream: The Quest to Solve Problems Before They Happen*.[54] Heath examines the way various countries budget for specific social welfare problems, and finds that countries that allocate more budget towards initiatives that prevent the problems occurring – rather than on programs that address the problems once they have already happened – have much better success at alleviating problems than countries that spend the same amount overall but allocate more resources to "downstream" problem-solving.[55]

The difficulty is that there are hurdles to viewing and addressing problems using an upstream approach – or embracing an "upstream mind-set". The types of problems that can be solved upstream often appear to be inevitable – something that Heath calls "problem blindness".[56] People believe that the negative outcomes they are seeing are natural and out of their control. Market downturns and the ensuing impact on business is an example of this type of problem, but although the negative business impact might appear to be inevitable, it isn't, necessarily. These types of problems also rarely have a single cause, which means that it's easy for people to look at them and think, "That doesn't fall within my remit to solve" – there is a lack of ownership over the problem and therefore no one steps in to try to solve it.[57] At law firms, rather than bringing all stakeholders together to deal with data holistically in a way that allows for genuine data-driven decision-making, it's simply easier for individual departments to apply "band-aid" solutions that allow them to access the sub-set of data they need for the small part of the firm in which they operate. These individuals, if asked, would likely agree that dealing with data at a higher, upstream level would prevent the problems they are facing downstream, but the problem seems too big and too unwieldy for them to deal with, especially if it might appear to be "above their pay-grade". Another difficulty is that these types of problems tend to be bigger, more complex problems, and people in typical organizations are so busy trying to solve smaller, everyday problems that they don't spend the time or the resources to address the larger problems – even though doing so would have a bigger impact than the collective time they're spending on smaller problems.[58] This is why, for example, a problem like climate change can seem to impossible to address, but dealing with skin cancer by topically applying sunscreen feels manageable – even though the skin cancer might have been alleviated altogether had climate change been tackled first.

Upstream problem-solving can be difficult to do, but it's an approach to keep in mind as you look at problems that are identified by your team. If you can examine the root causes of a problem and then find ways to address those so that the problem doesn't arise or need to be dealt with downstream, that's a powerful way to work.

Pre-mortems
One practical way of implementing an upstream mind-set in your team is by conducting a pre-mortem at the beginning of any major project. Where a post-mortem or after action review helps you log mistakes or issues that arose over the course of a project and learn from them so they are not

repeated, a pre-mortem requires you to consider ahead of time all of the ways that a project might go wrong and then mitigate those risks so that they don't happen in the first place.[59] In addition to reducing project risk, pre-mortems have other benefits, including:

- Getting stakeholders aligned around project vision and objectives;
- Helping those involved approach the project realistically;
- Getting those involved prepared to deal with potential issues upfront; and
- Providing a safe space for people to raise the specter of project failure.[60]

This last point is valuable because it introduces into the project team an open and honest channel of communication. Talking about failure and risk should not be taboo – it should be welcomed as part of project planning so that hurdles and potential roadblocks can be warded off early.

Conducting a pre-mortem looks a lot like conducting a design thinking exercise. In order to do so:

1. Schedule a time when all key stakeholders and the project team can be present, ideally in-person in one room.

2. It's best if a pre-mortem is conducted in an organized fashion. This means one person should be assigned the responsibility for leading the discussion.

3. Either the discussion lead or another individual can be individually responsible for whiteboarding or note-taking, or participants can use post-it notes to jot down their "failure" ideas and throw them up on a wall.

4. As a team, brainstorm all the risks or potential issues that might arise during the project, and all the reasons it might fail. Taking the team through the different project phases will help to ensure that weaknesses are being examined throughout the life of the project.

5. Once you have a list of failure ideas, group these together thematically, and begin to consider the kinds of things you could do upfront to ensure that those things don't happen, or to mitigate their impact if they do.

The notes from a pre-mortem should be collected and then used as part of project planning. Some of these ideas will end up shifting the way the team approaches parts of the project. Others will be fed into a risk mitigation plan (seen in Table 10), which becomes a tool that the project leader should regularly review with the project team to determine whether mitigation actions need to be taken as the project progresses.

Table 10: Project risk mitigation plan.[61]

ID	Theme	Sample risks	Sample mitigations	Status	Owner
1	Data access	We do not get suitable data to test the extraction models.	• Define the data request in the first week. • Communicate when the data is required by, and the consequences if we do not get it. • Explore the use of dummy data.	Open	Delivery lead
2	End users	End users to not commit sufficient time to the project.	• Define how much time is required and when it will be. • Schedule this time as far in advance as possible. • Ensure senior stakeholders highlight the importance of participation.	Open	Delivery lead
3	Scope	The project scope is unclear	• Clearly define and document which is in scope and out of scope. • Ensure senior stakeholders prioritise the sope items. • Sequence the project deliverables to align with the priority scope items.	Open	Delivery lead

Upstream thinking and pre-mortems can help empower you and your team by making you not just problem-solvers, but problem-preventers.

Two root cause analysis tools you can use now

One of the most challenging aspects of a DMAIC exercise, an upstream approach to problem-solving, or any type of process improvement cycle is uncovering and understanding the root cause of a problem or an inefficiency. Here are two methods you and your team can use immediately in getting to the root cause of a problem.

The five whys

Developed by Sakichi Toyoda, a Japanese inventor who founded Toyota, the original purpose of the five whys was to understand the root cause of a defect by iteratively asking "why" questions. In most circumstances, asking the question five times is sufficient to provide insight into the origins of the problem.

When you are trying to understand why someone does something a particular way (or why they think they need to do something a certain way), try meeting with them and asking them the question "why" at least five times during the session. This can also be used when someone comes to you or your team with a problem, and you need to understand what the core of that problem really is. Imagine a partner came to you to say she needed a better way of tracking the work her team was doing. Instead of jumping to build a solution, imagine the following discussion taking place:

You: "Why do you need a better way of tracking work?" (Why #1)
Partner: "Because the systems we have are not good enough."

You: "Why aren't they good enough?" (Why #2)
Partner: "Because they don't show me enough information about my team."

You: "Why do you need more information about your team?" (Why #3)
Partner: "Because I need to understand the work they're doing."

You: "Why do you need to understand they work they're doing?" (Why #4)
Partner: "Because I'm worried some of them are being overworked."

You: "Why does this worry you?" (Why #5)
Partner: "Because I'm worried about their wellbeing and concerned they may leave the firm."

In a real conversation, you may have interspersed some of these "whys" with some whats – such as "What type of information do you need about your team?". Notice, though, how the example reveals that it's entirely plausible that the root cause of the problem will not be uncovered until you dig really deeply into it. Those five whys were necessary to get at the emotional need that the partner wants to resolve. Understanding that emotional need sets up you and your team for success as you go out to build a solution, because you're armed with the right information.

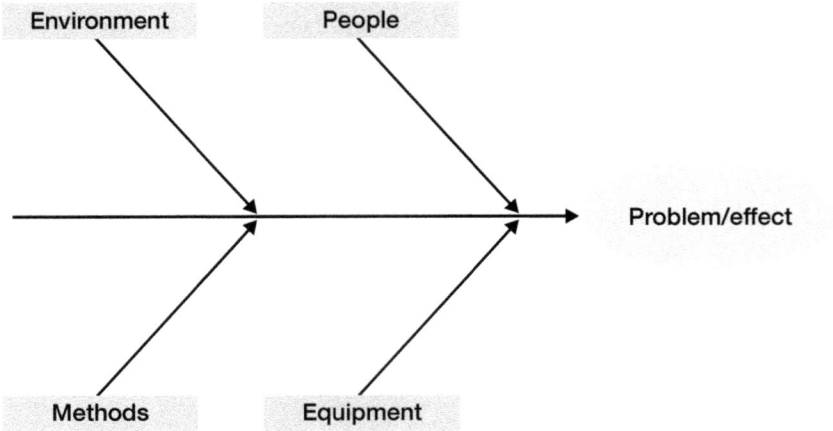

Figure 36: Fishbone analysis mindmap.[62]

Fishbone analysis technique

For larger problems that affect multiple parts of an organization, the five whys technique might fall short because there are so many stakeholders. It is still a technique that can be used during stakeholder analysis and user discovery, but for larger projects that are trying to solve the root cause of a problem that affects the whole organization, the fishbone analysis technique allows for a more collaborative approach to problem definition.

Developed by another Japanese manufacturer, Kaoru Ishigawa, the fishbone diagram – also known as a cause-and-effect diagram – is a visualization tool that helps teams analyze the cause of a problem or defect within an organization.[63] Fishbone analysis uses guided brainstorming in combination with the fishbone mind-map shown in Figure 36.

The problem is written at the front end of the diagram (like the head of a fish), with a horizontal arrow crossing the line of the page to point at the head.

During a fishbone analysis session, stakeholders brainstorm the major causes of the problem, which are grouped thematically. Often, major causes will involve things like the context or environment, the people, the process, or method. These are drawn as the fishbones pointing to its backbone.

Stakeholders are then asked to dig deeper into each of these major themes to examine them more closely and identify all possible sub-causes related to these themes that are giving rise to the problem, which are listed along each fishbone and depicted as layered branches in the diagram.

Using the diagram allows for focused, guided brainstorming and discussion on each aspect of a larger problem, illustrating the many facets of it and allowing for solutions to be developed that address the complexity of the problem.

Examples of problems for which you might use the fishbone technique include:

- Determining why a legal department is consistently late in delivering work to a part of the business;
- Understanding why a law firm's business development plan is not working to bring new business to the firm from the right types of clients; or
- Uncovering the root causes of a broken process that has become a bottleneck.

Deploying these root cause analysis techniques when you are examining a problem, and training your team to "stick with the problem" and understand it properly before moving to a solution, will ensure you are approaching problem-solving the right way.

Checklist: Problem-solving and process improvement techniques

☐ Train your team to approach problem-solving deliberately and to understand a problem properly before attempting to solve it.

☐ Put the end user's needs at the center of all of your problem-solving efforts, embracing empathy as an approach that will serve your organization well.

☐ Train your team to remain open during problem-solving exercises and projects, rather than shutting down ideas and options.

☐ Leverage ideation and the concept of exploring a wide solution space during brainstorming sessions with your team or other stakeholders. Consider starting a timer and asking everyone to either individually jot down as many ideas as they can or to shout them out for someone to record – the pressure of the timer will encourage a higher volume of ideas.

☐ As you develop solutions or progress on a project, continue to engage the end users and seek their feedback so that the solution can be improved upon iteratively in direct response to what the end users need from it.

☐ Consider leveraging design thinking as a method for collaboratively solving problems and developing solutions, and as a practice that will help improve your organization's approach to innovation and new ways of doing things.

☐ Before improving any process, map it first and establish a baseline so that improvements can be properly measured.

☐ Work with project managers on process improvement efforts where possible, as they are likely to have experience with DMAIC and other key methodologies.

☐ Train your team on the DMAIC methodology, and consider having some members of your team certified, especially if you do not have project managers with relevant experience who can support your projects.

☐ Practice employing the five whys in conversations with lawyers who have raised problems, or when examining the reasons for an inefficiency or pain-point, and train your team to do so too.

☐ Leverage root cause analysis discussions with stakeholders when undertaking a broader, enterprise-wide process improvement initiative.

☐ Wherever possible, embrace an upstream problem-solving mindset, and evaluate situations to determine whether the problem can be prevented earlier than where it is currently being addressed.

☐ For large-scale projects, use pre-mortems and risk mitigation planning to ensure that the project goes as smoothly as possible.

☐ Once a process has been improved, monitor it and put in place controls to ensure it does not slide backwards.

References

1 See Linna, D. (2017), *Learn Fast: Start with Scientific Thinking and a Canvas.* LegalTech Lever, www.legaltechlever.com/2017/09/innovation-learn-fast-start-scientific-thinking-canvas-90minuteblogpost/ and Kennedy, D. (2019), *Successful Innovation Outcomes in Law: A Practical Guide for Law Firms, Law Departments and Other Legal Organizations.* Self-published on Amazon.com.

2 Kennedy, D. (2019), *57 Tips for Successful Innovation Outcomes in Law,* www.denniskennedy.com/wp-content/uploads/sites/445/2019/08/57-Tips-for-Successful-Innovation-Outcomes-in-Law-Dennis-Kennedy.pdf

3 Allain, R. (2013), *What's Wrong With the Scientific Method?* www.wired.com/2013/04/whats-wrong-with-the-scientific-method/

4 See, for example: Fisk, P. (2017), *Design thinking in action… 35 great examples of companies using "design thinking" to drive innovation and growth*, www. peterfisk.com/2017/05/design-thinking-in-action-35-great-examples-of-companies-using-design-thinking-to-drive-innovation-and-growth/; Rauch, S. (2022), How Top Companies Are Using Design Thinking Techniques, www.simplilearn.com/top-companies-using-design-thinking-techniques-article; McKendrik, J. (2020), *These Days, Everyone Needs to Engage in Design Thinking.* Forbes.com, www.forbes.com/sites/joemckendrick/2020/08/28/these-days-everyone-needs-to-engage-in-design-thinking/?sh=92b61bd1e2d3

5 Sheppard, B., Sarrazin, H., Kouyoumjian, G., and Dore, F. (2018), "The Business Value of Design". *McKinsey Quarterly Report*, 25 October 2018, www.mckinsey.com/capabilities/mckinsey-design/our-insights/the-business-value-of-design

6 Di Russo, F. (2012), *A Brief History of Design Thinking: How Design Thinking Came to 'Be'*, https://ithinkidesign.wordpress.com/2012/06/08/a-brief-history-of-design-thinking-how-design-thinking-came-to-be/

7 See International Service Design Institute at https://internationalservicedesigninstitute.com/.

8 https://internationalservicedesigninstitute.com/.

9 Digital.gov.nz. 2021. Service Design – Overview, www.digital.govt.nz/standards-and-guidance/design-and-ux/service-design/service-design-overview/

10 Interaction Design Foundation (2020), *The Principles of Service Design Thinking – Building Better Services*, www.interaction-design.org/literature/article/the-principles-of-service-design-thinking-building-better-services

11 Voltage Capital (2022), *5 Steps of the Design Thinking Process: a Step-by-Step Guide*, https://voltagecontrol.com/blog/5-steps-of-the-design-thinking-process-a-step-by-step-guide/

12 Rittel, H. W. and Webber, M. M. (1973), "Dilemmas in a General Theory of Planning." *Policy sciences*, 4(2), 155-169, https://urbanpolicy.net/wp-content/uploads/2012/11/Rittel+Webber_1973_PolicySciences4-2.pdf

13 Voltage Capital (2022).

14 IDEO (2020), Design Thinking Process, www.ideou.com/pages/design-thinking

15 Plattner, H. (2010), "An Introduction to Design Thinking". *d.School Process Guide*, https://s3-eu-west-1.amazonaws.com/ih-materials/uploads/Introduction-to-design-thinking.pdf

16 *Ibid.*

17 *Ibid.*

18 *Ibid.*

19 *Ibid.* Also see the excellent book *This is Service Design Doing: Applying Service Design Thinking in the Real World* (1st ed) by Stickdorn, M., Hormess, M, Lawrence, A., and Schneider, J. (2011, New York: NY, John Wiley & Sons) for a breakdown of how to plan for and hold various ideation exercises.

20 *Ibid.*

21 *Ibid.*

22 IDEO, 2020.

23 IDEO (2020), *Design Thinking Process*, www.ideou.com/pages/design-thinking

24 Note that design thinking is infinitely preferable to the nebulous concept of "hackathons" that have also entered legal organizations. Hackathons do not deploy the kind of consistent methodology that defines design thinking, nor do they put the user first or encourage an empathetic mindset. Some may prefer the name "hackathon" than design thinking, and indeed many innovation leaders shy away from the notion of empathy that rests at the heart of design thinking. However, the user-centered approach of design thinking has far greater potential to impact and change the culture of an organization – precisely because it requires practitioners to think about the people affected by a problem and what their needs are. For lawyers, this means they have to think about their clients first, which is a beneficial mindset to introduce in any legal context.

25 Hagan, M. (2017), Law by Design, https://lawbydesign.co/legal-design/

26 Kohlmeier, A. and Klemola, M. (2021). *The Legal Design Book: Doing Law in the 21st Century.* Lightning Source Inc: Chapter 2.

27 Gillespie, A. (2022), "Design thinking vs legal design: what's the difference?" *Legal Evolution*, 306, www.legalevolution.org/2022/06/design-thinking-versus-legal-design-whats-the-difference-306/

28 Innanen, A., The Business Case of Legal Design. .Dot, https://medium.com/legal-design/the-business-case-of-legal-design-6560fd17b70

29 Meadows, 2008.

30 Kaoru Ishikawa, Cause and Effect Analysis, 1960s.

31 The Systems Thinker, 2018.

32 Morris and Martin, Complexity, Systems Thinking and Practice.

33 This passage and the pages that follow is an adapted version of text that was first published in *Design Thinking for the Legal Profession*, 2018, Ark Publishing.

34 Travelers (2022), *20 Risks Facing the Manufacturing Industry and How to Help Protect Your Business*, www.travelers.com/resources/business-industries/manufacturing/20-risks-facing-manufacturing-industry

35 Daniel, D. (2021), *Kaizen (Continuous Improvement)*. TechTarget Network, www.techtarget.com/searcherp/definition/kaizen-or-continuous-improvement

36 *Ibid.*

37 *Ibid.*

38 Green, S. (2021), *A Simple Guide to Lean Process Improvement*, https://blog.hubspot.com/marketing/lean-process-improvement

39 Rastagi, A. (2020), *A Brief Introduction to Lean, Six Sigma, and Lean Six Sigma*. Grey Campus, www.greycampus.com/blog/quality-management/a-brief-introduction-to-lean-and-six-sigma-and-lean-six-sigma

40 Arthur, J. (2008). *Want to Know Enough About Lean Six Sigma to Get Started?* www. qimacros.com/lean-six-sigma-articles/lean-six-sigma/

41 SSGI (2020), *Lean Six Sigma: The Definitive Guide*, www.6sigmacertificationonline. com/lean-six-sigma/

42 Purdue University Lean Six Sigma Blog (2021), *Six Sigma Versus Lean Six Sigma: What's the Difference?* www.purdue.edu/leansixsigmaonline/blog/ six-sigma-vs-lean-six-sigma/

43 GoLeanSixSigma (2017), *DMAIC – The Five Phases of Lean Six Sigma*, https:// goleansixsigma.com/dmaic-five-basic-phases-of-lean-six-sigma/

44 Purdue University, 2021.

45 Six Sigma. (2022). *DMAIC: Approach to Continuous Improvement*, www.6sigma.us/ dmaic-process/

46 *Ibid.*

47 *Ibid.*

48 *Ibid.*

49 *Ibid.*

50 *Ibid.*

51 Legal Lean Sigma (2021), *Why We Do What We Do*, https://legalleansigma.com/ about-llsi/

52 *Ibid.*

53 See www.Seyfarth.com; Seyfarth Labs at www.seyfarth.com/services/consulting/ seyfarthlean-consulting/seyfarth-labs.html

54 Heath, D. (2020). *Upstream: The Quest to Solve Problems Before They Happen*. New York, NY: Simon & Schuster.

55 Heath (2020), p. 14.

56 *Ibid.*, p. 23.

57 *Ibid.*, p. 42.

58 Heath calls this phenomenon "tunneling": p. 60.

59 Duffy, P. (2023), *Pre-Mortems: How Imagining Failure Can Avoid Project Disaster*, Legaltech Hub, www.legaltechnologyhub.com/contents/ pre-mortems-how-imagining-failure-can-avoid-project-disaster/

60 *Ibid.*

61 *Ibid.*

62 Lewis, S. (2020), *What is a Fishbone Diagram (Ishikawa Cause and Effect)*. TechTarget, www.techtarget.com/whatis/definition/fishbone-diagram

63 *Ibid.*

Chapter 12:
Approaches to work and ways of working

In law firms and legal departments, our ways of working have remained stagnant for decades, while in many other industries new methods and approaches have been tried and tested and implemented that help teams function better. Some of these are ways of looking at work and strategy, and others are actual ways of operating. In this chapter, we explore business theories that will help you refine your work by looking at it in the context of competitive forces in the market, and software development methodologies that will help your team work more effectively together.

Law as a business

Legal partnerships have not historically viewed themselves as businesses. They have instead operated as though they stood outside the realm of business. As a result, with the exception of those firms who have hired COOs or other leaders from the business world, most firms have had little exposure to business theory. Not all of that theory will be applicable to law firms, or to the work that innovation teams do, but some of it is highly relevant. Below, we will briefly scan some of the more important business theories that can usefully be applied in order to provide a clearer lens within which to operate your legal innovation programs.

Michael Porter's Five Forces

Michael Porter is an American academic who is one of the most influential writers on economics and business theory. Most significantly, in a 1979 article in the *Harvard Business Review* and further in his 1985 book, *Competitive Advantage*, he set out a framework for evaluating competitive forces in the market.[1] Porter asserted that although every industry is different, the underlying drivers of profitability are the same.[2] These drivers of profitability are what he called "the Five Forces".

In brief, Porter's Five Forces are (1) the bargaining power of buyers, (2) the bargaining power of suppliers, (3) the threat of new entrants, (4) the threat of substitute products or services, and (5) rivalry among existing competitors.[3] Analyzing the way that the Five Forces work together in an industry can help companies anticipate shifts in competition and find better strategic positions within that industry.[4] For an innovation leader, analyzing your firm's competitive position in the industry provides a useful lens through which to develop the strategies and tactics that are likely to be most effective in helping your firm navigate the competitive landscape into the future.

1. The bargaining power of buyers

Large customers or clients can use their influence to force prices down or demand more services at existing prices. Buyer power tends to be higher when buyers are collectively organized and large relative to the competitive companies serving them, when products are undifferentiated and represent a significant cost to the buyer, and when the cost of switching business from one competitor to another is low.[5]

In legal, the bargaining power of clients has never been higher than it is currently. Clients are advocating for change and more willing to shift providers to those who are operating efficiently and leveraging innovative technology to support services.

Questions to ask:

- Are existing clients likely to move to another firm if they are not satisfied by your firm's prices or modes of operating?
- Is there anything your team can be doing to be make this less likely?

2. The bargaining power of suppliers

In industries where companies purchase inputs from suppliers that account for differing proportions of cost, suppliers can use their negotiating leverage to charge higher prices or demand more favorable terms.

Although this force may seem less relevant to the legal industry, it's important to break it down in terms of what a supplier provides – the ability for a company to develop the core product or service that generates revenue. In legal, then, the critical suppliers to law firms might be viewed as the lawyers themselves.

Questions to ask:

- Are qualified lawyers in short supply?

- Are there practice areas where your firm is at risk of losing key partners?
- Are associates engaged at work?
- Is there anything your team can do to improve lawyer satisfaction and retention in the practice areas that are at risk?

3. Threat of new entrants

The threat of new entrants to an industry can force existing players to keep prices down. When new entrants do enter the market, it can put pressure on prices and costs, which caps the profit potential of an industry.

In legal, new entrants are being seen in some jurisdictions in the form of the Big Four. In all jurisdictions, alternative legal service providers (ALSPs) have been exerting price pressure on incumbents for years now, and as the ALSP market grows, this pressure does too. Another threat is the increased tendency of corporate legal departments to keep work within the department.

Questions to ask:

- Are there pockets of practice that are particular targets for new entrants?
- Are there automation efforts your team could undertake, or partnerships with internal or external ALSPs you could enter into that might reduce price pressure and allow the firm to compete better against these new entrants?
- Would improving efficiency and reducing costs in certain areas allow the firm to take on work that might otherwise go to an ALSP, such as repapering exercises?

4. Threat of substitute products or services

Porter defined this as the risk arising when a new product or service meets the same basic need in a different way, reducing profitability of the industry as a whole.[6]

In legal, we are seeing this pressure exerted by technology providers themselves, with the lines between legal advice and legal information increasingly blurring and consumers more able to avail themselves of both through digital products and offerings. As advanced technology such as generative AI and large language models evolve, the pressure from this kind of competition is likely to become even greater.

Questions to ask:

- Can your team use technology to develop products that provide the same or better benefits than what is emerging onto the market, so that the firm is less at risk?

5. Threat of rivalry from existing competitors

When rivalry between existing competitors is intense, it can drive down prices in a "race to the bottom", with companies competing away the value they create.[7] This force is more likely to matter when competitors are of roughly equal size and industry growth is slow, and where other forces make for a highly competitive market.

The legal market is highly competitive and, especially in smaller markets, winning work away from competitors is one of the only ways to grow (at least around core business).

Questions to ask:

- What are the key competitive firms to yours?
- In what ways can your team support the firm in standing above those competitors, so that a race to the bottom is unnecessary?

A Five Forces analysis often gives rise to a strategic decision to either differentiate key services from competitors, or reduce or adjust costs in order to better compete. Although a Five Forces analysis will usually be done at the senior leadership level, the questions set out above provide a framework that you can work through with your team – in collaboration with the leadership team – to further refine your innovation strategy and identify the kinds of initiatives that will make a difference, not just internally, but more broadly in the way that your firm is able to position itself in the market. In order to answer these questions in relation to your firm, you have to know your firm well enough to know, for example, whether it is subject to price pressures and competition from peers, and to understand what the specific competitive set is for your firm. Just as we caution lawyers that they must deeply understand their client businesses in order to adequately serve them, so you should deeply understand the challenges faced by your firm in order to provide the kind of innovation program that will make a difference. Having a solid understanding of Porter's Five Forces and the way that they operate in the industry and apply to your firm will improve your efficacy as an innovation leader and allow you to work more strategically.

Red and blue ocean theory

Another business theory that innovation teams should have regard to in legal organizations comes from W. Chan Kim and Renee Mauborgne, who coined the terms red ocean and blue ocean to describe the market universe and establish a framework for different types of business strategy.[8] They defined red oceans as industries that are currently in existence, making up the known market space. By contrast, blue oceans are all industries that do not exist today. Blue oceans, therefore, denote unknown market spaces, as yet untainted by competition.

In red ocean space, the boundaries of an industry are already defined and accepted, which means that the competitive rules within that industry are known. Companies that are situated within known industries have to grab a greater share of existing demand in order to outperform rivals. As the market gets crowded, profits and growth are reduced and competition increases. Products become commodities. This crowded industry space becomes cut-throat, or "bloody" – hence the term red ocean. The increased competition in the legal market outlined in the introduction to this book, with new entrants fighting with incumbents for a decreasing market share, indicates that the legal industry as a whole is in red ocean space. Companies within red oceans have limited strategic options available to them. They need to beat the competition by exploiting existing market demand. The two key ways of doing this, in line with Michael Porter's strategies, is for a company to either differentiate its products and services from those of its competitors, or to compete on cost by lowering prices beneath those of its competitors.

Blue ocean strategy looks completely different. Because the industry is as-yet undefined, the onus is on companies to create demand rather than fight over it. In blue ocean markets, there is ample opportunity for growth that is profitable. Competition is irrelevant because the rules of the game haven't even been set yet. Organizations seeking to enter blue ocean space need to create an uncontested market, however – which is not an easy thing to do. As Kim and Mauborgne somewhat poetically write, blue oceans represent all the industries that are not in existence today. The benefits of uncovering one of these, of course, are huge – it breaks the need for a narrow strategic decision between lowering costs or increasing differentiation and opens up new opportunities for customer demand.

Table 11: Red Ocean versus Blue Ocean Strategy. Source: Kim, W. C., and Mauborgne, R. (2004), Blue Ocean Strategy.

Red ocean strategy	Blue ocean strategy
Compete in existing market space	Create uncontested market space
Beat the competition	Make the competition irrelevant
Exploit existing demand	Create and capture new demand
Make the value/cost trade off	Break the value/cost trade off
Align the whole system of a firm's activities with its strategic choice of differentiation or low cost	Align the whole system of a firm's activities in pursuit of differentiation and low cost

While the legal industry is a deep red ocean, that doesn't mean there isn't the possibility of creating blue ocean space within it. To the extent this is possible, the innovation team within a law firm is well suited to carve it out. Kim and Mauborgne assert that there are only two ways of doing this. One is by uncovering an entirely new industry, like eBay did with online auctions. This is rare, however. It's more common for a blue ocean to be created from within a red ocean when a company fundamentally alters the boundaries of an existing industry. Kim and Mauborgne's research in this area is interesting. Contrary to what one would expect, they found that incumbents are more likely to create blue oceans than new entrants. When incumbents do create blue oceans, they tend to do so within their core business (instead of creating a highly differentiated product). They also found that, although technology innovation is sometimes involved in creating a blue ocean, it is not a defining feature of them. Blue ocean creation also tends to be the result of a series of strategic moves – the "right" strategic moves – rather than being a consequence of superiority. In other words, "superior" companies are not necessarily those that will create the blue ocean within an industry. The move can come from unlikely places.

The defining features of successful blue ocean creation, according to Kim and Mauborgne, are exactly what distinguish their work from Porter's philosophies. Creators of blue oceans do not use their competition as a benchmark. They make that competition irrelevant by creating a leap of value for buyers and the company itself; instead of choosing either to differentiate or to adjust costs, they employ strategic moves that do both. By increasing value for customers at the same time as they drive down costs, they vault over competitors, creating an entirely new space. Creators of blue ocean are able to do this because they are not constrained by the existing boundaries of their industry. The benefits are significant – companies that create blue oceans generally do not encounter real competition for ten to 15 years after the blue ocean space is first created.

In their follow-up book to the original article, Kim and Mauborgne provide advice on how to actually create blue ocean space.[9] First, you need to select the scope for your blue ocean initiative, and understand which part of your business, product, or service you will tackle. Here, you may want to examine your firm's various practices, for example, and determine whether you want to focus on any one of them in particular. Second, you need to understand the current strategic landscape really well, and determine what it is about that landscape that causes the red ocean. In law, firms of a particular size offer similar services to the same set of clients, those services being necessary and there having been (until recently) little alternative to law firms for the provision of those services. If your scope is narrower and you are focused on a particular practice area, understanding the nature of strategy and competition in the market for that practice will be critical. Third, look at the constraints and pain-points in the industry. Are there boundaries that are causing pain-points for clients? These are opportunities lying in wait. An example here might be the fact that clients must wait for a lawyer to be available in order to get an answer to a particular question. Another might be that the billable hour means clients are less likely to reach out with basic questions because they're concerned about incurring costs. Finally, Kim and Mauborgne advise that you generate some blue ocean options that pursue both differentiation in the market and lower costs. Evaluate these, and you will be ready to launch a blue ocean play that could set your firm or organization up for success.

Many of the law firm subsidiary launches we have seen over the past few years are no doubt attempts at blue ocean plays. Managed services and repackaged legal services, along with new pricing models, probably also represent strategic attempts to develop blue ocean space.

As you and your team work with leadership to expand your innovation program, the notion of blue ocean strategy should be something you keep in mind. Where are there opportunities to differentiate the firm's services and improve value? This is the exact question innovation teams are brought in to consider, and working with a focus on that question and an eye to creating blue ocean space will help you succeed.

The Innovator's Dilemma

Everyone involved in leading or working in innovation should read Clayton Christensen's book, *The Innovator's Dilemma*.[10] Christensen was a professor of business administration at Harvard Business School, who spent his career researching and working in business innovation. *The Innovator's Dilemma* is essential reading, and I would argue it is particularly relevant when working in an environment like a law firm (especially large, successful law firms).

Christensen's main thesis is that competent, experienced executives of very successful companies sometimes unwittingly lead their companies to failure by driving towards profit and growth using tried-and-true managerial methods, because they do not allow for the types of structures that foster disruptive innovation. The very organizational structures, capabilities, resources, and decision-making processes that make those companies successful in the first place do not allow for disruptive innovation.[11] This is because those structures cannot at once support current profit models and sustaining innovations, and at the same time nurture disruptive technologies. The channels necessary to do the latter are completely different than what is necessary to support the former. Moreover, the market or client base in which the disruptive innovation is likely to first gain ground will not be the same client base to which the company is able to profitably sell its current product – the products are relevant in, and serve, different value networks. As a result, unless incumbent companies change the way they approach disruptive innovation – and set up the structures and space to do so – they are not the ones who will succeed with it. Instead, they will ultimately be leap-frogged by smaller, more nimble companies who have been able to gain traction with a disruptive technology with a different client base, and then achieve exponential growth that overtakes any steady growth in existing markets.[12]

The innovator's dilemma, like blue ocean strategy, is concerned with finding an uncontested space in a particular market. Both are critical theories for anyone trying to drive transformative change in commercial legal organizations. The resistance by incumbent leadership in large law firms towards certain innovation initiatives – particularly client-facing ones – is cast in a fresh light when you understand the innovator's dilemma. The perspective should allow you to empathize with the leaders who stand in your way as you push for disruptive innovation, because their resistance makes sense on the face of it. They are simply doing exactly what they've always done to be successful. The disruptive innovation you seek support for will seem counter-intuitive to them in all kinds of ways, and you need to be able to explain to them why they need to make room for a completely different approach.

Many of the truths that are found in *The Innovator's Dilemma* contradict the wisdom I have tried to impart in this book. I will explain this as we explore each of the key take-aways from Christensen's text, and the ways in which they apply to the legal industry and to your mandate.

1. The Status quo is not equipped to nurture disruptive innovation (especially disruptive technology innovation).[13]

The decision-making processes that are key to the success of established companies (and law firms) are set up to reject disruptive technologies.[14] Established companies are profitable because they respond to client needs. But products or services that do not seem to be useful for clients today might address their needs tomorrow.[15]

After all of the advice I've provided about identifying use cases upfront, ensuring there is a demand for a new technology or product before you invest in it, empathizing with end users and responding to those needs as your innovate and build, Christensen points out that with disruptive technology, customers often might not know that they need it, either until it has been created (like the iPhone), or until society has developed and the need suddenly arises.[16] In either case, if you wait until the customer asks for it, you will be too late. As Christensen says, "We cannot expect our customers to lead us towards innovations they do not need".[17] As a result, listening to customers and tracking their needs and competitors' current actions might help with sustaining innovation, but will not serve you as well if you are seeking transformative, disruptive innovation. In fact, the data gathered from listening to what your clients are currently saying might be misleading when it comes to disruptive innovation.

What does this mean for you?

Some of your work, or your team's work, should be focused on areas of innovation that do not yet seem urgent, and that are not responsive to existing client demands. Yes, for sustaining innovation it is critical to bring client voices to the fore and educate your organizational leadership about the new demands clients now have. But client voices should not be our only guide to the future. I remember sitting in a meeting with the managing partner and other rainmaker partners at a firm, in which they were discussing alternative fee arrangements and a move away from the billable hour. I distinctly remember the firm's most profitable partner saying, "My clients just aren't asking for it yet". I also remember thinking (and unfortunately not saying) "…but they will be soon". The key is to recognize those inflection points, and push for change anyway. The fact that clients don't want it now doesn't mean they might not demand it tomorrow, when it's too late for the firm to capitalize on having driven the disruption.

2. In a traditional organization, resources won't be readily available for disruptive innovation efforts, but you need resources to succeed.[18]

Resource allocation in established organizations such as large law firms is the responsibility of staff whose understanding of what projects should be resourced stems from their knowledge of and experience with the company's mainstream value network. They understand what the company should do to improve profitability now, but they do not know – and are likely to undervalue – initiatives that are put forward now but are unlikely to be profitable until a later stage (if ever). One of the characteristics of disruptive innovation efforts is that you cannot know if they will be successful – until they are.

What does this mean for you?
Unless there are no other projects that are clearly financially attractive or where there is a clear return on investment (unlikely), you will have difficulty obtaining resources to support disruptive innovation efforts. Many firms have launched online platforms providing automated templates and guidance to support start-ups and emerging growth companies. In one firm I worked at, the excellent emerging growth company resource center that included helpful advice and automated documents for start-ups a was almost impossible to find from the firm's main website. My team suggested plans to develop and promote it. We were told that as the platform did not generate significant revenue or profit, it wasn't worth putting the effort into it and we were unable to obtain the resources necessary to market it. It seemed a bizarre decision to me at the time, given that by its very nature the initiative – targeting emerging companies – was a long play, and one that was the brain-child of several partners. In light of Christensen's text, however, it makes sense.

The key to dealing with this inability to understand long plays or third horizon planning is to insist on having a bucket within your departmental budget that is allocated to "innovation" generally, without being tied to individual projects. This bucket should be substantial enough to allow your team to pursue initiatives that other functions or departments at the firm may not understand or view as worthwhile. It may take you some time to build up the credibility necessary for senior leadership to approve a meaningful sum for your innovation budget, but pushing for it from the get-go will help.

3. The market for the main offering of your organization or firm is unlikely to be the best market for your disruptive innovation.[19]

Trying to shape a disruptive offering to the current needs of existing customers or clients almost always leads to failure.[20] Instead, if a company is developing a disruptive innovation, it should identify the customer base to whom the defining characteristics of that innovation appeal now, and sell there (rather than to the company's current core customer base).[21]

What does this mean for you?

Large law firms in particular have a specific client base to which they predominantly sell their services. These firms are successful because they have defined that client base. These days, they likely use data to understand exactly which clients in what markets generate the greatest profit for them, and then direct business development efforts there. Those clients are unlikely, however, to be the same clients to whom your disruptive technology or innovation appeals. The firm may therefore reject your disruptive initiatives because it focuses on a market that is perceived to be smaller, less profitable, with less attractive margins than the well-established market in which they've succeeded for years.

You have no doubt had experiences where a potential initiative has been rejected because it is for a practice group where the work is viewed as less profitable, or that automates a process to pull in work from a client base that might otherwise engage an alternative legal services provider to undertake that same work. I have been told, in these instances, that it's not worth continuing the initiative because "that's not the kind of work we want". In other words, those clients are not seen as fitting within the desired class of client for the firm.

Ironically, the hesitation on the part of leadership to pursue these initiatives likely means you are heading in the right direction for disruptive innovation, and it's important to continue driving them forward. One law firm subsidiary has recently emerged with the aim of targeting small law firms as a potential client base. Another law firm subsidiary sells software to other law firms. These are entirely new client markets for those firms. If successful, these subsidiaries will dramatically increase profitability and expand the total client base for their respective firms.

4. The kinds of capabilities and structures an established company has developed to successfully sell its core product or service will not serve it well in developing and selling something else.[22]

The expertise at your firm that allows it to succeed in doing legal work and selling it to clients does not provide the capabilities to develop and sell other types of services or products.

What does this mean for you?

Consider the capabilities your team needs in order to pursue the initiatives you are undertaking that fall within the potentially disruptive category, and find a way to obtain these. If you are intending on developing knowledge products to sell on a subscription basis, for example, you will need not just the capabilities and skill sets to build those products but also:

- The ability to design them so that they are appealing to customers;
- The ability to price them appropriately;
- The ability to financially manage annual recurring revenue and manage subscriptions; and
- The ability to market and sell products (which is entirely different from the capability to sell services).

To the extent that you are able to develop the relevant skill sets on your team, you should do so – and hire the best professionals you can. Law firms often tend to push down salaries of professionals who are not legal practitioners, but if you are managing disruptive innovation you need talented professionals on your team just as the firm needs talented lawyers. You should be able to compensate them accordingly. To the extent that the capabilities required for your efforts cannot be housed within your team, manage expectations and budget for what you will need to outsource. Product design agencies, product marketing consultants and more may be necessary as these are not innate capabilities at a law firm.

5. In order to develop successful disruptive products, an organization has to be able to move fast and fail fast, but established companies are rarely able to operate in this way.[23]

Failure and iterative progress are necessary on the journey to finding a successful disruptive innovation. Established companies, and law firms in particular, are not good at accepting failure. Large companies also find it difficult to move quickly, pivot, and iterate.

What does this mean for you?
You need to carve out a space where failure is allowed and your team can move quickly. Typically, this will be an R&D function, ideally situated outside of the business model of the firm, that is not subject to the same structural hurdles. For example, in a law firm, the information security team is not used to moving quickly to allow for experimentation that might give rise to disruption. That team is instead set up to protect the law firm within the boundaries in which it operates. Another example is the liability insurance your firm must have, which will cover its core work but is unlikely to cover consulting work or product development work by professionals who are not practicing law. These structural pillars do not allow for the kind of work that your team will have to do if it is to have a chance at building something truly disruptive. In order to succeed, you will need to find a way of operating around or outside of them. This doesn't mean cheating or obstructing security practices, it means finding a safe space where you and your team are able to experiment.

6. Established companies adopt broad technology strategies that do not allow for the type of movement disruptive technology requires.

In particular, Christensen cautions against any "blanket technology strategy to be always a leader or always a follower".[24] Disruptive innovations, like blue ocean plays, generally involve "first-mover" advantage. Established companies are rarely comfortable being the first mover.

What does this mean for you?
If you have worked in a large law firm or have ever sold technology to law firms, you know that law firms typically take exactly the kind of broad stance Christensen warns against, and refuse to ever be first in adopting a new technology.

If any law firm is going to have a chance at succeeding with a disruptive innovation, it will have to become comfortable with being first occasionally. Finding a way to train your firm's leadership to recognize the benefits in first-mover advantage – and educating them on when it makes sense to be the first mover – will help you on your journey.

7. The companies that tend to be successful building disruptive technologies and defining emerging markets are successful because they are operating in a way that simply does not make sense for established companies.[25]

This is a tricky one to overcome. Good managers at established companies will find it difficult to do things that don't fit their existing model for how to make money – because it's counterintuitive to do those things. They have been successful because they are good at what they do, so persuading them to make decisions that go against their own proven best practices will be difficult. Christensen points out that "disruptive technologies rarely make sense during the years when investing in them is most important".

What does this mean for you?
Christensen argued that it is possible for managers to overcome this boundary if they recognize it as a conflict, and consciously work towards developing a context within the company that allows for the structures and resources to support both sustaining and disruptive innovation. Towards the beginning of this book we looked at strategy and the importance of buy-in from leadership. Ideally, as an innovator, you want to work at a firm where that buy-in is so significant and your relationship with senior leadership is so strong that you can have conversations about the innovator's dilemma, and work towards a context that allows room for disruptive innovation. For many firms, this has taken the form of developing a subsidiary structure that sits outside of the firm but is related to it, where disruptive innovation can be pursued within a business model that supports it. This is a goal that you might consider aiming for too. Whether or not you are given leeway to pursue that, the ability to have this type of open discussion with leadership is critical.

Understanding the innovator's dilemma will help guide the way that your team interacts with senior leadership and other parts of the organization, and will provide some clarity on the kinds of initiatives on which your team needs to hold firm in order to make sure it does not become one of the incumbents riding the waves of steady profits and sustaining innovation towards obsolescence.

Software development methodologies

In exploring new ways of working with your team, I'm going to turn now to the world of software development. In some ways, software development might seem like an obvious industry to draw from, given how much of legal innovation is concerned with the implementation of technology and automation. The way that lawyers work, however, and the way we generally operate within law firms, is very different from the ways that modern software developers typically work. In some ways it is analogous to how software developers used to work before an overhaul of the industry in the early 2000s.

The Waterfall days

In the 1970s, a model for software development originated called "Waterfall", or the Staged Gate Process. The Waterfall model brought a sequential approach to product development, which was linear and non-iterative in nature. During a Waterfall-type development, progress moves in stages (like falling water over a cliff) through conception, design, development, testing, and release (or production). Once development has moved to the next stage, there is no going back. For many years, this is how software developers operated.

The problem with the linear nature of Waterfall, however, is that it made it difficult to change requirements once the process was underway. The assumption was that all product requirements were defined upfront, and development was then followed through all the way to release. This meant that there was a high risk of product failure, or developing a product that did not meet market needs. If developers realized halfway through a Waterfall process that the market or the requirements had changed, it was hard to go back. In other words, Waterfall made it hard to accommodate change.

In addition to the shortfalls of Waterfall, the world of software development was plagued by unhealthy, extreme work practices. With the rise of personal computing, product development had undergone significant change and many developers felt the status quo was no longer working. The lag time between the definition of business needs and the release of a product had grown, which meant that by the time a product was released it was less useful to customers than it should have been. The processes of development were characterized by unwieldy documentation, and developers were under intense pressure to work around the clock in order to increase speed of production. I've heard some developers describe it as a time of near-crisis, when they were reaching burn-out levels of stress on a regular basis. This is not dissimilar to the state of the legal industry right now, with work regularly running late into the night and unduly high levels of mental health, depression, and addiction.

The Agile Manifesto

In February 2001, 17 developers calling themselves the "Agile Alliance" met at a lodge in Utah to develop and set down a new methodology for software development. The principles of this new way of working were memorialized in a document that is called "The Agile Manifesto", which can be accessed and read by all.[26] I highly recommend reading the entire Agile Manifesto, which is not a very long document but has become central to the way not just software developers now work but also the way work is conducted in all kinds of industries.

At its core, the Agile Manifesto encompasses the following principles:

- The top priority is satisfying customers through early, continuous delivery of value.
- Changing requirements are welcomed at any time.
- Shorter timeframes for turnaround are preferred.
- Collaboration between business-people and developers is a daily requirement.
- Hire great people, give them what they need, and trust them to get the work done.
- Face-to-face conversation is the best form of communication.
- Developers and other stakeholders should be able to sustain the pace at which they work.
- Working software is the best measure of progress.
- Attention to excellence and good design improves agility.
- Simplicity is essential.
- The best work comes from self-organizing teams.
- Teams should meet and regroup at regular intervals to continuously improve processes.[27]

The Agile Manifesto is designed to empower developers, speed up processes, and help to develop practices that focus more directly on the user and user needs.[28] The principles behind the Agile Manifesto are intended to allow teams to be more adaptive, respond more quickly to changes or directives, and develop products that are therefore more effective.[29] They allow developers to operate in a state of constant reimagination, underpinned by frequent customer feedback. Underlying the principles of the manifesto lie the following four values:

- Individuals and interactions over processes and tools.
- Working software over documentation.
- Customer collaboration over contract negotiation.
- Responding to change over following a plan.[30]

Rather than providing a rigid structure for how to work, Agile is a philosophy. Over the 20-some years since the Agile Manifesto was released, it has had a huge impact on the way people work – not just in the software industry, but in other industries too, with courses and certification programs available to help people organize their working practices through Agile teams.

Application to legal

Similar to software development during the Waterfall days, lawyers often work in linear ways, and the industry suffers from working practices that frequently cause burn-out.

Agile provides a philosophy for ways of working that might be hugely beneficial in legal environments. For your team, keeping the principles and values of Agile at the heart of the way you operate is likely to allow for more sustainable and collaborative work practices than those that generally characterize legal practice. Some of the ways that the Agile philosophy might manifest in the way you work include:

- Keep your end users central to the work that you do, whether they are lawyers or clients or both;
- Share your work early and often with those end users so that you ensure it remains responsive to their needs;
- Focus on user outcomes and build accordingly;
- Expect to receive change requests and be flexible enough to accommodate them;
- Release a working product, prototype, or configuration as soon as you can, and seek relevant feedback;
- If users provide feedback, heed it in further, iterative development;
- Hire the best team you can and trust them to perform well; and
- Make consistent and regular communication a central part of how you work with your team.

Since the release of the Agile Manifesto, there have also been a number of specific work practices developed that translate the principles of Agile into concrete actions. It's worth considering whether some of these could be adopted by your team and even beyond your team, by some of the legal practices you support.

Sprints and Scrum

Scrum project management, which has evolved out of Agile, is a framework that focuses on iterative or incremental work, allowing for optimal business value to be delivered in the shortest time possible.[31]

Every incremental step in a project should have a well-defined goal (though this can change throughout the project). The product (or project) owner who leads the team – known as the "Scrum Master" – works closely with the team to create a backlog, which is a list of items that must be done in order to achieve the goal of this particular incremental step in the project.[32] The items or tasks in the backlog are prioritized, and the team then works together to deliver a result. Teams are organized cross-functionally, and work collaboratively in short spurts called sprints that usually last two to four weeks. Sprints are focused on completing (or delivering) one aspect of the work at hand.

During a sprint, the teams will meet daily for a "stand-up", which is a very short meeting during which workers share where they are up to and what they will be focusing on that day. At the end of a sprint, the teams meet for a retrospective, which allows them to identify any areas for improvement in the way they work together. Work is organized on "scrum boards", which are available for the whole team to see throughout the sprint, and which categorize tasks into "to-do", "in-progress", and "done".

Kanban

Kanban is another project management framework to have evolved out of Agile. Kanban means "visual signal" or "billboard", and work in this framework is organized around a visual board.[33]

In the Kanban methodology, a board is used to visualize and track progress, leveraging cards (upon which tasks are defined), and columns (in which task status is organized). Horizontal swim-lanes can be added to further organize work into themes.

During Kanban projects, team members are restricted to working on only a few "work-in-progress" or WIP tasks at one time (usually three). Team members are allocated their WIP tasks and they work on these until they are finished, at which point they are allocated new items from the board.

Kanban is predicated on the notion of continuous improvement, so the board is flexible, allowing for new tasks and changes to tasks at any time.

A lot has been written about whether Scrum or Kanban is the more effective methodology, and the reality is that it depends on the organization and the type of work being undertaken. In your environment, there are aspects of both methods that you can usefully employ in order to get your team working more productively. Ways in which you can gain value from these frameworks in the way you run your department or function include:

- Organize into smaller teams focused on specific work – either individual projects, or parts of larger projects.

- Teams should be cross-functional, and should work together on tasks and share their knowledge and expertise as they work. This improves the overall quality of the work, and the efficiency of how the teams operate.

- These smaller teams should be constantly reassessing progress, and are thus less likely to get stuck in a rut or miss a deadline.[34]

- Break down work into smaller pieces to help teams stay focused. This helps individual workers understand what needs to be done and makes it less likely that work will be forgotten or left unfinished.[35]

- Rather than thinking of project work as linear, think of it as iterative and continuous. Allow flexibility to accommodate changes throughout the course of a project.

- Consider holding regular stand-up meetings to check in with where things stand and what needs to be done next. These don't have to be daily, but should occur more regularly than, for example, monthly status meetings. On a large project, daily stand-ups can be very useful. Make sure you keep these short – "stand-ups" where people actually stand can be helpful in that no one wants to stand for too long so there is innate motivation to keep the meeting short.

- Introduce the notion of a backlog and categorizing tasks visually to move them through "in-progress" to completion. Allocating responsibility for tasks on a board is also useful – if you work in an office environment, a white board can be turned into a Kanban board (either with dry-erase markers or post-it notes). Otherwise, looking into project management software such as Asana or Trello is valuable.

I have introduced legal innovation teams to Kanban boards and regular stand-up meetings in the past, and these proved to be helpful ways of organizing work. The stand-up meetings had additional benefits for collaborative work because they provided the opportunity for cross-functional members of the team to routinely share what they were working on. Often this sparked ideas and team members would take some of the wins they learned about that had occurred in different parts of the team, and consequentially deployed them in their area of responsibility. The result was scaled success – we were able to get more traction with projects than we would have otherwise, across a wider swathe of the population of the firm.

For legal teams, the principles of Agile might be similarly beneficial, and it's one reason why Agile-trained project managers can be so influential when they work with matter teams. There will be significant effort involved, however, in getting lawyers who are used to working in traditional ways to instead work collaboratively in cross-functional teams, continuously evaluating a backlog of tasks and iteratively releasing work to clients. That requires the overhaul of structures at a law firm, and might be something you work towards with other firm leaders for many years (if it is accepted as a valuable goal).

In smaller corporate legal departments, however, or in new, small firms that are being established with modern work practices at their core, Agile methodologies could prove highly effective.

Regardless of how the lawyers around you work, keeping Agile principles in mind as you organize work with your innovation colleagues is likely to improve the focus, quality of output, and the engagement of the team.

Checklist: Effective ways of working

- [ ] Consider working with senior leadership to periodically undertake a Five Forces analysis that will help drive the strategic direction of the firm as a whole.

- [ ] Keep Porter's Five Forces of competition in mind as you generate strategies for your team and/or department and use these to help you prioritize projects and approach new initiatives.

- [ ] As you evaluate potential projects, consider whether there are opportunities to generate an entirely new competitive space. In doing so, consider whether there are areas you can help to differentiate services and also increase value to clients.

- [ ] Although many of your innovation efforts should be focused on client needs, some should be focused on good ideas and technology innovations that clients are not yet asking for but that seem likely to succeed in the future.

- [ ] Reserve some of your innovation budget for as-yet-undefined projects so that you can resource potentially disruptive initiatives that other purse-string-holders at the firm will not understand.

☐ When pursuing disruptive innovations, don't worry if the client base for these is not the same as the client base for your firm's core work. In fact, there is scope for success at a greater scale if it is not.

☐ Understand that the capabilities and resources you need on your team are different than the capabilities and resources your firm needs to undertake legal work. Enumerate these needs and find a way of getting them.

☐ Carve out a safe space for your team to experiment, fail, and iterate. This will likely need to sit outside the existing structures and business model of the firm.

☐ Educate your senior leadership that if they want the firm to survive in the context of disruptive innovation in the legal industry, they will have to occasionally be first in trying new technologies and products.

☐ In strategy meetings with firm leadership, explain the innovator's dilemma and the conflicts that will therefore naturally arise as you do your work, so that you and your team can operate with critical support from above.

☐ Train your team on Agile principles and values, with the understanding that iterative, continuous delivery, and cross-functional collaborative work is more likely to offer value than linear, documentation-driven work.

☐ Introduce a Kanban board or project management software to help your team manage, assign, and track tasks, and prioritize the backlog of work.

☐ Consider holding regular stand-up meetings with your team, at least during significant projects.

☐ To the extent that your team works with lawyers on legal matters, introduce iterative development principles and customer-focused project management values.

☐ If your authority extends to legal project management, recruit project managers with knowledge of Agile methodologies and encourage them to leverage these with lawyers to encourage more sustainable work practices and prevent burn-out.

☐ Embrace the philosophy of continuous improvement in all that you do as a team.

References

1 See Porter, M. E. (1979), "The Five Forces That Shape Strategy", *Harvard Business Review*, 86: 79-93, and Porter, M. E. (1985), *Competitive Advantage: Creating and Sustaining Superior Performance*. New York, MacMillan.

2 Harvard Business School: Institute for Strategy and Competitiveness. (2021). *The Five Forces*, www.isc.hbs.edu/strategy/business-strategy/Pages/the-five-forces.aspx

3 Porter, 1979.

4 *Ibid*.

5 *Ibid*.

6 Harvard Business School, 2021.

7 *Ibid*.

8 Kim, W. C., and Mauborgne, R (2004), *Blue Ocean Strategy*. Harvard Business Review, October 2004, https://hbr.org/2004/10/blue-ocean-strategy

9 Kim, W. C. and Mauborgne, R. (2005), *Blue Ocean Strategy: How to Create Uncontested Market Space and Make the Competition Irrelevant*. Boston, Massachusetts: Harvard Business Review Press.

10 Christensen, C. M. (1997), *The Innovator's Dilemma: When New Technologies Cause Great Firms to Fail*. Boston, Massachusetts: Harvard Business Review Press.

11 Thrasyvoulou, X. (2014), *Understanding the Innovator's Dilemma*, www.wired.com/insights/2014/12/understanding-the-innovators-dilemma/

12 Christensen, p. 41.

13 *Ibid*., p.226.

14 Thrasyvoulou, 2014.

15 Christensen, p.226.

16 *Ibid*.

17 *Ibid*.

18 *Ibid*.

19 *Ibid*.

20 *Ibid*., p.227.

21 *Ibid*., p.226.

22 *Ibid*., p.227.

23 *Ibid*.

24 *Ibid*., p.228.

25 *Ibid*.

26 The Agile Manifesto, https://agilemanifesto.org/principles.html

27 *Ibid*.

28 Airfocus (2022). *What is the Agile Manifesto?* https://airfocus.com/glossary/what-is-agile-manifesto/

29 *Ibid*.

30 Fedorska, A. (2021), *How the World Has Changed Since the Agile Manifesto*, https://bigpicture.one/world-since-agile-manifesto/

31 Clesham, M. (2022), *Agile Methodologies – Scrum and Kanban*. Brightwork, www.brightwork.com/blog/agile-methodologies-scrum-and-kanban

32 *Ibid.*

33 *Ibid.*

34 Kanjilal, J. (2022), *Best Strategies for Organization Agile Teams*, www.developer.com/project-management/organize-agile-teams-strategies/

35 *Ibid.*

Chapter 13:
Product management

Traditionalists might say that law is a services business, rather than a product business, and as such, product strategy has no place in legal. In fact, product strategy and product management philosophies are essential reading for anyone working in legal innovation or digital transformation, for numerous reasons.

First, product offerings are becoming increasingly common in law. As firms grapple with new demands and competitive forces, one of the clear ways to differentiate their offering is by turning what has always been a service into a product. Products have innate advantages over services:

- An expert does not have to be available or even awake for a client to access expertise from a product.

- Unlike a service, which is often bespoke and must be sold to one client at a time, a product can be built once and then sold a thousand times – in other words, it can be scaled in a way that services cannot be.

- Because products do not need to be recreated every time they are sold, they provide a means to offer high value at a lower cost.

For law firm leaders and innovation teams looking for potential disruptive moves, product development is ideal because it allows for both differentiation and reduced costs.

Second, parts of legal work lend themselves to repackaging as a product, charged out at a flat rate. Even though the work still involves the provision of a service, or a combination of services, those services are offered in a consistent, streamlined manner, delivered within an agreed-upon timeframe, and charged out at a fixed fee, like a product.

Imagine if you could shop for legal services like you shopped on Amazon. Instead of buying a book, a planter, and a new lunchbox for your child, you might see and be able to choose from a list of products such as:

- Employee handbook;
- Business formation – LLC; and/or
- Claim for unpaid wages.

Although this is happening to some degree in the business-to-consumer space, and in deregulated jurisdictions, we haven't yet reached this level of productization for most commercial business-to-business legal services. As law firms re-evaluate how they price work, however, it will be helpful for them to think of certain standardized types of work as legal products, and to approach these from that perspective.

Third, even in the absence of either product development or packaged services, law firms should pay heed to product management strategy as it will inform the way that the firm works with third party products, providing guidance for configuring and implementing solutions for use by either internal professionals or clients.

Like agile and design thinking, product management is focused on the user or client experience. It provides the necessary structure within which successful products can be planned, developed, and sold. There has been a wealth of material written about product management and product strategy, and much of this work is useful in driving impactful innovation. Product management as a discipline has given rise to many tools and resources that can be useful in framing innovation efforts broadly. Looking to product management strategy as part of your overall approach to innovation will therefore give you and your team a better foundation from which to lead.

Product strategy

A product strategy is the plan a company develops to define the vision for a product and how that vision will be realized.[1] Although a product can be scaled easily and requires fewer ongoing resources than a service offering, developing the product in the first place is resource-heavy and risky. Products that don't meet customer needs or achieve "product-market fit" will not succeed. Unless you pause to develop a plan around the development of a product, you risk rapid failure.

A product strategy will provide the big picture overview of a product idea, setting out why it should exist and how users will benefit from the product.[2] Having a good product strategy in place will ensure that:

- Everyone is working towards the same high-level business goals;
- There is a clear product vision (which is consistent across all stakeholders);
- The product represents strong customer advocacy;
- The product is aligned with the organization's business strategy; and
- There is effective collaboration across functions.[3]

It also gives everyone involved in the development of the product a focus, which should remain clear throughout the course of development to ensure that the final product is in line with the original vision for the product. That focal point is called the value proposition and, without one, product teams are prone to over-emphasizing product features with a lack of understanding around:

- Who the product is for;
- How and where it will be used; and
- Why customers or clients will pay for it (or, in an internal legal environment, why lawyers would use it).

Anyone working in innovation at a law firm will recognize these considerations as being equally valid whether bringing on new technology or deploying and re-configuring third-party technology.

Product strategy frameworks

If you are, in fact, developing a product or productizing a service, having a product strategy is essential. An effective product strategy provides a concrete framework to your development work. Instead of being vague about what you want to accomplish in building a product, or a managed service, it helps you set down in concrete terms the goals you seek to reach and the actions you'll take in getting there. The product strategy should form the bridge between the vision for your product and the tactical steps to fulfil it.

The best-known product strategy framework, called the V2MOM, was developed by Mark Benioff from Salesforce, who is widely regarded as a marketing genius.[4] The V2MOM is one of the easiest strategic planning frameworks to employ in order to ensure operational alignment around product development.[5] It is made up of the following elements:

- Vision – what do you want to accomplish?
- Values – What's important about it?
- Methods – How will you realize your vision?
- Obstacles – What might stand in the way of your reaching the vision?
- Measures – How will you know when you have achieved it?

Far from being restricted to products, a V2MOM framework can be established for anything from individuals and their goals to a service offering or an entire company. It will help to align daily actions with long-term goals and increase business transparency. As you embark on a new project, especially if that project involves building something, consider sitting down with your team and creating a plan that encompasses the elements of a V2MOM.

Vision
The vision aspect of any product strategy is similar to the vision discussed at the beginning of this book in relation to what your team sets out to accomplish, and the vision discussed in chapter nine that pertains to a particular project. You and your organization should have a very clear vision for every new product (or service). This vision should set out what you (or your team, or the firm) want to accomplish from this product or service, what impact it will have on the company or the firm, and how you can make it inspiring and engaging. The vision for your product should sit at the heart of your product strategy.

Values
What are the core values that are most important as the product team pursues their vision for the product? Are there values that you can use to guide your everyday decisions over the course of the project?

An example might be the value of simplicity – in executing your vision, the product team seeks to make sure that the design is elegant, simple, and user-friendly. This type of value will generally stem from what the customer wants or needs, and therefore helps to guide the project or product development in a way that aligns with the target customer.

Methods
Think about what specific actions your team and company need to take in order to achieve your vision. Consider how you will prioritize these tasks, and balance between the team's work and the broader company's work that is involved in the product development.

Obstacles

It's important to consider upfront what obstacles you and the product team might encounter in accomplishing your vision and how you'll overcome these. Consider what hurdles might stand in your way, and what is going to make it difficult to accomplish your vision and execute on your methods as you plan to. What specific things can you do or plan for to help overcome these things?

Measures

The "M" in the V2MOM refers to Measures, but it may as well refer to metrics. This aspect of the framework encourages proponents to consider how you will define success. More specifically, it requires product teams to consider ahead of time how they will measure success, and what specific tracking they will employ to understand whether or not they are executing on their vision once the product is released.

There are other product strategy frameworks, but these simply provide different ways of thinking through and capturing the same types of information at the outset of your product initiative. Working through the steps of a V2MOM framework will provide you with a strategy that brings clarity to your product development efforts, helps you prioritize what needs to be done and where to focus your resources, and provides a guide that will help inform tactical decisions as you develop the product.

A product strategy will look different depending on the context in which it's being used, so it's important to make the effort of reviewing the V2MOM elements specifically in relation to your organization, and the product you are planning for.

The Business Model Canvas

After establishing a framework and strategy for your product offering, you will need to decide what kind of business model will work to drive its success.

A business model, according to Alexander Osterwalder, describes "the rationale of how an organization creates, delivers, and captures value".[6] The Business Model Canvas (as depicted in Figure 37) is one way of setting out these aspects of a venture in order to determine whether a business is truly viable.[7] Although it can be used in relation to an entire new business, the Business Model Canvas can also be extremely helpful as you plan for an individual product or service offering. The Canvas requires you to understand who your target customers are, in which market they are situated, and will help you check the business logic around why customers would buy your product or service.[8]

After setting out all the relevant information in a Business Model Canvas, it provides a visual shortcut to showing all stakeholders and everyone involved with the development of the product how the different essential elements will come together to deliver your products, establish the cost structure, prove the value proposition, serve the relevant customer segments, and generate profits.[9] Once you start using the Business Model Canvas, you'll find that it can be just as useful for services and process improvement projects as it is for straight products.

The Business Model Canvas can be used to analyze potential competitors as well as for developing the business model for your product (or service, or business). Unless you understand the market, you won't know whether your business model is unique and valuable.

Business Model Canvas				
Key Partners Who are your key partners?	**Key Activities** What are the activities you perform every day to deliver your value proposition?	**Value Proposition** What is the value you deliver to your customer? What is the customer need your value proposition addresses?	**Customer Relationships** What relationship does each customer segment expect you to establish and maintain?	**Customer segments** Who are your customers?
	Key Resources What are the resources you need to deliver your value proposition?		**Channels** How do your customer segments want to be reached?	
Cost Structure What are the important costs you make to deliver the value proposition?		**Revenue Streams** How do customers reward you for the value you provide for them?		

Figure 37: Business Model Canvas.[10] *Source: Wikimedia Commons.*

In order to use the Business Model Canvas, you will ideally work through each element of it with your team. Using the canvas itself really works to help tighten up the rationale around a new product, and will help ensure it is successful.

Customer segments and personas

Who are you aiming your product or business at? Understanding this will be critical to its success. Ask yourself who are the target customers, but also, what do they think, see, and feel? Similar to a design thinking exercise, you should start from the perspective of the customer and take into account their needs in the area of their lives that is affected by your product or business idea.

Traditionally, product managers would approach customer segments through building and breaking down customer personas, much in the same way that personas would be approached in communications planning, as discussed in chapter ten.[11] In product management, a persona is used to help understand the key traits, goals, behaviors, responsibilities, and needs of a specific type of user or buyer – each persona is a profile of the typical customer for a product.[12] In identifying relevant buying personas, you would visualize the people who will actually buy your product and how they would go about doing that. Ideally, you would be able to spend time surveying those people, in order to get a real sense of what the persona groups are that are relevant to your product.

Personas will usually include a significant amount of detail about the type of person, both personal and professional. The following types of information are likely to be relevant:

- Their age, geographic location, and education level;
- Socioeconomic status;
- The goals and dreams they have for both their professional and their personal lives;
- Their day-to-day challenges, frustrations, and fears;
- Any potential biases for or against your product, firm, or organization;
- How the person deals with the problem today that your product plans to solve; and
- What the person would need from your product to deem it worthwhile.[13]

As you gather information about the personas who would buy and/or use your product, you might find that you end up with several different types of personas, each of whom are relevant to your product development in different ways. In your project team, for example, consider whether the product you're developing is intended for clients or internal lawyers, and if for clients, what exact type of client. If possible, again just like a design thinking exercise, you will need to observe, interview, or survey people to establish this.

Questions to ask:

- Will you be targeting this product at clients of the firm only, or are there potential customers beyond that populate who may be targeted users of your product?
- What are the specific needs of each customer segment in relation to the area where you are building a product? (Consider creating a survey canvassing them for the types of information summarized above and collecting responses to develop the relevant personas for your product.)
- How would they prefer to access the type of product you're building?
- How do they currently operate, what do they currently use, what would make your product a viable alternative?

The desired outcome of this process is to have a clearly defined segment with a number of personas that delineate sub-segments within your target demographic and describe your customer profile, including their behaviors, problems, and current workarounds and alternatives.

Value proposition
The value proposition describes the detail of how the value of your product interacts with your customer segment. It should be captured in a statement that explains what benefits your product provides for and how your product or business does that uniquely well.

Questions to ask:

- What pain-point does your product or business solve for your ideal target customer?
- How does your product solve that problem for the target customer in a way that is better than the alternatives the customer currently has available to them?

Channels

The channels in your business model canvas are the methods that you will use to reach your customers. This is a term that comes from marketing, and usually refers to all the different ways that you can communicate with your customer.

In planning for your product, consider whether you intend to communicate with clients or customers through lawyers, through your internal marketing team, or through specific business development campaigns that sit outside the framework of your organization. For each of your customer segments, you should end up with a list of potential channels that can be used to reach them.

Questions to ask:

- Will you use social media channels, email campaigns, or direct mail-outs?
- What channels will you use to reach each customer segment?
- Are there different channels that will be more useful for reaching different customers? For example, perhaps for existing clients of the firm you will ask lawyers to send them emails, and for other customer segments you will drive interest through social media.

Customer relationships

In this block on the Business Model Canvas, you will be considering the relationship between the customer and the product, and the relationship the customer will have with you as the business or product developer throughout the sales and product lifecycle.

Questions to ask:

- What is the customer journey through the product?
- What parts of that journey are most important and how can you make sure the customer's journey at those times is smooth?
- How will you support the customer?
- How will the customer contact you?

Revenue streams

This is perhaps the most critical aspect of the Business Model Canvas. For each customer segment you want to get a sense of how many potential customers there are in the segment, and the potential revenue to be generated from that customer base. Effectively, you are calculating total market size by segment.

Questions to ask:

- What is the estimated size of each customer segment?
- What is the realistic adoption of the product from within each customer segment?
- How many early adopters and how many mainstream customers are there within each customer segment?
- What are the revenue streams you will drive through the product, and what is the total projected revenue based on market size?

Key activities

Here you will be considering what you or your team (or the broader organization) has to do in order to deliver the product to market and make it successful. These activities likely involve not just designing and building the product but also the affiliated activities that will make the product viable.

Questions to ask:

- How will you test iterations of the product with end users?
- Will you need to develop test plans for quality and user acceptance testing?
- Will maintenance of any data or information be required?
- Will lawyers need to lend their time to provide their expertise to maintaining the knowledge architecture of a product?
- What other activities will be necessary to ensure the product can deliver the value proposition to the customers?

Key resources

After identifying the key activities necessary to produce, deliver, and maintain the product, you will need to understand what resources you need in order to undertake those activities. You will be considering the strategic assets you have in place, and what assets you need to have in place in order to deliver on your product in a way that is competitive.

Questions to ask:

- What roles do you need on the team in order to deliver on the product?
- Do you have those roles now or will you need to recruit/bring on contractors to support?
- If lawyer expertise is required, do you have access to lawyers who will support the product?
- Do you have access to the technology that you need?
- Does any of your technology need upgrading in order to ensure quality of product outcome and ensure it is competitive in delivering on the value proposition?

Key partnerships

The Business Model Canvas helps you think through the various aspects of your product vision and business in a way that might highlight some gaps. If there are any activities for which you don't have resources, one of the ways to address this is through developing strategic partnerships with other companies.

Questions to ask:

- Are there any partnerships you could develop that would help you to deliver the product in the most competitive way?

For legal products, one obvious partnership might be with a vendor who provides some of the underlying technology and customer support (or even overflow development support). Another might be with an ALSP who could share the burden of maintaining knowledge assets.

Cost structure

It's important to understand what the costs will be to build and deliver the product, and how and when these arise during the product development lifecycle. Some of these won't be obvious as you first plan for development of a product, but it's important to uncover those hidden costs early in the process so that the total cost of development and delivery are clear and a meaningful return on investment can be calculated.

Questions to ask:

- What are the costs of designing and developing the product?
- Will there be ongoing costs associated with maintenance or license fees for underlying technology?
- Do you need to pay external or contract engineers or other resources?
- Are there fees for data storage or hosting? Ideally you should be able to generate a realistic picture of costs associated with the product development that are tied to key activities.

Once you have worked through the Business Model Canvas, you can review it with your team to evaluate whether it makes sense to build and deliver the product in this way, or whether there are aspects that should be tweaked or improved. Does the business model make sense? Will revenue off-set costs? Do you have most of the resources you need to support key activities? Is the value proposition sufficiently meaningful to your target market?

The Business Model Canvas exercise will ultimately help you build a product that is more competitive and more likely to succeed in the market. It can also be used outside of product development, for almost any business endeavor. If you run an internal innovation team, but especially if you are planning to launch a law firm subsidiary, the Business Model Canvas can help you identify weaknesses in your strategic planning so that you can address them upfront.

The product development lifecycle

If you are going to develop products as part of your innovation strategy you will ideally be working with a product manager and software development professionals who deeply understand the product development lifecycle (PDLC) and can support the team through product builds. My advice to you is that you hire someone with this professional background, rather than try to become a product professional yourself. However, it's useful for anyone working in innovation to understand the PDLC at a high level. In practice, the PDLC also looks a lot like some of the service design frameworks we explored in chapter 11, with many of the same steps involved. In brief, the PDLC typically involves the following steps:[14]

1. *Develop the idea.* Usually through brainstorming for solutions[15] (of course, anyone educated in design methodologies would say that customer discovery and customer needs analysis should come first, as does understanding the problem you are trying to solve!).

2. *Validate the idea.* Is there a market for this idea? Do some market research to validate whether it is an idea that would gain traction in the market. Speak to potential customers in order to ascertain if this is a product they would want to buy.

3. *Build a prototype or proof of concept.* Establish through a proof of concept whether the idea will work in reality. Is the idea feasible, could it be a real product?

4. *Develop a marketing plan.* What is the messaging you will use to explain the value of this product? How will you get that message out?

5. *Build the minimum viable product.* The minimum viable product (MVP) is a light-touch version of the product that does what it needs to do but does not necessarily have all of the features that the final product will have. It should be sufficient to show customers what the product can be, so that customers can use it and provide feedback for further development. The idea is to get a working product into the hands of end users as quickly as possible. (Agile principles underpin the entire PDLC, so shipping a working product rapidly is critical.)

6. *Release the MVP to ascertain market interest and obtain feedback.* Release the product and market it so that potential customers hear about it. What is the initial response to the product? Is the market excited by it? Are customers interested in using it? Gather feedback from users on how the product could be improved.

7. *Improve the product.* Iterative development and continuous improvement, as established by Agile principles, will lead to a successful product. The product should be constantly improved as user feedback comes in.[16]

Note that at almost any point in the PDLC, the product can be scrapped. The concepts of releasing MVPs and working through continuous improvement allow product managers to be nimble in the way they approach product development. If a product release is not well received, they can go back to earlier versions of a product and move in a different direction that might be more successful with the customer base.

Product management tools

Ultimately, some of the most useful aspects of product management for innovation strategy are the tools that have been developed to support product development. We will review some of the most important such tools below.

Jobs To Be Done

One of the key frameworks in product management is the Jobs To Be Done Analysis. This framework can be used as a way of deeply understanding a problem and understanding how to start solving it. It also provides a lens that will help you see and understand problems more clearly.

Initially developed by Clayton Christensen in a course on marketing malpractice he taught at Harvard Business School,[17] and subsequently developed by Tony Ulwick (who had already coined the phrase "Outcome Driven Innovation"),[18] and later Jim Kalback,[19] the Jobs To Be Done (JTBD) framework turns classic product development on its head by focusing on the outcomes customers are looking for, instead of making products and then marketing them to make customers want them. In the PDLC above, the idea comes first, and messaging is later developed to help customers want the product. In a JTBD framework, products are developed in order to serve the customer by doing the core job the customer is trying to get done, rather than pushing products to them that they may not need.[20]

Christensen, along with Taddy Hall, Karen Dillon, and David S. Duncan wrote an article introducing the JTBD framework, explaining that they had watched many companies fail and had examined the reasons for that.[21] Ultimately what they realized is that companies needed to focus on what "progress" the customer was trying to make in a given situation, or what the customer hoped to accomplish. Solving for that, rather than trying to observe customers and understand everything about them, was more likely to lead to successful products. Ulwick described JTBD as:

"A perspective or lens through which to observe markets, customers, needs, competitors, and customer segments differently and by doing so, make innovation far more predictable and profitable."[22]

In the JTBD framework, the unit of analysis that is most important to product designers is not the customer or the product but instead the "core functional job" the customer is trying to get done.[23] Ulwick created a company, Strategyn, that works with businesses to transform the way they built and looked at products.[24] Over 86 percent of those companies have had success applying the JTBD framework to develop and improve their product,[25] with the result that the framework is widely accepted as a model for successful product innovation.

There are several classic customer stories that can help illustrate the benefits of the JTBD framework and how it works so well. The most famous is this: Imagine someone comes to you and says they want a quarter-inch drill. In traditional product development paradigms, the developer would go off and build a drill to those specifications, thinking they were doing the right thing in responding to what the customer needs.

In fact, the customer does not need a drill. The JTBD framework would ask instead, What is the outcome the customer is seeking? By asking this question, you will quickly find that the customer is not seeking a drill at all – the outcome they're seeking is a quarter-inch hole in the wall. Take that one step further, and perhaps you'll find that they are seeking to hang a particular picture on the wall, which they think can best be done by drilling a quarter-inch hole for a screw that will hold up that picture. With this information, product developers can identify a solution that will work better to deliver the customer's sought-after outcome than the drill would have. It might not even involve a hole in the wall!

JTBD is a framework that runs parallel to root cause analysis and fits well within service design philosophy. It's a useful tool to have up your sleeve because, in almost any situation, it will ensure you are responding better to customer (or client) needs. It can be surprisingly difficult, however, to get to the root of what the desired customer outcome is in a particular situation. The "job" a customer is trying to achieve is not necessarily obvious to the observer, which is why traditional user discovery methods often do not succeed at getting to the heart of a problem.[26] There are also different types of jobs – functional jobs (like hanging a picture on a wall), emotional jobs (for making you feel a certain way), and ancillary jobs (outcomes that a customer wants before, during, or after they get their main job done).

In order to determine the desired outcome in the JTBD framework, jobs will often be analyzed until the product designer has a written statement in the following form:

Situation ⟶ Motivation ⟶ Outcome

Visual frameworks that require product designers or problem-solvers to ask specific questions can help uncover the core job to be done (see Figure 38): in which situation do you need to get this done? What is it exactly that you want to do? What is the outcome you seek from doing that?

WHEN I ...	I WANT TO ...	SO I CAN ...
Situation	Motivation	Desired outcome
WHEN I use a drill	I WANT TO make a hole	SO I CAN hang a picture

Figure 38: Jobs To Be Done Analysis.[27]

The JTBD analysis is a useful lens for you and your team to bring to any problem-solving exercise, and especially to deploy when you are considering launching a product. Even outside of the context of product development, thinking about your lawyers' and clients' problems from the perspective of jobs that need to get done will help you make more of an impact as an innovator.

Product opportunities

There is some overlap between the way product theory views product opportunities, and the way that design thinking looks at iterative problem-solving. If instead of starting with a problem to be solved, you were seeking to find an opportunity for a product that would be viable and generate revenue, you could use the JTBD framework and approach your strategic planning in the following way in order to uncover product opportunities:

1. Choose a specific target customer demographic (in the context of a law firm innovator, this could be the firm's client pool within a particular industry or practice area).

2. Identify the jobs customers are trying to get done within that persona group.

3. Categorize the jobs to be done into themes.

4. Create job statements for each of these that make it clear what the product would have to do in order to hit the mark.

5. Prioritize JTBD opportunities in the chosen market/customer segment.

6. Select the job you will address with your product.[28]

In reality, most firms are not yet in a position where they are so product-driven as to have to generate new opportunities for products. Most product opportunities in current commercial legal contexts arise because there is a clear problem to be solved. Understanding that problem from the JTBD lens, and proceeding to develop a product that will help the customer get the job done, is then more likely to ensure your work is successful.

Product-market fit

Product-market fit is a process or framework that evolved out of the Lean Startup principles made famous by Steve Blank.[29] In 2013, Blank introduced a new way for entrepreneurs to start businesses, which upset conventional wisdom and allowed for faster business model innovation to fit customer and market needs.[30] The product lifecycle and product management guidance that has been shared in this chapter stem largely from Lean Startup principles, which adopt Agile methodologies such as continuous improvement. For example, the PDLC laid out above, which includes the early release of an MVP and iteration upon client feedback, is part of the Lean Startup process. The Business Model Canvas is a tool used by lean start-ups, where former start-ups would instead have focused on developing a lengthy business plan.

Originally developed by VC executive Andy Rachleff, product-market fit is the process of evaluating the success of a product in its target market based on user feedback, and being able to recognize its potential profitability.[31] Rachleff referred to product-market fit as a value hypothesis that articulates the key assumption underlying why a customer is likely to use your product.[32] Product-market fit identifies the features you need to build, the audience that is likely to care, and the business model required to entice a customer to buy your product.[33] It can be looked at as an analysis with three requirements:

1. A product that solves a problem.

2. Customers who need to have the problem solved.

3. A market that is open enough to allow for the entry and growth of a new product.[34]

Some commentators have proposed visual frameworks such as the one in Figure 39 to help entrepreneurs or business owners identify product-market fit when they launch new products.

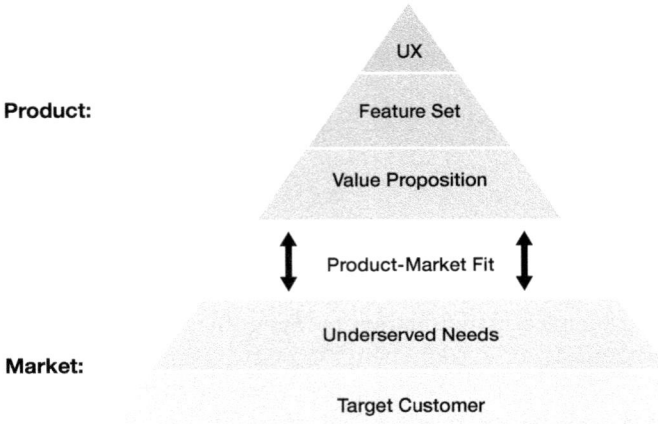

Figure 39: Product-Market Fit Pyramid by Dan Olsen.[35]

In reality, if you have product-market fit, most commentators suggest that you will recognize it immediately. Product-market fit occurs when customers rapidly start using your product without you or the business having to spend on marketing or promotion. It will be evident when your target customers are buying, using, and telling others about your product in significant enough numbers that the product appears to grow organically. The success of a product that has achieved product-market fit occurs because the product owners have pitched it right – they have successfully evaluated a particular market as being ready and eager to receive the type of product they developed. As Rachleff said, "Nothing is as irreplaceable as a great market".[36]

It's worth knowing about product-market fit because although achieving it is to some extent a matter of luck (we will not always have great markets into which to launch products), watching for it will give you good insight into whether or not your product is likely to succeed in its current iteration. If you release an MVP to a target customer (or client) base and you have to work extremely hard on advertising and marketing in order to earn new customers, you have not yet achieved product-market fit. It's then worth tweaking the product in light of customer feedback and releasing an improved product, or ultimately, it might be an indication that you need to pivot entirely and either build a different product or target a different part of the market.

Build, Partner, Buy

Another framework from the world of product management that is essential for any innovation, legal operations, or digital transformation team in law firms and corporate legal departments, whether or not they are concerned with developing products, is the Build, Partner, Buy framework. Although this framework stems from product management philosophy, it should be widely applied whenever decisions are being made about how to develop the solution to a problem.

Whenever a product or a solution to a problem is planned, and the various aspects of a product strategy have been evaluated, a decision will need to be made about how to approach that development.[37] As we discussed briefly in relation to partnerships in the Business Model Canvas, it is not necessarily the case that a business will take on all aspects of the development of a product themselves. If resources are scarce in certain areas, it might be worth partnering with another organization in order to achieve some of the activities necessary to build the whole product. Whenever a company makes this kind of decision, however, there are trade-offs to be had.

Decisions like these are covered by the Build, Partner, Buy framework. A company will need to decide whether to build the product entirely themselves, partner with another vendor in order to build the product, or buy a third-party solution to solve the problem. The choices are not mutually exclusive. Many companies use all three strategies at different times to meet different needs.

For technology organizations or businesses whose core model is the development of products for sale to customers, the most obvious choice is usually that they should build the product or solution themselves from scratch. Doing so provides them with a competitive advantage – they will then own the IP associated with the product, and may be able to patent aspects of the engineering that goes into it, which will give them a lasting competitive advantage. For these types of organizations, buying or licensing a third- party solution can seem unnecessarily expensive (because their core business is development).

Law firms and legal departments are in the opposite position. Their core business is not technology development or product development. Even as law firms explore disruptive innovation offerings and branch out into the productization of legal services, their core business remains the practice of law. Accordingly, law firms typically do not have the resources to capably build successful products from scratch – and certainly not many such products. Nor should they have to. Most legal products are applications that allow for the self-service of legal information, or workflow solutions that automate parts of legal work. In both of these instances, there are numerous third-party tools on the market that can support firms in developing the products. Workflow automation solutions such as expert systems, for example, provide modular capabilities that allow innovation teams to develop applications that serve multiple product use cases. Using these solutions can provide law firm innovation teams with a shortcut towards successful product development. Persisting in building from scratch in spite of the availability of these solutions makes little sense. Building from scratch in an environment that is not set up for custom development is likely to be more expensive than licensing third party solutions, and gives rise to technical debt stemming from the need to maintain and continuously update the homegrown products. Organizations like law firms also lack the kinds of internal processes that would enable the effective ongoing development of a homegrown product: they are notoriously bad at maintaining information about software versioning and custom configurations, and often fail to ensure appropriate knowledge transfer as IT professionals come and go.

Generally speaking, law firms should not build a product from scratch unless there is no other option available, or there is a real competitive advantage to be had from doing so. In the absence of a third-party solution that is currently available on the market, your next most sensible options will be to approach vendors with whom you have a good relationship to determine whether you could partner with them to develop the capability you need to build the desired product. Only once these options have been explored and sensibly rejected should custom development be entertained.

For law firms, although a strategic evaluation should be undertaken in relation to each such project, the most sensible order of decision-making around product development is:

1. *Use.* Look at your current software licenses and capabilities, not just in your own team but across the firm, to determine whether you can use or combine existing tools in new ways to develop the solution or underpin the product.

2. *Buy.* Examine the market to see if there is a third-party solution you don't yet have but can license, that will provide you with the capability to develop the product.

3. *Partner.* In the absence of either of the above, consider whether there is a software vendor with whom you can partner, where they either develop the technology themselves or will provide the development resources necessary for a custom build.

4. *Build.* If all other options have been exhausted and the value of the product combined with its strategic impact is worth it, either hire an external development team to build for you or, if you have them, leverage internal resources to build the product in-house yourselves.

What law firms need to think about as they move towards productization

As discussed above, there are significant benefits for legal organizations in moving towards productization. Doing so does not mean that all services of a law firm can or should be productized. Instead, it means that there are opportunities to generate substantial additional revenue by creating products for sale, and this is a competitive advantage that firms should be aware of and considering.

Law firms are used to thinking of value in terms of the time it takes to deliver on a piece of work. The difficulty is, some people will take longer to complete that work than others. Is the value of a memorandum of advice worth less if someone is able to get it done in less time? It will obviously take a senior partner less time to complete a memo than it will a junior associate, because the partner's expertise means she doesn't have to research as many issues and knows how to write an effective memo with fewer drafts. To account for this evolution in expertise, law firms charge more for partners' time than they do for an associate's time. However, beyond hierarchical pricing, law firms are not good at evaluating value differentials in other ways.

If a senior partner uses her expertise to populate knowledge graphs that sit in the back end of a product that is then sold to clients, that partner's time has only been leveraged once – and yet multiple clients can access the expertise she has shared by buying the product. In spite of the fact that the partner spent no active time developing the product when it was sold the second time or the third time – or the 100th time – the value those subsequent clients get from it is the same as the value the first client got from it, and the product should be charged accordingly This scale in product sales, being able to repeatedly leverage the same expertise without additional input from humans, is a highly profitable exercise, and explains why law firms should be exploring product offerings.

Law firms need to become comfortable thinking about value in these terms. The value lies in the output, not in the hours required to deliver that output. Only once firms are able to re-assess their estimation of value will they feel comfortable charging for products the way they should, or charging for work at a flat fee. Once this re-assessment has occurred, auto-mation and efficiency will be viewed by law firms through a different lens. If value is attached to the output of the work rather than the work itself, then it will become obvious that it's beneficial for the firm to generate that output as fast as possible. Doing so will enable the firm to make more money (whereas in the billable hours model, inefficiency can be rewarded).

Product philosophy can help innovation teams to shift the culture and perceptions of a firm around value, because the conversations that must be had around scale and pricing of a product force leadership to look at work in new ways.

A note on value-adds

Many law firms have recognized that products in legal are valuable to clients, but because these fall out of the traditional relationship between clients and lawyers, or because they fall outside of the scope of work it is expected that a law firm will charge for, they have opted to give these away for free. This has been happening for many years. Document templates, client alerts, or updates on pertinent areas of law, newslet-ters with market updates, access to data analysis tools that provide the ability to track legislation or trends, even products that enable clients to self-serve legal information – I've seen all of these given away for free as part of existing client engagements. The typical explanation for this behavior is that doing so strengthens the client relationship to make it "stickier". If you dig deeper with the lawyers who make the decision to forsake potential revenue from charging for these products, you will often hear an argument that clients won't pay for these things. Often, however, the reality is that the conversation about whether a client would consider this worth paying for – over and above the traditional service offering of the firm – has never happened. Lawyers are not good at selling products. They worry that selling a product to their clients will cheapen their relationship and potentially scare the client away.

Unfortunately, by giving away these products for free, lawyers are making a far greater mistake. Anything that is given away for free is devalued by the people who receive it. It's human nature to assume that if something is free, it can't be worth much. The lawyers giving away these "value-adds" therefore dig themselves – and their firms – into a hole, because if this type of product has been free before, it's hard to suddenly start charging clients for products later. This is a shame, because the development and scaling of legal products is a real opportunity for firms to differentiate themselves and create distance between them and their competitors.

Perhaps worse, giving the products away for free also devalues the work of the people who spent their time building those products, and who likely will have to continue spending time to maintain the information in the products and the engineering that sits behind them. Devaluing their work serves to increase the divide between lawyers (whose work is revenue-generating and therefore considered valuable) and non-lawyers (whose work is considered to be neither of those things). The fact that revenue adheres to lawyer work and not other work has downstream impacts on compensation and benefits, and therefore affects engagement and limits the ability of firms to hire good talent for allied professional roles. Yet, as we have discussed, the most effective law firm teams of the future will be multi-functional, where every type of worker on the team is talented and highly skilled. By reinforcing a divide that does a disservice to people without a law degree, law firms are shooting themselves in the foot, making it harder for them to hire really good talent on the business side.

Moral of the story – charge for your legal products. They are valuable, and most clients will recognize this. If you are in a structure that makes it difficult to charge for products, continue to agitate for this and in the meanwhile attribute value to the products through measuring the costs associated with their development. Convey the message to clients that the product they are enjoying "on-the-house" is worth X amount and is a perk of their relationship with the firm.

Checklist: Building successful products

☐ Consider working with your team to develop legal products or productized services that will generate revenue and provide new strategic offerings for clients.

☐ Even if your team is not involved in product building, develop product strategies in relation to any project involving technology in some capacity.

☐ For any product or solution your team develops:

- Identify the vision for the outcome.
- Undertake planning upfront and understand the aspects of the project covered by a V2MOM strategy.
- Leverage the Business Model Canvas to evaluate the potential success of the project and plan for its complexity.
- Use the Build, Partner, Buy framework to decide how you will develop the product in a way that makes sense for your organization.
- Use surveys and listening sessions to understand the buyer and user personas for your product, and build for those persona needs.
- Taking into account those customer needs, develop an MVP for early release that can be tweaked in light of customer feedback.
- Ensure that you know enough about the client base to which you're releasing the product and the market in which you're releasing it to understand whether there is likely to be product-market fit.
- If there is not good adoption among customers after release, consider tweaking the product and re-releasing it, or pivoting.

☐ Whenever you are evaluating a problem or considering developing a product, use the JTBD framework to identify the actual outcome that the customer seeks, and orient development accordingly.

☐ If your team is involved in developing products, push leadership to charge for them.

☐ If you are unable to charge revenue for products, ascribe a value to each of them and ensure clients who receive the benefit of those products understand that there is a dollar value associated with them.

References

1 Selden, C. (2022), *What is Product Strategy? Framework and Examples*, https://amplitude.com/blog/product-strategy-framework

2 *Ibid*.

3 *Ibid*.

4 Zaveri, P. (2021), *Best Marketing Strategy CMOs Learned from Salesforce CEO Mark Benoff*, www.businessinsider.com/best-marketing-strategies-cmo-marc-benioff-salesforce-cloud-confluent-twilio-2021-11

5 Mitsis, C. (2022), *The V2MOM: Overview, How to Use It, Examples*, www.cascade.app/blog/the-v2mom-framework

6 Osterwalder, A. (2010), *Business Model Generation: A Handbook for Visionaries, Game Changers, and Challengers*. Hoboken, New Jersey: Wiley & Sons.

7 *Ibid*.

8 Fox, G. (2021), *How to Use the Business Model Canvas: A Step by Step Guide*, www.garyfox.co/canvas-models/how-to-use-business-model-canvas-guide

9 *Ibid*.

10 Osterwalder, p.44.

11 Fox, 2021.

12 ProductPlan. (2021). Personas. https://www.productplan.com/glossary/persona/

13 *Ibid*.

14 ProductPlan (2021), Product Development Cycle, www.productplan.com/glossary/product-development-cycle

15 *Ibid*.

16 *Ibid*.

17 Christensen, C. M., Hall, T., Dillon, K., and Duncan, D. S. (2016), *"Know Your Customers' 'Jobs To Be Done'"*, *Harvard Business Review*, September 2016.

18 Ulwick, T. (2016), *Jobs to be Done: Theory to Practice*. Idea Bite Press.

19 In his book with Michael Schrage: Kalback, J. and Schrage, M. (2020), *The Jobs to Be Done Playbook: Align Your Markets, Organization and Strategy Around Customer Needs*. Two Waves Press.

20 Ulwick, 2016.

21 Christensen *et. al*, 2016.

22 Ulwick, T. (2017), *What is Jobs-to-be-Done?* https://jobs-to-be-done.com/what-is-jobs-to-be-done-fea59c8e39eb

23 *Ibid*.

24 *Ibid*.

25 ProductPlan (2021), *Jobs-To-Be-Done Framework*, www.productplan.com/glossary/jobs-to-be-done-framework/

26 *Ibid*.

27 Pedicini, A. *Product Frameworks*, www.product-frameworks.com/Jobs-To-Be-Done.html

28 Gecis, Z. (2015), *Eight Things to Use in "Jobs-To-Be-Done" Framework for Product Development*, https://uxdesign.cc/8-things-to-use-in-jobs-to-be-done-framework-for-product-development-4ae7c6f3c30b

29 Blank, S. (2013), "Why the Lean Start-Up Changes Everything", *Harvard Business Review*, May 2013.

30 *Ibid.*

31 bCombinator (2021), *What is Product-Market Fit and Why Is It So Important*, www.bcombinator.com/what-is-product-market-fit-and-why-is-it-so-important

32 Griffin, T. (2019), *12 Things About Product-Market Fit*, https://a16z.com/2017/02/18/12-things-about-product-market-fit-2/

33 *Ibid.*

34 *Ibid.*

35 Dan Olsen: https://dan-olsen.com, "The Lean Product Playbook", https://amzn.to/1EYCUdP.

36 Griffin, 2019.

37 Henken, D. and Watenpaugh, N. (2018), *Build, Buy, Partner: The Challenges of Product Management*, https://developmentcorporate.com/2021/06/28/product-managers-build-buy-partner-do-you-really-have-a-choice/

Chapter 14:
Incentives and adoption

As discussed in part one, innovation cannot be deemed to have happened unless there has been widespread adoption of the new solution or the new way of doing things by the desired group of people. Adoption is one of the most critical aspects of any innovation program, and should be considered first, rather than last. The adoption of new innovations fails at an astonishing rate in the industry at large.[1] It should be no surprise that law firms and law departments have a hard time gaining adoption of new processes and solutions: there is a psychological cost for people in changing their behavior to adopt something new. This cost is increased in an industry where work has been conducted in mostly the same way for generations.

Adoption is also integrally tied to, and in some ways almost synonymous with, change management. Change management, after all, is a methodology for getting people to change from the old way of doing things to the new. A successful change management program results in strong adoption, so change management tactics are also adoption tactics.

In this chapter, rather than re-hashing the guidance provided on change management in chapter nine, we will be exploring the psychology behind adoption, specific strategies for adoption, and the incentivization of adoption of new processes and technologies.

Strategies for adoption

If you have an effective organization-wide innovation strategy in place, there should not be a need for a separate adoption strategy because adoption will be a core tenet of that innovation strategy (as we saw with the 3Es Innovation Strategy in chapter three). Similarly, with any individual project, if you have developed a change strategy that includes a communications plan, then adoption should be folded into it as one of the key components.

Adoption should not be regarded as distinct from the way that your team approaches innovation or change. It is not an add-on to be considered at the end of a project like an addendum. Instead, strategic adoption approaches should govern all of the innovation initiatives you and your team undertake. Every action you take, every decision you make to address a pain-point, take on a project, map a process, or implement a technology, should be made strategically in light of whether or not there is a relevant need for the action or decision from your end users and a high likelihood that your users will adopt the solution. Firms that have embedded the values of innovation and digitization into the fabric of how they operate will have greater success in achieving adoption of new solutions because the context and structures of the firm promote innovative ways of doing things and celebrate people who adopt innovations. Lawyers who work in an environment where their performance reviews and bonuses are tied to innovation efforts, where firm leadership regularly talks about the importance of digital workflows, and where there are internal incentives for creativity and experimentation, are much more likely to show curiosity and interest in a new solution than lawyers in a firm where the innovation teams sit off to one side and everywhere else business is done as usual. To the extent possible, firm-wide innovation strategies should seek tangible buy-in from leadership such that incentives and structural support for innovative initiatives and adoption of new solutions is seen as mission-critical to success at the firm. This holistic support will help you drive adoption in every project your team takes on.

Case study: Strategizing for adoption at King Wood Mallesons (KWM)

KWM is an example of a firm that has implemented a firm-wide innovation strategy with adoption built into every element. Michelle Mahoney, the firm's executive director of innovation, points out that holistic innovation and digital transformation are a long game, relying on systemic enablement and culture change to create momentum and progress. Taking a whole-firm approach to these initiatives requires patience and a clear vision linked to the firm's overall strategy to sustain and deliver lasting change and impact.

KWM's innovation strategy is designed to grow and defend the firm whilst fostering an innovation mindset across all personnel and lawyers. The firm expects innovative behavior to be business as usual, and a willingness to try new things has been identified as a core competency expected of all employees. Michelle recognizes the need to provide a reason upfront for why people should be motivated to change their behavior. "To achieve scaled innovation", she says, "the approach needs to be holistic and begin with education and culture change. People need clarity as to why the firm is changing and innovating."

KWM has implemented systemic programs around education and enablement to create new capabilities and to change mindsets. Lawyers are encouraged to try new things and the firm promotes an openness to exploring or applying new ways of working. In order to get lawyers on board with this holistic initiative, the firm formally recognizes people who succeed in the innovation space, and has put in place certifications and recognition for success on qualifying initiatives. Recognizing the pace and demands of modern lawyering, KWM's innovation team works to link innovation efforts to client engagements wherever possible. Lawyers on those matters can then roll their innovation work into client work, reducing the need to find additional time in the day. It also means that lawyers know they are spending their time on already highly valued activities.

Prior to rolling out the program, KWM undertook a year of research into its people and clients to determine drivers, blockers, incentives, and limiting factors. The results of this research informed the program design for the digital literacy program. Culturally, this program has created an environment where exploration and capability building in digital literacy is expected, rewarded, and recognized. Critically, Michelle points out that the further engrained the narrative becomes, the greater the adoption of the supporting initiatives. Creating interconnected reinforcing initiatives that develop openness to new ways of working encourages digital literacy, improves client outcomes, and ultimately creates value for all involved.

Planning for adoption

Not all firms are progressive enough to put innovation at the core of their operational identity. When it comes to adoption at a more discreet, project basis, however, forward planning remains essential. Each project should be evaluated at the outset for its likelihood in being adopted, and projects that are highly unlikely to result in broad adoption should not be attempted until a later stage. Once the overall culture of the firm has changed, you may find that some of these projects become feasible.

As discussed in chapter 11, human-centered design approaches provide a good test for whether a project or initiative is likely to be adopted. Solutions that have a high likelihood of strong adoption bring together what is desirable from a human perspective with what is both economically viable and technologically or operationally feasible (see Figure 40).[2]

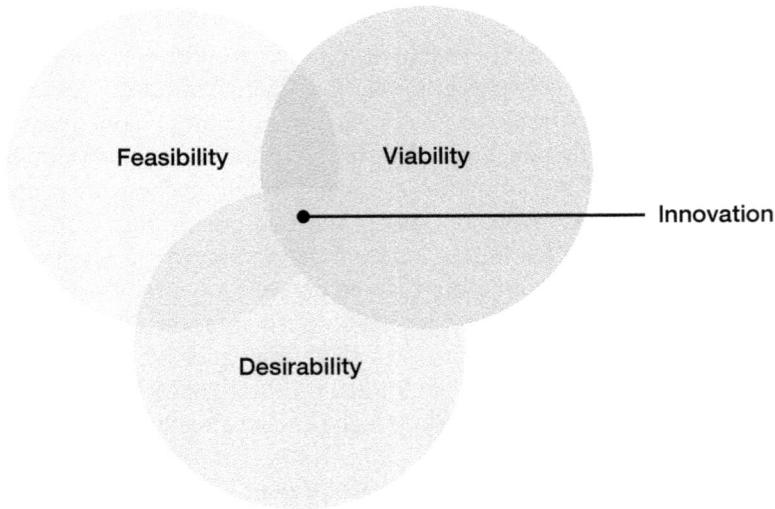

Figure 40: The Innovation Sweet Spot.[3]

Desirability asks the question of whether the product or solution is solving key customer problems.[4] Feasibility asks whether you are working within your operational strengths (in terms of technological capabilities, human and budgetary resources, and so on) to develop the solution.[5] Viability asks whether the business model for the solution sets it up for success or long-term growth.[6] As we explored in relation to design thinking, the nexus between that human desirability, operational feasibility, and economic viability is considered to be the innovation sweet spot.[7] It's a sweet spot not just because these are solutions for which the resources and capabilities exist that allow them to be effectively built, but also because they will delight users in a way that maximizes the potential for adoption. In some ways, this assessment of a solution acts as an early litmus test for adoption, and projects should be approached with this in mind.

Beyond solving a genuine problem, what does it mean for a solution to "delight" its end users?

The word "delight" denotes greater pleasure than the mere satisfaction that's gained from a process that works well, and that hyperbole is deliberate. Research has shown that the users of a new solution will typically underestimate the benefits of a new product by a factor of three, while they overestimate the costs of giving up the current solution by the same factor. People evaluate and compare things to the status quo, and they are risk averse (especially lawyers). As a result, a new solution has to be a whopping nine times better than the current one in order to succeed in gaining adoption – see Figure 41.

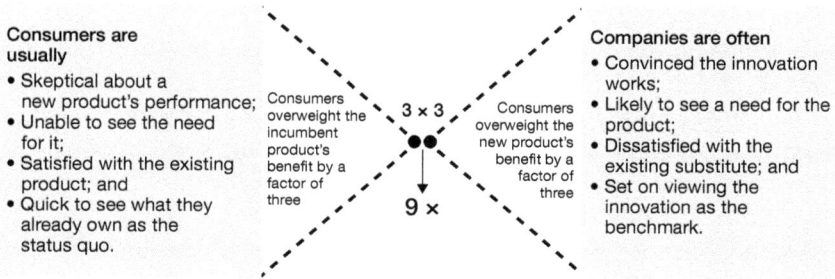

Consumers are usually
- Skeptical about a new product's performance;
- Unable to see the need for it;
- Satisfied with the existing product; and
- Quick to see what they already own as the status quo.

Consumers overweight the incumbent product's benefit by a factor of three

3 × 3

9 ×

Consumers overweight the new product's benefit by a factor of three

Companies are often
- Convinced the innovation works;
- Likely to see a need for the product;
- Dissatisfied with the existing substitute; and
- Set on viewing the innovation as the benchmark.

Figure 41: The 9x Rule.[8]

Companies used to assume that adoption of new products would be driven by people's belief that these delivered improved value or utility over existing products.[9] If true, this would mean that businesses need to focus on developing innovations that are simply objectively superior to the status quo. The assumption was that the mere fact that a new product was better than the existing one would create a desire within the consumer to purchase it. Communications scholar Everett Rogers calls this the concept of "Relative Advantage", and considers it the most critical driver of new-product adoption.[10]

However, Relative Advantage does not take into account some of the more complex psychological biases involved in decision-making. In fact, people's responses to alternate choices before them have four distinct characteristics:[11]

1. *Perceived valuation* – the attractiveness of an alternative is not evaluated based on its actual value but on the subjective or perceived value.[12]

2. *Relative valuation* – rather than viewing alternatives in a vacuum, people evaluate them in relation to a reference point. The reference point is almost always a comparison to products or solutions they already own or use.[13]

3. *Comparative evaluation* – any improvements to the reference point are seen as gains. All shortcomings compared to the reference point are viewed as deficiencies or losses.[14]

4. *Loss aversion* – people are impacted significantly more by losses than by similarly-sized gains.[15]

Psychologists Daniel Kahneman and Amos Tversky developed this framework for how individuals value choices in the marketplace.[16] They considered characteristic four, loss aversion, to be the most important. An example of this psychological response in action can be seen in gambling – a person is unlikely to accept a bet where there is a 50 percent chance of winning $100 and a 50 percent chance of losing the same amount. The gains from the bet have to outweigh the losses by two or three times before it is deemed attractive by most people.[17]

Another scientist, Richard Thaler, published research on this topic way back in 1980.[18] He found that people will demand much more to give up an object than they will in order to acquire it. For example, someone who collects wine might initially buy it at a significantly lower price than it is valued at after they've cellared it for a number of years, but would be unwilling to buy or sell the same wine at the appreciated price. Say a bottle that was bought for $10 can sell for over $200 at auction ten years later. Although the original buyer might drink some of the wine after it has appreciated in value, Thaler found that the same buyer was generally unwilling to sell the wine at the new auction price or to buy more of that wine at the auction price.[19] He called this the "Endowment Effect".[20] Repeated experiments have shown that they irrationally overvalue the items in their possession over those they don't have by a factor of between two and four.[21]

Building on Thaler's research, a number of economists have demonstrated a concept related to the Endowment Effect, called Status Quo Bias, meaning that people tend to stay with what they have even in circumstances where a better alternative is offered to them.[22] Economist Jack Knetsch illustrated the Status Quo Bias in an experiment during which he gave a control group of students the choice between a nice coffee mug and a bar of Swiss chocolate.[23] The split of choices between the students was almost even – about 50 percent chose the mug and 50 percent chose the chocolate.[24] Knetsch then unilaterally gave all of the subjects in another group a mug, and all of the subjects in a third group bars of Swiss chocolate. The subjects in both of the latter groups, who had not initially been given a choice between the mug or the chocolate, were later offered the opportunity to exchange their gift for the alternative item. Based on the control group, one would assume that about half of the subjects in each of the latter groups would choose to exchange their gift when given the opportunity. However, this did not happen; instead only approximately ten percent of the subjects in these groups chose to exchange their products.[25] The experiment indicates that most of the students felt that it would be painful or undesirable to give up what they already had – even if they would initially have preferred the other item.

The Status Quo Bias has been confirmed in many subsequent experiments. It has been shown to adhere to people's choices in all kinds of areas of their lives, including choices related to their careers, their choice of car, and financial investments.[26] Over the years, researchers have also found that the magnitude of Status Quo Bias increases the longer a person has held onto the thing they are being asked to give up. Thaler's experiments revealed a bias of a factor of two in favor of already-owned products. Subsequent research has found that over time this bias rises to a factor of approximately four.[27] Also interesting is that people seem to be unaware of the presence or workings of the Endowment Effect or Status Quo Bias, and can even act defensively if the subject is raised with them.[28] Even though these are innate behavioral tendencies, we typically deny they are influencing our decision-making.

What do all of these psychological theories mean for the way that we choose projects and introduce change? While people might gain highly desirable features by adopting a new solution, they often have to give up some of the benefits of the status quo. Psychologically, people don't see or feel these changes as mere behavioral adjustments. They view them as gains and losses. A new feature might be seen as a gain, and the absence of an existing feature in the old solution will be seen as a loss. Losses are defined by the brain, however, as broader than losing something tangible in the existing solution. Losses include the amount of time it takes to switch from one solution to another and the hurdles involved in transitioning to a new way of doing things. Due to the Endowment Effect and Status Quo Bias, the longer someone has been using something or doing something a certain way, the greater the psychological impact will be if you take that tool away or ask them to do something a different way. They will overvalue those losses by at least a factor of three. It's therefore not enough for a new tool or solution to be better. Unless the gains significantly outweigh the losses, it will be difficult to get people to adopt the new way of doing things.

If you start to look at the change you're introducing through the psychological lens of the person who is experiencing it, you will be able to better understand its impact. When selecting products and choosing projects for the year, think about how much behavior change they will require. Consider how long the lawyers have been using the product you're asking them to give up, or how many years they've been doing things the same way. These considerations don't mean you should shy away from change that disrupts well-established ways of doing things, but it does mean you need to consider certain factors in order to ensure adoption:

- Is the new solution a factor of nine or ten times better than the old one? A solution that introduces a marginally improved way of working might not be worth bringing on if the intent is to dislodge habits and preferences ingrained over 20 years.

- Are there any greenfield areas where you will be introducing a type of solution for the first time rather than replacing an old one? Projects that involve adopting a new solution without giving up an old one will not suffer from the Endowment Effect. Though you will still be dealing with Status Quo bias and the way things have always been done, projects where you are introducing something entirely new may shift the ratio around behavioral losses and gains and make it easier to gain adoption.

- Are there ways to minimize the behavior change involved in transitioning to a new solution? Rather than introducing entirely new workflows, for example, can you build the new solution into existing workflows? The more you align a new solution with existing ways of working, the more likely it is to be adopted.

- If you can't build it in to existing workflows, can you find ways to make it a natural extension of existing workflows, or to show where the new workflow should sit within current workflows? If you are introducing an automated review solution, can you provide guidance and signposts to allow people to easily understand at what stage during their usual matter workflow they need to take a step left and access the new solution to undertake that part of the process, and then how they afterwards get back to their standard matter workflow? Helping users understand exactly where within their regular habitual patterns the new solution fits in will minimize the disruption caused by a new process or solution.

- Can you introduce change in steps, so that rather than replacing an entire platform or solution or workflow you begin by replacing only one part of it? Think of the way social media platforms introduce change. They don't change the whole interface all at once, they change one page or aspect within it at a time so that once you've adopted those and the new look and feel has started to feel less strange, they can move on to the next change.

- How can you frame the gains in a way that emphasizes their significance and improves the overall ratio of losses and gains in relation to the behavior change?

- Can you add a degree of autonomy to the change so that people feel they are choosing it themselves? Some software releases within existing products are introduced in a way that allows the users themselves to voluntarily elect to adopt it. On your home screen, for example, you might see a button that encourages you to try the new version of an existing product, or to adopt the new look for a page. Teasers of the benefits of the new version are presented to the user, and eventually, especially with word of mouth from other users, many users will choose to upgrade voluntarily.

- As people come on board with the new solution, can you phase out the old one gradually? Removing it swiftly all at once is likely to cause high levels of anxiety, but if users are given the option of gradually moving to the new solution and the incumbent option is eliminated bit-by-bit, the anxiety can be reduced and adoption elevated.

Assessing the behavior change necessary for adoption

Whenever you're faced with an adoption problem, remember that your users are being asked to change their behavior. Resistance to a new way of doing things will be proportionate to the size of the behavior change required of them. John Gourville proposed a matrix that can help teams introducing new products and solutions assess the likelihood of whether users will adopt those solutions and shed light on how long such adoption might take (see Figure 42 on the next page).[29] When regarding a new technology or a new process, Gourville's matrix suggests you look at the extent to which the innovation introduces new, beneficial change against the degree of behavior change required.[30]

- *Easy sells* are those solutions that provide limited new benefits but also require limited behavior change. An example of an easy sell might include a new feature in Word that automatically appears in an upgrade. It's easy to adopt because it's right there in Word, but it also won't change a huge amount about the way someone works. These micro-innovations represent the most common category of new products on the market broadly – like familiar candies that now have all organic ingredients, or the same toothpaste brand that now comes with a whitening agent. Innovation teams can get good traction internally by introducing more micro-innovations within existing workflows and products, but they won't be the kind of big bang innovations that lead to disruptive change.

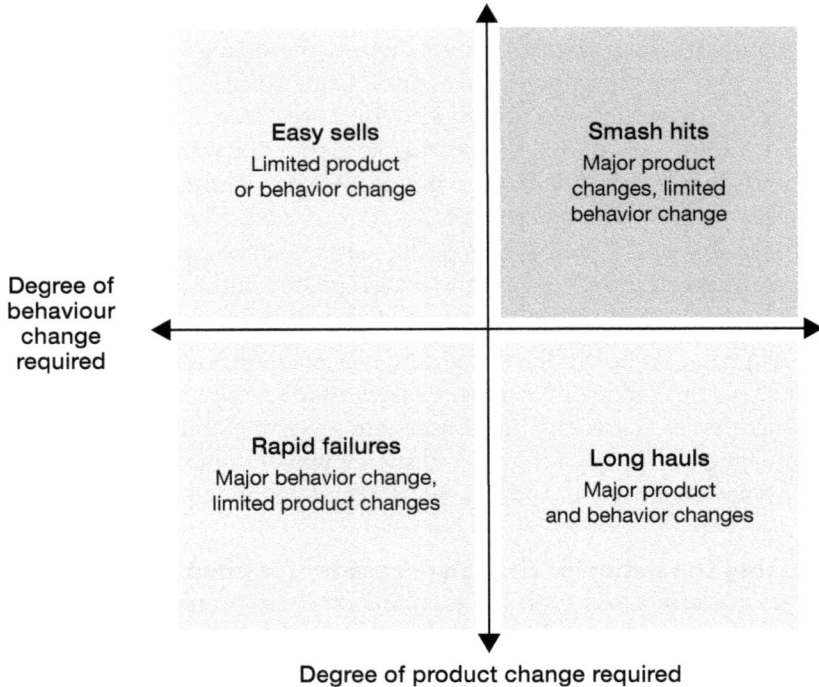

Figure 42: Assessing behavior change necessary for adoption. Adapted from Gourville.

- *Sure failures* are changes that provide limited new benefits or change but require a huge amount of behavior change. A new word processing app that marginally improves version control but requires lawyers to move out of Microsoft Word might be an example here. It's unlikely to be adopted because it requires so much behavior change from the lawyers but doesn't offer them much in return. Needless to say, these types of projects should be identified upfront and avoided.

- *Long hauls* are innovations that offer vast benefits and create great value but also require substantial behavior change. These are worth undertaking, but the change and adoption program has to have a long tail – it will require ongoing work over many years to generate significant adoption. An example of a long haul innovation is introducing a document management system if previously everyone in a legal team has saved locally or on SharePoint. The centralization of documents and departmental knowledge is worth the disruption, but the massive change in how people save documents and use taxonomies will need to be carefully managed. The introduction of a contract lifecycle management system in a large organization is another example of long haul change.

- *Smash hits* are projects that offer substantial benefit and require minimal behavior change. These are the projects that are most likely to succeed in both the short- and the long-term. An example of a potential smash hit solution is a smart drafting tool that is embedded within both Word and the document management system or a knowledge repository, offering lawyers the ability to save and utilize high quality precedent clauses in real time as they're drafting. The solution operates within Word as a side panel to the document they are drafting, so behavior change is minimal, and yet it completely transforms the way that they are able to draft.

Planning for adoption at the project level should involve a review of the new solution at the outset to really understand the ratio of losses to gains that users will experience if they adopt it. This calculus may change over time as the firm's culture gradually changes, and as products evolve, so it's worth re-visiting projects you put on the back burner from time to time. However, taking on projects that should be recognized at the outset as sure failures from an adoption perspective is an easy way to lose credibility in your firm, and for your team to feel ineffectual. Firms with a lot of unused software products lying around – or "shelfware" as it is colloquially called – have not planned well for adoption.

The adoption curve and the virtue of patience

Even beyond behavioral psychology, there are some people who simply won't adopt any product easily or rapidly. Conversely, there are others who will consistently adopt new solutions rapidly. Everett M. Rogers, in his book *Diffusion of Innovations*, set out a lifecycle for consumer adoption of products that is helpful in the context of solution adoption generally.[31] In his research on innovations in the market, Rogers found that once a new innovation is launched, it takes a number of years to fully penetrate or "diffuse" the market.[32] The adoption timeline over that period typically looks like an S-curve, as shown in Figure 43 on the next page. The reason for the disparate adoption levels over time is that different types of people adopt solutions at varying rates.

The adoption curve depicts those adopter categories, which Rogers defined as "the classifications of members of a social system on the basis of innovativeness".[33] The classifications include innovators, early adopters,

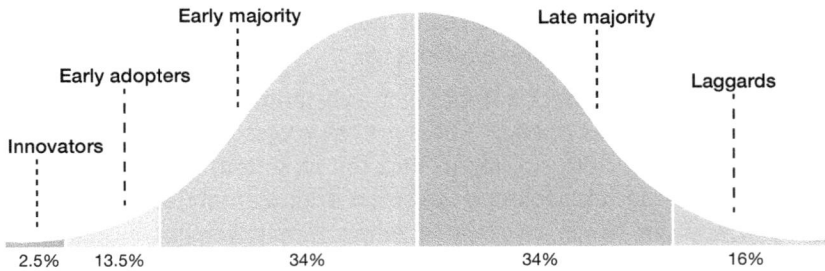

Figure 43: The product adoption lifecycle.[34]

early majority, late majority, and laggards. In each adopter category, individuals grouped together are similar in terms of their innovativeness, which Rogers defined as "the degree to which an individual or other unit of adoption is relatively earlier in adopting new ideas than other members of a system".[35] The adopter categories can be defined as follows:

- *Innovators* are the first group to adopt new solutions. These tend to be highly curious people who are passionate about technology and like experimenting or "playing" with something new. They are often technologists themselves.[36] Innovators represent only a small percentage of a target user base.[37]

- *Early adopters* also jump in early to a new technology or solution, but their motivation is different. Unlike innovators, they tend to adopt because they're interested in using the solution to address their actual problems – not to play. Early adopters generally represent about ten percent of the user population.[38] They are unlikely to be decision-makers, but can be opinion influencers and might be part of extensive communication networks, which means their word of mouth support is critical for later adoption.[39] Once a critical mass of early adopters has developed, Rogers' process of "technology diffusion" hits a tipping point and spills over to the early majority. At this point, the adoption process is somewhat self-sustaining.

- The *early majority* of adopters typically makes up about 40 percent of the target user base.[40] These are people who like to "wait and see" about a product or a solution until there is an evident stream of satisfied users and technical standards have been clarified.[41] Members of the early majority need to be convinced by references before they invest time or money into a new solution.[42] They are deliberate in their adoption of new solutions and take more time to make an adoption decision.[43] Large law firms are generally part of the early majority or later on the adoption curve when it comes to procuring technology products.[44]

- The *late majority* is similar to the early majority in terms of what they expect from a solution, but they are generally more risk-averse and potentially less confident in their own ability to master a solution (if they are users) or to deploy and implement it successfully (if they are buying organizations).[45] The late majority is characterized by "followers" and represents about 30-40 percent of the total user base. Although they are skeptical about the innovation and its outcomes, they can be susceptible to peer pressure.[46] To reduce the uncertainty of the innovation, interpersonal networks of close peers should persuade the late majority to adopt it.[47] Word-of-mouth will make the late majority feel "safe" enough to adopt a new solution.[48]

- *Laggards* are resistant to change and generally technology-averse. If they buy or use a solution at all it will be because it has become so ubiquitous that they have little choice but to do so.[49] They are difficult to deal with, requiring a low price (if they are buyers) and a lot of hand-holding and support (if they are users). Laggards constitute about ten percent of the user base.[50]

There are two important things to note with this breakdown of adoption personas. One is that each persona group has unique characteristics, so different adoption and communications tactics will be successful with each one.[51] Understanding these personas will help you think strategically about your roll-out plan, and how it might affect each of these groups. Innovators just need to be handed the keys to the new solution and encouraged to play with it. Early adopters need to be shown how the solution addresses their specific problem. The early majority needs references from existing users proving that the solution works and adoption won't be a waste of their time. The late majority need more cajoling, a groundswell of word-of-mouth peer pressure, and reassurances that there is nothing to fear from the new solution. Laggards will always take the longest to adopt and will need the most white-glove hand-holding and support. If you and your team can identify upfront who in the targeted user group for a new solution is likely to fall into each group, it will help you to direct the appropriate type of communications and tactics to the right people. Failing that, as different categories of adopters come on board at different times over the adoption process, you can schedule the appropriate types of communications and tactics to occur at the right times during the adoption curve so they have the greatest impact.

The second thing to note is that Roger's research, and the many years of research that have since been done to confirm his models, proves that adoption will *always* take time – no matter what. One of the most important things you can teach your team is that they will need to have patience and brace for slow adoption on every project. To be successful, any roll-out program around a new solution or process must take into account a long, drawn-out adoption process, managed accordingly.[52] If you or members of your team wrongly assume that the adoption of new solutions will be rapid, you will run the risk of depleting your resources too quickly, and become despondent in the face of slow change, even though the pace of change you're dealing with is perfectly normal.

The qualities of adoptable innovations

In addition to his research on the adoption curve, Rogers looked at the qualities of products that were most likely to be adopted. Unlike behavioral psychologists such as Kahneman, Tversky, and Thaler, Rogers didn't focus on the psychological obstacles people endure when being persuaded to change. Instead, he focused on the evolution or reinvention of products and services so that they become a better fit for users.[53] In other words, in his research it's not the people who change – it's the products that change to become a better fit for the people.

In examining what characterized the innovations that were more likely to be adopted than others, Rogers identified five influential attributes:[54]

1. *Relative advantage.* A corollary to the endowment effect, relative advantage describes the degree to which a product or process is perceived by users to be better than the solution currently being used.[55] The greater the improvement, the greater the likelihood of adoption.

2. *Compatibility.* This characteristic measures the extent to which an innovation is considered to be consistent with existing values and ways of doing things.[56] A new solution that is incompatible with existing systems and workflows is less likely to be adopted than one that is compatible with users' current experiences and ways of working.[57]

3. *Complexity.* New solutions that are easier to understand and more intuitive will be adopted faster than those that require users to master new skills and behaviors. Complexity therefore measures the degree

to which an innovation is perceived as difficult to comprehend and use.[58]

4. *Trialability.* This characteristic measures the degree to which an innovation can be experimented with on a limited basis; in other words, how easy is it to pilot the solution to determine whether it will work for the user or not.[59] An innovation that is "trialable" represents less uncertainty and lower risk to the individual who is considering it.

5. *Observability.* If users are able to see or visualize the (positive) results of a new solution, they are more likely to adopt it.[60] Being able to show visible results – especially within the end user's specific environment – has the effect of lowering uncertainty about the solution. Role modeling (or peer observation) is the key motivational factor in the adoption and diffusion of technology.[61] It also has the effect of stimulating peer discussion about a product ("word of mouth"), which for Rogers represents one of the most important factors leading to adoption.[62]

According to Rogers, these five characteristics can predict the rate of adoption of a new solution. Together, they determine between 49 and 87 percent of variations in the adoption of new solutions.[63]

By examining the solution you are rolling out (or propose to roll out) in light of these five characteristics, you will be able to identify weaknesses in your offerings ahead of time and limit the risk of low adoption. Hopefully you have not chosen to implement a solution that is not compatible with your organization's existing system, or where the vendor will not permit you to trial it, but the other factors are a little more nuanced and require some upfront consideration as you review potential projects. Rogers' five characteristics of innovation should be one of the guides you consistently use in evaluating solutions before making a procurement decision.

But what do you do if, upon reviewing a solution you have developed or configured internally, you recognize that it is likely to be viewed as too complex, or too much of a departure from the status quo to be adopted well?

Rogers considered reinvention to be critical to successful innovation.[64] The success of an innovation, according to Rogers, depends on how well it is able to evolve to meet the needs of demanding and risk-averse users in the market.[65] Many of the more successful products on the market continue to succeed because they involve end users in the process of evolving, or reinventing, the product.[66] As you develop or customize solutions internally, remember that going back to users frequently to find out what makes most sense for them, or what would solve their problems best (as the problems, too, evolve over time) will help you ensure that the solution you're providing is suitable and will be used. Rogers held the view that no product or process is ever completely finished; continuous improvement is the key to spreading an adoption.[67]

Locking in the old with the new

In chapter nine, locking in the old with the new was mentioned as a critical aspect of change management that would be addressed later in this chapter. Generally speaking, a change cannot be said to have happened until it has become the "new normal". Status quo bias adheres to the old way of doing things, but as people's behavior changes, the new ways of doing things will eventually become the status quo. People who join the organization after the change has been introduced will never know the old way of doing things – the new way will simply be business as usual for them.

Kurt Lewin, a pioneer of organizational and social psychology in the United States, developed a simple model of change management involving just three steps – unfreezing, changing, and refreezing.[68] In the unfreezing stage, because many people will naturally resist the change, the goal is to make people aware of how the status quo is unacceptable or how it is preventing the organization from moving forwards or being as competitive as it could be.[69] Similar to Kotter's burning platform, the aim is to make people feel a sense of urgency in order to encourage them to shift out of complacency and become willing to make a change.[70] Once they become "unfrozen", they will be willing to move with the right motivation. The changing step, which is the transition period from the old to the new, is when the new solution or process is implemented. It's when most people struggle, and when resistance really becomes an issue. During this time, as discussed in chapters nine and ten, people need education, strong communications, support, and the time to learn new processes, behaviors, and ways of thinking.[71]

Once people have moved through the change, however, the new state has to be frozen into place (for the time being, until another change comes along). Lewin's term "refreezing" refers to the act of reinforcing the change but also stabilizing it and solidifying it after the transitional stage.[72] Although some commentators feel that refreezing is unnecessary in the modern corporate world because things are constantly in flux and there is a stream of continuous change, this critique is unfounded. Refreezing does not mean that you are instigating stagnation. Rather, each progressive change made must be cemented into the organization's culture or else people will revert back to the old way of doing things – the common "one step forward, two steps back" phenomenon. Along the path to full digital transformation, for example, you are likely to have many discrete changes over a period of years. Each of those must be widely accepted as the right way of doing things before you move onto the next step of the transformation journey. There is no reason to invest time, effort, and resources into a change project if you are not going to take it through to the end by ensuring it is accepted as the new normal.

Locking in the new with the old can mean that you build new processes into existing workflows. It might mean that you ensure that easy links to the new solution appear in all of the relevant systems that your lawyers regularly use. It means that any system or process that touches the new solution is adapted to accommodate the new solution, so that the integration or connection between them is seamless. It also likely means using structural incentives to build the new solution into the culture of the organization in other ways.

Incentives

In order to lock in a change, reinforcement through positive rewards, acknowledgement of outstanding individual efforts, and other incentive programs are often used to define the new normal. Positively reinforced behavior is more likely to be repeated.[73]

Organizations have numerous measures available to them to incentivize adoption. The hierarchy, status, and rigidity that make law firms run can serve them well when it comes to recognizing and rewarding their staff. The KWM case study included earlier in this chapter illustrates concrete ways that a firm can leverage internal structures in order to create an environment where capability building around new solutions is expected, rewarded, and recognized. As innovation leaders, part of your job is to find ways of building these rewards and recognitions into the fabric of the firm so that contribution to innovation initiatives and effort spent taking up new solutions is understood to be expected from all employees. Examples of tried and true incentive programs include:

- The most obvious incentive: awarding prizes (gift cards, even Starbucks gift cards, have been shown to work) for hitting certain targets in the new solution. Providing free lunches, pizza parties, cookies or doughnuts in exchange for word-of-mouth stories, or to get people along to training, is a well-trodden path to generating engagement around a solution. These sorts of incentives are not structural in the same way that some of the other incentives are below, but rewards can be effective nevertheless.

- Billable hours credit or forgiveness: make it easy for people to spend the time getting training and learning how to use the system by giving them billable hours credit for that time. Firms that have the kind of deeply entrenched support from above that allows for a billable hours credit program, whether it provides associates with a set number of hours across the board for innovation work or allows them to apply for credit where relevant to their practice, are more likely to get traction with their innovation initiatives both because of the incentive this constitutes, and because the kind of top-down buy-in reflected by such a program sends a message to everyone at the firm that innovation is important.[74]

- Performance and bonuses: if you are able to do so, make training on and adoption of new systems relevant to performance tracking for professionals at the firm. Spending some small percentage of time over the year on innovation efforts should represent one of the key performance indicators for all members of the firm. Contribution to or attending training on new systems can even be built into the considerations determining end-of-year bonuses. If an associate knows that failing to attend training on a new solution, or failing to adopt the transaction management system that his or her practice is now using, may lead to a smaller bonus, they are much more likely to change their behavior.

- Certification programs: develop certifications for internal (or external!) distribution, that celebrate people who have undertaken the training and hit certain milestones in the new solution.

- Build a leader board or a competitive element into the tool, so that when people log in they can see where they stand compared to others or at least track their own performance as they chart towards performance milestones.

- As your adoption program ensues over time, hold events that gamify adoption in a fun way. You can stage these in person or virtually. Time-bound initiatives like week-long boot camps and summer camps with advanced training and games that get people using the system are examples. Another idea is holding a game show night with your managing partner as host, featuring the product and involving your power users competing to display their advanced knowledge of it. Your creative innovation team will be able to brainstorm many other such concepts.

A note on disincentives

It has been common in corporate culture for many years to talk about motivating people with the "carrot and the stick" approach. This term is derived from the old analogy of motivating a donkey to pull a cart either by hanging a carrot in front of it or hitting it with a stick from behind. The carrot denotes positive reinforcement while the stick represents punishment, which the corporate world has widely assumed equates to negative reinforcement. In fact, the concept of motivating behavior through positive and negative reinforcement has its origins in the psychological field of Applied Behavior Analysis (ABA), and negative reinforcement is not intended to be synonymous with punishment. Instead, negative reinforcement refers to the practice of reinforcing desired behavior by removing something (rather than by giving something, which is positive reinforcement).[75] ABA proponents suggest that both negative and positive reinforcement are necessary to produce a desired behavior.[76] Many of the adoption tactics used in corporate environments are in fact negative reinforcement tactics, though we might not recognize them as such. For example, removing access to a shared drive as people start to save documents into a document management system is a negative reinforcement. When it comes to punishment, which is different from negative reinforcement, it has been found to be less successful at generating desired behavior in the workplace.[77] Although good behavior might be generated in the short-term, the long-term psychological effects of punishment outweigh these immediate wins.[78] Employees who are penalized for lack of adoption or performance are likely to feel isolated and unsupported, resulting in hostile behavior, lack of engagement, and heightened anxiety.[79] It is therefore recommended to discontinue adoption tactics that draw upon the notion of a "stick" to drive compliance with desired behavior. Reinforcement, both positive and negative, should provide a rich enough toolkit to draw upon without needing to resort to outright penalties for non-compliance.

Remedial adoption

Regardless of how well you develop a strategy for holistic adoption, or plan your projects with adoption in mind, it's almost inevitable that you will end up with some projects that are not well adopted. This means that, at the end of a project, in spite of your best efforts to plan for adoption and implement change programs throughout the project, you are left with lower usage rates than you wanted. In these circumstances, taking on adoption as a project in and of itself may make sense in order to specifically address the low usage. See the case study below for an example of a firm that was able to get great traction with a core system that had low adoption rates by designing a five-month program to drive adoption. Note that there is a difference between this type of program and ongoing promotion around a solution, which should continue for more than a year after launch. Note also that remedial adoption is only worth attempting where you know the solution is the right one and lack of adoption is not indicative of a failed initiative. There is no shame in pivoting away from a solution that was rolled out and never got adoption because it turned out to be the wrong product for your users. In those circumstances, by far the best response after your team has done what it can to turn the situation around, is to recognize it for the learning experience it is and move in a different direction.

Case study: Adoption success story at Nauta Dutilh

Large Benelux law firm Nauta Dutilh recognized that its core operational tool (governing timekeeping, conflicts, and intake workflows) was being under-utilized, to the detriment of the firm. In order to generate better adoption of this tool across every part of the firm, the leadership team launched a dedicated project focused entirely on driving adoption.

Project Professionalize was put in place to generate business transformation and improved performance in five key business areas – client focus, business integrity, working capital management, matter lifecycle, and employee engagement. In relation to each of these areas, the firm defined metrics that allowed for the tracking of performance. At that stage, an innovative system was put in place to publicly measure adoption and compliance. A color system was introduced that clearly signaled the performance of each practice group:

- A red score illustrated the performance was below standard;
- Orange meant that performance was below standard but within an acceptable range; and

- Green showed that performance was meeting – or exceeding – the standard.

The performance of each practice group and business department was regularly measured against the metrics during a five-month period, and the scores for each group were available across the firm, enabling benchmarking and giving rise to healthy competition. Each group's score was regularly compared against their scores for the previous month, so they could also easily see what progress they were making. During the tracking period, lawyers and staff were also supported with guidance including advanced training, suggested actions for increasing performance, and research to overcome change resistance.

Outcome: Lawyers and other employees became competitive and interested in seeing whether their improvement increased from month to month, and what their progress looked like in comparison to other groups. Vital insights into the drivers and barriers of success were collected by the firm. An important objective of the Professionalize team was to generate insights into the context of why people do what they do, and to develop an understanding of the drivers and barriers of standard-compliant behavior. The main learning was that sustainable improvement could be successfully achieved if the organization provided support along the path to habit formation, thus making it easier for individuals to comply.

Project Professionalize and the associated adoption processes made a significant impact at the firm in three main areas. Overall performance increased in all five business areas due to continued monitoring across the board. In particular:

- The backlog in timely handling of so-called Party Verification Requests (KYC) decreased by 80 percent;
- The backlog in time entry decreased by 31 percent; and
- The use of a particular function in the intake software grew from two percent to 70 percent in one of the practice groups.

At the completion of the five-month roll-out, a complete picture of overall performance was generated using a heat map, enabling the project team to prioritize and focus ongoing actions. Instead of deeming the project over or complete, they continued to work on driving adoption, for example by amplifying small wins to drive better behavior and further accelerate improvements.

For the first time, an overall view and understanding was generated of the role that people, process, and technology played in the key business areas highlighted by Project Professionalize, enabling the executive committee and board to improve coordination of future initiatives at the firm.

Adoption metrics

One of the aspects of Project Professionalize that made it so successful is the fact that the firm's leadership team sat down ahead of time to map out exactly what it wanted to accomplish and how to measure progress. It focused on five key business areas and defined metrics to track and measure performance in each of those. "You can't manage what you don't measure" is a common management adage that is often attributed to Peter Drucker. Although in fact Drucker did not write these exact words, and though as it pertains to people management this adage has since received criticism,[80] it remains true when it comes to adoption. Unless you measure the extent to which people are using a new solution, you will be unable to tweak your methods and adjust tactics to improve adoption. Measuring user adoption will also give you deeper insight into how your users are leveraging the solution and allow you to continuously improve and tweak it to ensure ongoing usage.

As part of any project, metrics should be defined in advance that will help you track and record not just adoption, but also performance of the solution in the key areas of business transformation that it is designed to tackle. Processes to measure and track these metrics should also be developed, with responsibility allocated for ongoing recording and evaluation. Part of a post roll-out plan should involve checking in on a regular basis to look at adoption and other metrics in the system to determine (a) how usage is evolving over time, and (b) whether other performance metrics in the system indicate ways that you could increase usage by tweaking configurations in the system. An example of the latter can be seen in the roll-out of an enterprise search system. One of the metrics you should build in relation to such a project is the ability to see what keyword searches are being conducted most regularly. Once you understand that, you can perform those searches yourself to see whether the right type of content – the best and most useful content – is appearing at the top of the results page. If it is not, you may need to tweak the relevancy in the search system to make sure that users will find what they're looking for during their most regular searches. Doing so will build credibility in the system and help increase adoption.

Of course, tracking adoption metrics will also help you to understand whether there is a serious problem with adoption that requires remediation planning, and it can demonstrate success and value in a new solution that will then allow you to prove to management that there is good return on their investment. Metrics are therefore a vital part of adoption planning for a variety of reasons.

Training

Many firms equate adoption programs with training programs. They are not the same, but training on a new solution or process will almost always be part of the adoption phase of a change program. I do not intend to go into depth in this chapter (or, indeed, in this book) on the various types of training or experiential learning and their relative benefits. There is much written on the subject, and most law firms will have training staff who have expertise in this area. Those who don't have dedicated staff will usually license a third party to support training for a major initiative. However, innovation teams will often be responsible for some part of strategic planning around training for their own solution roll-outs, especially if these are not enterprise-wide, and there are strategic decisions to be made around training that can be instrumental in driving adoption. These include the following:

- Consider what type of training will best suit each persona group affected by the new solution and ensure that you provide a variety of training options that accommodates all of these.

- Offer basic training in short spurts that allow people to get started in the new solution quickly.

- Identify the key activities each persona group will need to undertake in the new solution so that they can continue to work efficiently, and make sure the basic training guides them through those activities.

- Provide this critical day-one training prior to launch, with multiple reminders, so that they can prep ahead for the day the change lands and will know what to expect.

- Create one-on-one appointments with people in the first week so that you can check in on them to make sure they are handling the change well.

- Set up multiple means for users who need help to rapidly contact support if they need it, and ensure the turn-around time is rapid.

- Guarantee that there are staff on call 24/7 (or as close to it as you can manage) during the first days of the change, so that lawyers working late can always reach someone for trouble shooting.

- Ensure that there are multiple training touchpoints and white glove support during the first day post-launch.

- Make users feel that there is excitement in the air, by celebrating the launch with balloons, welcome emails, even doughnuts and coffee, so that they are encouraged to take a positive attitude from the outset and are more likely to attend and embrace training.

- Provide video training options and written guidance, so that people who are introverted or particularly busy have in-office training available to them.

- Newer software often includes in-app training and guidance. Make sure this is switched on and working well so that your users can benefit from it. If the new solution does not include this innately, there are programs such as WalkMe[81] (a "digital adoption program") that allow you to build this type of real-time guidance into other systems. Though it requires significant pre-planning and resources to set up this kind of guidance ahead of time, the effort will certainly pay off for large, mission-critical launches.

Word of mouth

One of the most relevant insights derived from Rogers' research into adoption is that while marketing methods such as advertising can spread information, it is conversations that spread adoption.[82] When it comes down to it, the adoption of new solutions or processes involves risk and uncertainty. This is particularly pertinent for lawyers, whose profession requires them to be risk-averse. Because so much is at stake, users rely on people who they personally know and trust, and who have successfully adopted the new solution themselves, in order to provide them with the credible reassurances they need.[83] Rogers called these kinds of conversations Peer-to-Peer communication exchanges.[84] These channels are more trusted and have greater effectiveness in dealing with resistance or apathy. Only these real-life trusted individuals can satisfy the anxiety of the skeptical to convince them that their own attempts at change won't result in humiliation, wasted time, or other loss.[85]

While innovators and early adopters are not so reliant on these kinds of reassurances, most of your user group will see high risks in any change you introduce and will therefore require assurance from trusted peers that the benefits of a promoted solution are real and worthwhile.[86] One of the interesting aspects of this need for reassurance in our post-COVID, hybrid-working world is that in-person communications are more powerful in driving adoption for late adopters and laggards.[87] The body language and trust generated by face-to-face communications are more persuasive when it comes to adoption user stories than online communications.[88] Leveraging your network of change agents and plugging into the early adopter population to encourage conversation and word-of-mouth recommendations will be essential in propelling usage of a new solution forward so that it reaches a tipping point. Creating in-person opportunities for those conversations to occur will magnify their impact further.

Checklist: Adoption techniques

The checklist below summarizes information in the chapter as well as offering some ideas around adoption activities and events. It should not be viewed as exhaustive, nor do you need to do all of the things listed! There are countless adoption activities that will have a positive impact, and what works well will vary from organization to organization. The most critical thing to remember is that adoption takes time and requires planning. Launching an enterprise-wide solution with an announcement and a week of training will not lead to adoption. At a minimum, you should be planning a year-long calendar of adoption tactics and events that target different adopter personas in a variety of ways.

☐ Strategize for adoption upfront by developing an innovation strategy that builds techniques and a culture likely to lead to increased adoption of innovations broadly.

☐ Strive for 9x or 10x improvement. Wherever possible, choose projects and innovations that provide relative benefits so great that they overcome the user's overweighting of potential losses.

☐ Plan your projects with adoption in mind, taking on only those where the ratio of gains to losses is favorable for adoption. Use Gourville's Adoption Matrix to evaluate projects and prioritize smash hits and long hauls.

☐ Evaluate the solution you're introducing to ensure that it is compatible with the firm's culture and way of doing things, and that it is intuitive rather than complex to adopt.

☐ Where possible, build in the ability to trial a new solution and to visually demonstrate the positive impact of using the solution.

☐ Emphasize the benefits of a new solution or process over the losses of an old way of doing things; fold this into your messaging and signpost it in places where your lawyers work.

☐ Bake the new way of doing things into existing workflows or systems, to ensure that it is compatible with your users' ways of working and to minimize behavior change.

☐ Ensure the integrations between the new solution and any existing systems it touches are as seamless as possible.

☐ Signpost the places within matter workflows when it's appropriate to use the new system, so that users don't need to expend extra energy trying to figure out when to use it.

☐ If possible, introduce the new process or solution in stages, so that users can become comfortable with one aspect of the change at a time.

☐ Consider giving users the ability to self-select into the new system when they're ready, for example by providing access to the new interface or system through a button on a page in the old system. Ensure that you also communicate with users to let them know what to expect from the new system and why it's better, to encourage them to make the move.

☐ Build an adoption program that targets different messaging and support tactics depending on where users fall on the adoption curve.

☐ Utilize early adopters and your network of change agents and encourage them to engage in positive day-to-day conversations about the new solution in their practice groups or business units.

☐ Find ways to bring super-users and non-adopters together in person at events that promote discussion about the new solution.

☐ Celebrate super-users publicly, sending out emails or having law firm leadership announce their success in the new solution so that adoption becomes seen as desirable.

☐ Use senior leaders in the organization – practice group chairs, office chairs, influential partners – to vocalize their support of the new solution, so that users understand the firm has a vested interest in their adoption of it.

☐ Identify metrics related to usage of the new solution and use these to identify non-adopters and to tweak configuration in the system so that it is continuously improving in its ability to delight users.

☐ Create a rewards program for users who attend not just basic but additional levels of training, and who hit certain milestones in the solution.

- [ ] Allow users to access billable hours credit for the time it takes them to get on board with the new solution.
- [ ] Build success in the new solution into existing structural incentive programs such as performance and bonus reviews.
- [ ] Make adoption fun by gamifying it and adding a competitive element. Ideas include:
  - Like Nauta Dutilh, introduce a visual indicator such as the red-orange-green system to show lawyers how they're doing compared to others in their practice, or in other practices.
  - If working in an office space, create a sticker that goes on people's office door or cubicle once they have taken training or hit a certain adoption metric, so that people can see at a glance who has attended training or hit a milestone and who has not.
  - Create a competition with a deadline and have practice groups compete to achieve key metrics within the new solution by a certain date. The winning practice group gets bragging rights and a prize (a swanky dinner at a popular restaurant, for example).
  - Hold an in-person event and make it a big deal at the firm, with key personnel attending. Use a game show framework to have user contestants vying against one another for best use of or knowledge of the solution.
- [ ] Offer refreshments at all in-person training sessions.
- [ ] Make training accessible and offer a variety of types of training, including short videos, written instructions, in-app training, as well as in-person.
- [ ] Create training programs that include basic day-one training that allows users to immediately get going in the system, as well as advanced training spread out over time.
- [ ] Leverage user stories by finding pockets of success across the firm – lawyers who were initially reluctant but are now advocates, people whose use of the new solution provided unexpected success on a client matter, and so on. Record these as videos, podcast snippets, and as written quotes and distribute these regularly across the firm so that stories of happy adopters abound.
- [ ] Send regular newsletters out that include stories of adoption success in the new solution.

☐ Announce the new solution to clients and consider organizing an event where select clients attend to see the new solution in action, so that clients know what type of innovation initiatives their outside counsel have been undertaking. During the client event, have lawyers from different practices demonstrate the solution. Publicize the event and pictures of the event broadly so that non-adopters can see there is client buy-in for innovation initiatives generally, and this solution specifically.

☐ Organize a showcase event with super-adopters using the solution to demonstrate to non-adopters the kinds of things they are able to do in it. These can be undertaken either firm-wide or office by office.

☐ Select associates to attend the partner retreat (and attendant parties) to demonstrate the solution for the partners. Consider holding a competition for the few spots available at the partner retreat, with attendance dependent on milestones reached within the solution.

☐ Hold summer camps or boot camps focused on progression in the solution, with fun activities over a short period of time to draw people in.

☐ Don't stop promoting a new solution for at least a year after launch, or until it becomes fully baked into the existing way of doing things. Your adoption strategy does not end until that point.

☐ Once the tipping point of adoption has been reached, gradually phase out the old solution so that users don't have the option of going back.

References

1 Emmer, M. (2018), *95 Per Cent of New Products Fail: Here are 6 Steps to Make Sure Yours Don't*, www.inc.com/marc-emmer/95-percent-of-new-products-fail-here-are-6-steps-to-make-sure-yours-dont.html#.

2 Punatar, P. and Stewart, A. (2020), *To Succeed, Innovative Financial Products Must be Desirable, Feasible and Viable*, www.accion.org/to-succeed-innovative-financial-products-must-be-desirable-feasible-and-viable

3 IDEO Design Thinking, *Design Thinking Defined*, https://designthinking.ideo.com/.

4 Punatar and Stewart, 2020.

5 *Ibid*.

6 *Ibid*.

7 Rife, N., Syrett, M., Gardner, S., Kohse, J. Jarr-Koroma, S. (2021), "The Innovation Sweet Spot: The Innovation Sweet Spot Sits at the Center of Desirability, Feasibility, and Viability, the Three Tenets of Design Thinking." *The Jabian Journal*: Spring 2021. https://journal.jabian.com/the-innovation-sweet-spot/

8 Gourville, J. T. (2006), *Eager Sellers and Stony Buyers: Understanding the Psychology of New Product Adoption*. Published in Harvard Business Review, https://hbr.org/2006/06/eager-sellers-and-stony-buyers-understanding-the-psychology-of-new-product-adoption

9 *Ibid.*

10 *Ibid.* See also Rogers, E. M. (5th ed.) (2003), *Diffusion of Innovations*. The Free Press: New York, p. 229.

11 Gourville, 2006.

12 *Ibid.*

13 *Ibid.*

14 *Ibid.*

15 *Ibid.*

16 *Ibid.*

17 *Ibid.*

18 As cited in Kahneman, D., Knetsch, J. E., and Thaler, R. H. (1991). "Anomalies: The Endowment Effect, Aversion, and the Status Quo Bias." *Journal of Economic Perspectives*, Vol. 5, No. 1, Winter 2021: pp 193-206. https://pubs.aeaweb.org/doi/pdfplus/10.1257/jep.5.1.193

19 *Ibid.*

20 Kahneman, Knetsch, and Thaler (1991).

21 Gourville, 2006.

22 *Ibid.*

23 *Ibid.*

24 *Ibid.*

25 *Ibid.*

26 *Ibid.*

27 *Ibid.*

28 *Ibid.*

29 Gourville, 2006.

30 *Ibid.*

31 Rogers, 2003.

32 Investaura (2021), *The Art of Business Planning: The Adoption Curve*, www.business-planning-for-managers.com/main-courses/marketing-sales/marketing/the-adoption-curve/

33 Rogers (2003), p.22.

34 Smartsheet (2022), *How to Implement New Software Without Stressing People Out*, www.smartsheet.com/content-center/product-news/resource-management/how-implement-new-software-without-stressing-people

35 *Ibid.*

36 Investaura, 2021.

37 *Ibid.*

38 Rogers (2003), p. 283.

39 *Ibid.*

40 Investaura, 2021.

41 *Ibid.*

42 *Ibid.*

43 Rogers (2003), p. 283.

44 Investaura, 2021.

45 *Ibid.*

46 Rogers (2003), p. 284.

47 *Ibid.*

48 *Ibid.*

49 Investaura, 2021.

50 *Ibid.*

51 Smartsheet, 2022.

52 Schirtzinger, 2022. *An Overview of the Innovation-Adoption Curve.* High Tech Strategies, www.hightechstrategies.com/methods/technology-adoption-lifecycle/innovation-adoption-curve/

53 *Ibid.*, p. 180.

54 *Ibid.*, p. 219.

55 *Ibid.*, p 229.

56 *Ibid.*, p. 15.

57 *Ibid.*

58 *Ibid.*

59 *Ibid.*, p. 16.

60 *Ibid.*

61 Parisot, A.H. (1997), Distance education as a catalyst for changing teaching in the community college: Implications for institutional policy. *New Directions for Community Colleges*, 99, 5-13.

62 Rogers (2003), p. 16.

63 Schirtzinger, W. (2022), *An Overview of the Innovation-Adoption Curve.* High Tech Strategies, www.hightechstrategies.com/methods/technology-adoption-lifecycle/innovation-adoption-curve

64 *Ibid.*

65 *Ibid.*

66 *Ibid.*

67 *Ibid.*

68 Hartzell, S., *Lewin's 3-Stage Model of Change: Unfreezing, Changing & Refreezing.* Study.com, 11 September 2012, https://study.com/academy/lesson/lewins-3-stage-model-of-change-unfreezing-changing-refreezing.html

69 *Ibid.*

70 *Ibid.*

71 *Ibid.*

72 *Ibid.*

73 *Ibid.*

74 The notion of using billable hours credit as an incentive to increase adoption assumes that you work in an environment where lawyers bill by the hour. In legal departments, this is generally not the case. In firms, it largely still is, but some commentators dislike the notion of billable hours credit because it ties innovation work to the very business model that it is trying to disrupt. However, change is incremental, and locking in each change with the new requires using some of the old structures to embed change before moving to the next one. If you have to leverage existing structures in order to ensure a new solution is adopted, even if you dislike those existing structures, you should do so now. Eventually, when you get to the point where your next change can be eliminating the billable hour, you will have gotten there by virtue of the many changes along the way that had to be locked down first before moving onto the next one.

75 Dalphonse, A.

76 *Ibid.*

77 Milbourn, G. Jr. (1996), Punishment in the Workplace Causes Undesirable Side Effects, *Wichita Business Journal*: November 1996.

78 *Ibid.*

79 Assad, A. (2021), *The Effects of Punishment on Employee Behavior*, Chron, https://smallbusiness.chron.com/effects-punishment-employee-behavior-14302.html

80 Zak, P. (2013), *Measurement Myopia*, The Drucker Institute, www.drucker.institute/thedx/measurement-myopia/.

81 www.walkme.com/

82 Schirtzinger, 2022.

83 *Ibid.*

84 *Ibid.*

85 *Ibid.*

86 *Ibid.*

87 *Ibid.*

88 *Ibid.*

Conclusion

Most of this book has dealt with internal innovation leaders and teams, some of whom may also have responsibility for external or client-facing projects and initiatives. Although external teams have been mentioned, and the importance of working with clients has been emphasized, innovation groups that sit entirely outside of a firm have not been the focus of this handbook because most firms are still primarily intent on driving innovation from within their existing business structures. As the landscape around legal transformation evolves, however, it's important to end with some notes on these external innovation programs. This is where real, transformative change is likely to build momentum.

In 2022, Legaltech Hub conducted a significant amount of research on the market for legal innovation globally. We established a benchmark, based on our research, that can be used to evaluate and measure the maturity of innovation programs at law firms. Having regard to what initiatives are being undertaken by innovation, KM, and legal technology teams, we were able to identify ten key indicators of internal innovation maturity and ten indicators for external innovation maturity. Although each of these indicators is important and relevant for establishing a benchmark, one factor stands out as being the most critical for illustrating that a firm is a leader in innovation. That factor is what we call "freedom to act", meaning the ability for innovation teams and personnel to act outside of or independent of the structures of a law firm.

As discussed early in part one, a consistent challenge for internal innovation teams is that they are beholden to the existing business model of the firm or organization in which they sit. Although law firms and legal departments are recognizing the importance and increasing necessity to "go digital" by automating processes and systems and modernizing both the practice of law and the delivery of legal services, most law firm leaders and general counsel don't yet have a real appreciation of how deeply the organization has to buy into that change if it is going to have the desired effect. It is not enough to hire professionals with change management, technology, innovation, or legal operations skills, or to give them a trans-formation mandate. It's certainly not enough to hire some former lawyers and ask them to "innovate" so that a firm has a response when clients ask superficial RFP questions about the firm's use of technology. Digital transformation is exactly what it says it is – a transformation. Undertaking any kind of true transformation necessarily involves disrupting existing systems and processes. That means, as highlighted by Christensen's work on the innovator's dilemma, law firms must find a way to provide spaces for these efforts that are free from the constraints of the ordinary struc-tures that define them.

In 2013, Clayton Christensen and his colleagues Dina Wang and Derek van Bever wrote an article in the *Harvard Business Review* outlining the extraordinary success of McKinsey & Company's subsidiary entity, McKinsey Solutions, which was launched in 2007.[1] The authors defined McKinsey Solutions as comprising "software and technology-based analytics and tools that can be embedded at a client, providing ongoing engagement outside the traditional project-based model". They explained that at the time McKinsey Solutions was launched, the share of consulting work that remained "classic strategy" was on the decline, with management consulting firms seeing their competitive position eroded by "technology, alternative staffing models, and other forces".[2] As a result of these changes in the market, the authors posited, the industry of management consulting was on the verge of disruption. Initiatives like Mckinsey Solutions, which provides for ongoing engagement outside the typical project-based model of consulting, and puts the focus on "hard knowledge assets" and an "unbundling" of McKinsey's traditional offerings, were ideally situated to succeed in this market. Christensen et al. proceeded to discuss the legal industry, pointing to it as one facing similar pressures and that had reached a comparable inflection point. The authors' view was that consulting could learn lessons from legal, which was already seeing more alternative offer-ings and the unbundling of services.

Indeed, in 2013, the first law firm subsidiaries were already being launched.[3] Christensen et al. cite an AdvanceLaw survey of general counsel that found that 79 percent agreed that the unbundling of legal services would rise.[4] They also pointed to the Altman Weil survey of law firm managing partners and chairs, which found that though in 2009 only 42 percent expected to see more price competition, by 2012 that number had climbed to 92 percent.[5]

The legal pressures in the market that Christensen et al. pointed to in 2013 have only risen since then. As explored in the introduction to this book, regulatory changes, new competitors in the legal industry, advances in technology, and the practice by corporate legal teams of sending less work to outside counsel, or leveraging alternative legal service providers for some of the work that outside counsel used to do, have all given rise to a market that puts traditional law firm models under even more pressure. If Christensen et al. thought in 2013 that we were close to a tipping point for disrupting the practice of law, a decade later in 2023 we are on its very precipice.

Many firms globally appear to have recognized this. Subsidiary entities that serve as R&D entities, product development, and sales organizations, or that provide alternative legal services at lower price points than their parent firms have proliferated in the past ten years. In the UK, Allen & Overy's Aosphere, Eversheds Sutherlands' legal innovation consulting business Konexo, and Linklaters' Nakhoda are prime examples. In the US, Wilson Sonsini's SixFifty, Reed Smith's Gravity Stack, and Littler Mendelson's JV with Neota Logic, ComplianceHR, have all been successful endeavors. This kind of disruptive offering by law firms is not limited to the larger markets, however. Many of the Canadian top tier firms have established ALSPs or subsidiary entities. In Germany, a number of firms have established separate GMBH entities to undertake legal technology development. And the rate at which firms are launching these types of offerings is also increasing. In 2022, Cleary Gottlieb and Norton Rose Fulbright launched their subsidiary entities within a month of one another (Cleary X and LX Studio, respectively).

Law firm subsidiaries all look a little different, which is to be expected. The leadership of each firm envisages the impact of disruption in their own way and develops what they consider to be the most strategic response accordingly. Unlike McKinsey Solutions, and in defiance of Christensen's predictions, most of these subsidiaries are not yet significantly profitable. What they provide, however, is an alternative strategy, a new play in the market that gives the firms who have launched subsidiaries a chance at one day owning viable alternative legal businesses even as their traditional models fail. In short, it means they have a horse in the disruption race.

We are approaching the point at which law firms that have not yet considered or launched a competitive offering are at significant risk of falling behind or losing large chunks of business as the market continues to evolve. Running an internally focused innovation program will simply not be enough to compete with firms that have external subsidiaries providing legal or legal-adjacent services through an entirely different business model, delivering new types of products and services to clients in different ways and at greater value. Internal innovation is bound and confined by the structure of the traditional law firm offering, and it is almost impossible to develop or sell a disruptive offering from that position. This type of innovation is unlikely to result in transformative change.

If your role and that of your team is restricted to internal innovation efforts and you are not given leeway to interact with clients, charge for your work, or develop new revenue streams for the firm, it is incumbent upon you to challenge the status quo. That's what it means to be a chaos pilot. You will need to break things, occasionally. The fact that you were hired means the firm or organization understands there is a need for change. The consequent obstacles thrown in the way of disruptive efforts means you will need to find a way to show leadership what the benefits of real transformation might look like – and what the results might be if they fall behind while that transformation in the industry is led by others. Without the ability to actually do things in new ways, your impact will be minimal and the firm may not survive in the legal landscape of the future.

The guidance provided in this book will serve you well as you set out to develop a team and build a strategy for change. In order to truly future-proof your firm, however, you will need to look externally and burst free of the shackles of traditional legal models.

References

1   Christensen, C. M., Wang, D., and van Bever, D. (2013), "Consulting on the Cusp of Disruption", *Harvard Business Review*, https://hbr.org/2013/10/consulting-on-the-cusp-of-disruption

2   *Ibid.*

3   Freshfields Bruckhaus Deringer launched Freshfields Continuum in mid-2012 (*Ibid*).

4   Christensen et al., 2013.

5   *Ibid.*

Acknowledgements

This book took a long time to write. It was perhaps not advisable to take it on during a global pandemic and at the same time that I was also planning a leap from a steady, salaried job in a law firm into full-time entrepreneurship.

Juggling my day job, a side-gig, teaching classes, raising children and also writing a book meant that there were many weekends, late nights, and early mornings of writing – which took its toll not just on me, but on my loved ones.

My heartfelt thanks to my husband Chris, for supporting me through it all, bringing me cups of coffee and believing in me endlessly, and to my wonderful children Iggy and Lulu, for being my biggest, sweetest cheerleaders and giving me the snuggles I needed to get through. Thank you to my parents, Peter and Jenefer, to my brother Adam, and to Matteo. All of you have given me the encouragement I needed to persevere over the past few years, and have encouraged and applauded my endless curiosity and thirst for knowledge even when it sometimes led to left-field decisions.

Thanks also to my lovely, wise editor Alex Davies, who has had to exercise super-human patience with me and who remained calm, helpful, and resourceful throughout, and to the wonderful Sian O'Neill, who provided encouragement from the sidelines.

Imposter syndrome is real and I am indebted to the mentors, especially the female mentors, that I have been privileged to know and learn from. You have all taught me so much and allowed me to build expertise and confidence through your quiet coaching – Andrea Alliston, Kate Simpson, Carla Swansburg, Amy Wegener, Isabel Parker, and Caryn Sandler. Thank you also to Simon Wormwell and John Gillies for believing in me from the early days, and to Alex Smith and Nir Golan for endless product and service design discussions and for your friendship, especially when the world went dark.

Thanks to Jeroen Plink for throwing his weight behind me and all of my most radical ideas, for lifting me up and giving me the space to pursue my passions.

A special thank you to Oz Benamram, for his support from the moment I arrived in New York, and for his generous foreword to this book.

About Globe Law and Business

Globe Law and Business was established in 2005. From the very beginning, we set out to create law books that are sufficiently high level to be of real use to the experienced professional, yet still accessible and easy to navigate. Most of our authors are drawn from Magic Circle and other top commercial firms, both in the United Kingdom and internationally.

Our titles are carefully produced, with the utmost attention paid to editorial, design and production processes. We hope this results in high-quality publications that are easy to read and a pleasure to own. Our titles are also available as ebooks, which are compatible with most desktop, laptop and tablet devices. In 2018 we expanded our portfolio to include journals and Special Reports, available both digitally and in hard copy format, and produced to the same high standards as our books.

In 2021, we were very pleased to announce the start of a new chapter for Globe Law and Business following the acquisition of law books under the imprint Ark Publishing. Our law firm management list is now significantly expanded with many well known and loved Ark Publishing titles.

We are also pleased to announce the launch of our online content platform, Globe Law Online. This allows for easy search and networked access across firms. Key collections include the Law Firm Management Collection, Private Client and Energy and the Energy Transition. Email me at sian@globelawandbusiness.com for further details or to arrange a free trial for you or your firm.

Sian O'Neill
Managing director
Globe Law and Business
www.globelawandbusiness.com

Milton Keynes UK
Ingram Content Group UK Ltd.
UKHW021242111123
432390UK00002B/2